D0812611

HOMONYMS

A

Dictionary

of

Homonyms

---

by Louise Ellyson

FOR REFERENCE

*Not to be taken from Lib*rary

GARDNER WEBB COLLEGE LIBRARY

GARDNER-WEBB COLLEGE LIBRARY
P. O. Box 836
Boiling Springs, N.C. 28017

AMEREON HOUSE

MATTITUCK, N. Y.

Copyright   1977 by Louise W. Ellyson. All rights reserved.
No part of this publication may be reproduced, stored in
a retrieval system, or transmitted in any form or by any
means without prior written permission of the author and
publisher.

Ref.
PE
1595
.E44
1981

Library of Congress Cataloging in Publication Data

Ellyson, Louise.
  A dictionary of homonyms.

  Reprint of the ed. published by Banner Books, Sherman
Oaks, Calif.
  1. English language — Homonyms — Dictionaries.
I. Title.
PE 1595.E44   1981   423'.1   80-68951
ISBN 0-88411-136-9

For further information and ordering, contact:
AMEREON HOUSE, the publishing division of
Amereon Ltd.
Box 1200
Mattituck, New York 11952

Manufactured in the United States of America
by the Mad Printers

To

Samuel Johnson

Noah Webster

P. M. Roget

H. W. Fowler

and

Random House,

all of whom contributed substantially to this book, especially by not thinking of it first.

INTRODUCTION

This is a new kind of dictionary, one that depends upon sight and sound rather than root stems for its word patterns. It is the first serious collection of homonyms published in the English language.

A true *homonym*, which means "same name," is a word that is spelled like another and has the same sound, but a different meaning, as in *bear*, an animal, and *bear*, to carry. A *homophone*, "same sound," is a word that has the same pronunciation as another, but a different spelling, as *bear*, to carry, and *bare*, naked. A *homograph*, "same spelling," is a word that is written like another, but has a different pronunciation, as in *en'trance*, a doorway, and *en trance'*, to delight. The three categories of homonyms are not separated in these pages.

Since my purpose is to acquaint you with the complexities - and delights - of English-language homonyms, I have simplified their meanings and phonetic symbols as much as possible. You will note that the words are arranged in lists of two or more. The first entry is in large black type; the second, if there is a change in either spelling or pronunciation, is in large light type. SO sō adj. *thus,* is followed by SEW v. *to stitch* and SOW v. *to plant seeds* - same sound, no new phonetics. By adding a new phonetic sound to SOW sou, we get an adult female swine. Each entry, except the first, refers back to the preceding one.

(Entries are not in strict alphabetical order because we tried to put the better-known word first. For example, *cede* follows *seed.*)

A study of these words, especially the true homonyms, confirms that English is a vital and growing language. A *quisling* is a traitor, without benefit of even Judas's upper case.

A two-holed conduit for fire hoses is a *siamese,* named for the famous Siamese twins. To *preen* comes from an obsolete word meaning *pin* and describes an action of both humans and birds; in all likelihood it referred originally to a pointed beak. "See how Piers with his new leg ribbands doth preen himself like yon chanticleer," one of our ancestors may have said.

The process continues with language forming new patterns, often bubbling with laughter, not caring if its sources were Greek, Latin, Icelandic, or Frisian.

So much for the joys; there are also complications. Why should the adjective *general* mean common to most while the noun denotes a (most uncommon) military rank? This book does not attempt to answer such questions, but it does present the complexities of such duplications in a simplified manner for the beginning reader, the foreign student, and the frankly curious.

To the section of homonyms I have appended a list of words I call *Bruisers.* These are almost-homonyms, words that are often misspelled, misused, or confused. My experience in tutoring children with learning disabilities has taught me that those children's reversal tendencies are latent in even competent readers. What adult can state that he never confuses *through* and *thorough,* for instance? But this is not the place to go into problems of dyslexia. Let it suffice to say that *marital-martial* are *Bruisers,* while *copy-replica,* a confusion in concept, are not.

En'ē wā, I hōp ū lĭk hom'ə nimz nou.

Louise Ellyson
Richmond, Virginia
July, 1977

ABBREVIATIONS USED

adj.	adjective
adv.	adverb
art.	article
conj.	conjunction
interj.	interjection
n.	noun
p.p.	past participle
pref.	prefix
prep.	preposition
pro.	pronoun
u.c.	upper case
v.	verb

KEY TO PRONUNCIATION

a e i o u at, get, hit, not, up
ā ē ī ō ū āte, ēve, hīde, hōme, ūse
oo soon
o͝o bo͝ok
au bawl
oi oil
ou loud
er her
är bär
air māre

hw white
ng sing
sh shoe
th thin
t͟h than
zh azure
ch chat

The schwa (ə) is a vowel sound in unaccented syllables, as: away, ə wā′; event, ə vent′; easily, ēz′ə lē; gallop, gal′əp; circus, ser′kəs.

PART I

HOMONYMS

A

A ā
n. first letter of the English alphabet
indef. article: no particular person or thing
EH
interj. what?

ABACK ə bak′
adj. surprised
adj. toward the back

ABANDON ə ban′dn
v. to forsake, desert
v. to yield without self-control

ABDUCTOR ab duk′tər
n. a kind of muscle
n. a kidnapper

ABEL ā′bəl
n. (u.c.) son of Adam and Eve
ABLE
adj. having skill

ABLATIVE ab′lə tiv
adj. a case in grammar
adj. tending to remove by melting or erosion
ABLATIVE ab lā′tiv
adj. tending to meet

ABORT ə bort′
v. to miscarry
v. to stop before a mission or flight is completed, as of a missile

ABOUT ə bout′
prep. of, concerning
prep. near
prep. around

ABOVE ə buv′
adv. overhead
adv. north of
adv. foregoing

ABSORB ab sorb′
v. to drink in
v. to destroy

ABSTRACT ab′strakt
n. a kind of idea
- *n.* a summary

ABSTRACT ab strakt′
v. to steal

ABUSE ə būs′
n. improper use

ABUSE ə būz′
v. to harm, mistreat

ACADEMIC ak a dem′ik
adj. of a college or school
adj. not practical

ACCENT ak′sent
n. stress of a syllable in a word
n. a manner of speaking
n. a mark that indicates vowel quality

ACCESSORY ak ses′ər ē
n. an addition
n. an accomplice

ACCOMMODATE ə kom′ə dāt
v. to oblige
v. to have or make room for

ACCOUNT ə kount′
n. a narrative, story
n. an amount of money in the bank
n. consideration

ACE ās
n. a single spot on a card
n. a skilled person

ACERBATE as′ər bāt
v. to make sour or bitter
v. to exasperate

ACEROSE as′ə rōs
adj. needle-shaped, as pine leaves
adj. mixed with chaff

ACETIC ə sēt′ik
adj. of vinegar
ASCETIC
n. a recluse
adj. severe

ACRE ā′ker
n. a unit of land measure
ACHER
n. one who hurts or grumbles

ACTS aks
n. deeds
n. parts of a play
n. (u.c.) a book in the Bible

AX aks
n. a cutting tool

ACUTE ə kūt'
adj. sharp
adj. (of an angle) having less than 90 degrees
n. a kind of accent

AD ad
n. an advertisement

ADD
v. to sum up

ADDER ad'dər
n. one who adds
n. a kind of snake

ADDITION ə dish'ən
n. the act of uniting

EDITION
n. one of a series of printings

ADDRESS ə dres'
n. place where one lives
v. to speak
v. to prepare for mailing

ADDS adz
v. sums up, totals

ADZ
n. a tool

ADDUCE ə dūs'
v. to show evidence

EDUCE
v. to develop

ADE ād
n. a drink

AID
n. help

AIDE
n. a helper

ADHIBIT ad hib'it
v. to admit
v. to use
v. to attach

AD LIB ad lib'
n. an improvised statement
adv. at one's pleasure

ADMIT ad mit'
v. to allow to enter

v. to confess

ADVANCE ad vans'
v. to move or bring forward
v. to lend

AERIAL ā'rē əl
n. antenna
adj. of or produced by the air

ARIEL
n. (u.c.) a sprite in a play by Shakespeare

AERIE ē'rē
n. nest of an eagle or hawk

EERIE
adj. uncanny, weird

AFFECT ə fekt'
v. to influence
v. to pretend

EFFECT
n. consequence

AFFLUENT af'loo ənt
adj. wealthy
n. a tributary stream

AFGHAN af'gan
n. (u.c.) a native of Afghanistan
n. a kind of dog
n. a kind of blanket

AFTER af'tər
prep. behind
prep. in search of

AGAINST ə gānst'
prep. hostile, in opposition
prep. beside, near, before

AGAPE ə gāp'
adj. with the mouth wide open

AGAPE a'gə pā
n. brotherly love

AGATE ag'it
n. a playing marble
n. a type size

AGE āj
n. a length of time
n. the card player on the dealer's left

AGED ājd
v. became older

AGED ā'jid
adj. of advanced age

AIL āl
v. to be sick

ALE
n. a malt beverage

AIR air
n. atmosphere
v. to make known

ERE
prep. before

HEIR
n. one who inherits

AIRLINE air līn
n. a system of airplane flights
n. a hose for a deep-sea diver

AIRWAY air wā
n. an air route
n. a passage in a mine

AISLE īl
n. area for walking in some buildings
I'LL
v. I will or I shall

ISLE
n. a small island

AJAR ə jar'
adv. partly open
adv. in contradiction to

ALIEN ā'lē ən
n. one born in another country
adj. hostile, opposed

ALIGHT ə līt'
v. to settle, descend
adj. burning

ALL aul
adj. the whole of

AWL
n. a tool

ALLEY al'ē
n. a narrow street or walk
n. a large playing marble

ALLOWANCE ə lou'əns
n. a sum of money
n. tolerance

ALLOWED ə loud'
v. gave permission

ALOUD
adv. voiced

ALL READY aul red'ē
adj. completely prepared

ALREADY
adv. previously

ALLURE ə lūr'
v. to tempt, charm
n. a kind of passageway

ALTAR aul'ter
n. a platform or table

ALTER
v. to change

ALTOGETHER aul too geth'ər
adv. entirely

ALL TOGETHER
adv. in a group

ALUM al'əm
n. a chemical

ALUM ə lum'
n. a graduate

ALWAYS aul'wāz
adv. every time

ALL WAYS
adv. by every method

AMEND ə mend'
v. to change for the better

EMEND
v. to correct

AMENDS ə mendz'
n. payment for a loss
v. changes for the better

AMMONITE am'ən īt
n. a kind of fossil shell
n. a kind of fertilizer

AMOK ə muk'
n. a psychic disturbance

AMUCK
adj. frenzied

AMYGDALIN ə mig'də lin
adj. of or pertaining to an almond
adj. of or pertaining to a tonsil

ANALYST an'ə list
n. one who analyzes
ANNALIST
n. a chronicler of yearly events

ANATHEMA a nath'i mə
n. a curse
ANATHEMA a na thē'mə
n. a thing devoted to divine use

ANCHOR ang'ker
n. something that keeps a boat still
n. one who knows his field

ANEMONE ə nem'ə nē
n. a kind of flower
n. a kind of sea plant

ANGER ang'ər
n. wrath, displeasure
n. distress, pain

ANGLE ang'əl
n. a corner
v. to fish

ANGLER ang'lər
n. one who fishes
n. a kind of fish

ANIMUS an'i məs
n. hostile feeling
n. soul, purpose

ANOINT ə noint'
v. to put oil on
v. to dedicate to the service of God

ANOTHER ə nuth'ər
pro. something different
adj. one like the first

ANTE an'ti
n. a bet in poker
pref. before
ANTI
pref. against

ANTENNA an ten'ə
n. aerial
n. part of an insect

ANYONE en'ē wun
pro. any person
ANY ONE
pro. any specific person

ANYWAY en'ē wā
adv. in any case
adv. carelessly

APE āp
n. a kind of animal
v. to mimic

APOLOGY ə pol'ə jē
n. explanation, excuse
n. a poor substitute

APOSTROPHE ə pos'trə fē
n. a sign (') used when a letter is omitted
n. a kind of oration

APPETITE ap'ə tīt
n. a desire for food
APATITE
n. a common mineral

APPOSE ə pōz'
v. to place next to
OPPOSE
v. to act against

APPRESSED ə prest'
adj. fitting closely
OPPRESSED
adj. burdened

APPRISE ə prīz'
v. to inform
APPRIZE
v. to appraise

APPROPRIATE ə prō'prē ət
adj. suitable
APPROPRIATE ə prō'prē āt
v. to steal

APRON ā'prun
n. a protective skirt
n. a hard-packed area for airplanes

APT apt
adj. disposed, prone
adj. clever, bright

ARBOR är'bər
n. a leafy place
n. an axis

ARC ärk
n. part of a circle

ARK
n. a vessel

ARCH ärch
n. a curved structure
adj. sly
n. chief
pref. chief

ARMS ärmz
n. upper limbs of the body
n. weapons

ARMY är'mē
n. a body of trained warriors
n. a group of caterpillars

ARRAS ar'əs
n. a kind of tapestry
n. a kind of wedding gift

ARTICLE ärt'i kəl
n. a prose composition
art.: the, a, an
v. to bind by covenant

ASCENT ə sent'
n. movement upward

ASSENT
v. to agree

ASH ash
n. the residue of burned material
n. a kind of tree

ASP asp
n. a kind of snake
adj. quivering

ASPIC as'pik
n. a kind of jelly
n. the great lavender

ASS as
n. a kind of donkey
n. the buttocks

ASSAI ə sä'ē
adv. very (music)
n. a kind of palm tree

ASSISTANCE ə sis'təns
n. help

ASSISTANTS
n. helpers

ASSOCIATE ə sō'shē āt
v. to unite, connect

ASSOCIATE ə sō'shē it
n. a fellow worker

ASYLUM ə sī'lum
n. a kind of hospital
n. a refuge

ATE āt
v. did eat

EIGHT
n. a number

ATLAS at'ləs
n. maps in a book
n. (u.c.) a Greek giant

ATTEND ə tend'
v. to be present
v. to guard

ATTENTION ə ten'shun
n. awareness
n. politeness

ATTRIBUTE a'trib ūt
n. a quality

ATTRIBUTE ə trib'ūt
v. to see as coming from

AUDACIOUS au dā'shəs
adj. bold, fearless
adj. rebellious, shameless

AUDIT au'dit
v. to examine records
v. to attend classes as a listener

AUGER au'gər
n. a bit, brace, boring tool

AUGUR
n. a prophet

AUGHT aut
n. anything
n. zero

OUGHT
v. should

AUGUST au'gust
n. (u.c.) a month

AUGUST au gust'
adj. majestic

AUTARCHY au'tär kē
n. an autocratic government

AUTARKY
n. policy of economic independence

AUTHORITY au thor'i tē
n. power or right
n. a quotation from an accepted source

AUXILIARY augs il'i ā rē
n. helper
adj. additional

AWAY ə wā'
adv. from here to there

AWEIGH
adj. (of an anchor) free from the bottom

AWFUL au'fəl
adj. very bad, ugly
adj. inspiring fear

OFFAL
n. garbage

B

B bē
n. second letter of the English alphabet

BE
v. to exist

BEE
n. a kind of insect
n. a block on a bowsprit

BAA ba, bä
v. to bleat

BAH bä
interj. expression of annoyance

BACHELOR bach'ə lər
n. an unmarried man
n. a young male fur seal
n. a holder of a certain degree

BACK bak
n. the rear
v. to support
n. a kind of ferry
n. a kind of container for liquids

BACKBONE bak'bōn
n. spine
n. courage

BACKFIRE bak'fīr
n. an engine explosion, as in a car
v. to have a result opposite to the planned one
v. to start a counterfire

BACKGROUND bak'ground
n. the rear of a scene
n. a person's origin, education, experience

BACKHAND bak'hand
n. a stroke, slap, with the outer hand
n. writing that slopes to the left
adj. indirect, insincere

BACKLASH bak'lash
n. lost motion of machine parts
n. a sudden recoil or reaction
n. a snarled fishing line

BACKLOG bak'log
n. a reservation or accommodation
n. log at the back of the fire

BACKSET bak'set
n. a reverse
n. an eddy
n. part of a lock

BACKSTAIRS bak'stairz
n. stairs at the back of a house
n. a means of intrigue

BACKTRACK bak'trak
v. to return over the same route
v. to withdraw

BACKWARD bak'wərd
adv. toward the back
adj. slow, retarded

BACKWASH bak'wosh
n. water or air thrust backward
n. a condition remaining after an event

BACKWOODS bak'woŏdz
n. uncleared land
adj. unsophisticated

BAD bad
adj. not good

BADE
v. ordered

BADGER baj'ər
n. a kind of animal
v. to pester, nag

BADLY bad'lē
adv. in an incorrect way
adv. very much

BAFFLE baf'əl
v. to confuse, perplex
n. an artificial check for gas, light, or sound

BAG bag
n. a pouch
v. to kill or catch

BAGGAGE bag'ij
n. luggage
n. an immoral woman

BAGUETTE ba get'
n. a kind of gem
n. a small molding

BAIL bāl
n. money to keep someone out of jail until trial
v. to dip water out of a boat
n. handle of a kettle
BALE
n. large bundle

BAILIWICK bā'lə wik
n. the district under a sheriff or bailiff
n. a person's area of skill or knowledge

BAIT bāt
v. to prepare a line for fishing
v. to harass
BATE
v. to moderate

BALANCE bal'əns
n. an instrument to determine weight
n. the rest, remainder

BALD bauld
adj. with no hair on the scalp
BALLED
v. made into a ball

BAWLED
v. cried aloud

BALDPATE bauld'pāt
n. one who lacks hair on the scalp
n. a kind of widgeon

BALE bāl
n. a large bundle
n. a group of turtles

BALK bauk
v. to stop short and refuse to go on
n. beam, rafter

BALL baul
n. a round object
n. a dance

BALLOON ba loon'
n. a bag expanded with gas or air
v. to multiply at a rapid rate

BALMY bä'mē
adj. mild and soft
adj. fragrant

BALSAM baul'səm
n. a kind of fir tree
n. an ointment
n. a soothing agency

BAN ban
v. to prohibit or bar
n. a public proclamation

BAN bän
n. a coin of Romania

BAND band
n. a troop
n. a musical group
n. a thin, flat strip
BANNED
v. prohibited

BANDY ban'dē
v. to give and take
adj. bowlegged

BANG bang
n. a sudden noise
n. a blow
BHANG
n. a narcotic of hemp

BANGS bangz
n. noises
n. a fringe of hair

BANK bank
n. a business that deals with money
n. a slope by a stream
n. an arrangement of objects in a line
BANC
n. a judge's seat

BANKER bank'ər
n. one who works in the banking business
n. a bench used by masons
n. a vessel used in cod fishing

BANKRUPT bank'rupt
n. one who lacks money to pay debts
n. one who lacks a particular quality

BANTAM ban'təm
n. a small chicken
n. a small, quarrelsome person

BANTER bant'ər
v. to tease
n. one who is on a diet

BANYAN ban'yən
n. a kind of fig tree
n. a kind of wrapper worn by women

BAR bär
n. a rod, pole
v. a drinking place
v. to shut out
n. the law
BARRE
n. a rail for ballet dancers

BARB bärb
n. a pointed part behind a hook or arrowhead
n. a kind of pigeon
n. a kind of scarf
n. a kind of horse
n. an unpleasant remark

BARD bärd
n. a storyteller and singer
n. a thin slice of fat meat
BARRED
adj. striped
v. was kept out of a place

BARE bair
adj. uncovered
adj. just sufficient

BEAR
n. an animal
v. to give birth
v. to tolerate
v. to suffer

BARELY bair'lē
adv. only, no more than
adv. openly

BARGE bärj
n. a kind of boat
v. to force oneself upon rudely

BARK bärk
n. the cry of a dog
n. the external cover of a tree
BARQUE
n. a ship with sails

BARLEY bär'lē
n. a kind of cereal
adj. size of a small piece of coal

BARNACLE bär'nə kəl
n. a kind of sea animal
n. one who clings
n. an instrument used to control a horse

BARON ba'rən
n. a man of power
n. a cut of meat
BARREN
n. a group of mules
adj. sterile

BARONESS ba'rən es
n. wife of a baron
BARRENNESS
n. infertility

BARREL ba'rel
n. a wooden cask
n. part of a gun
n. trunk of a horse or cow

BARROW ba'rō
n. a frame used for carrying a load
n. an ancient burying mound

BASE bās
n. the bottom support
n. a goal in a game
adj. cowardly
adj. of little value

BASS
n. a low note
BASS bas
n. a kind of fish

BASED bāst
adj. supported by

BASTE
v. to sew loosely
v. to put liquid on food
v. to beat with a stick

BASIS bās'əs
n. the main element

BASES
n. corners of a baseball field

BASK bask
v. to lie in a warm place

BASQUE
n. (u.c.) one who lives in a country between France and Spain

BAT bat
n. a flying animal
n. a wooden club
v. to blink

BATE bāt
v. to worry
v. to flutter the wings, like a hawk

BATHOS bā'thəs
n. anticlimax
n. sentimentality
n. triteness

BATTEN bat'ən
n. a thin strip of wood
n. part of a loom
v. to grow fat, prosper

BATTER bat'ər
n. one who bats in a game
n. a mixture for bread or cake
v. to pound

BATTERY bat'ə rē
n. electric cells
n. two or more related things
n. act of pounding

BAY bā
n. a body of water
n. a sound of a hunting dog

n. a red-brown horse
n. a kind of bush
n. a compartment; bay window

BEY
n. a governor of a Turkish province

BAZAAR bə zär'
n. a market place

BIZARRE
adj. strange, odd

BE bē
v. to exist, live

BEE
n. a kind of insect
n. a block on a bowsprit

BEACH bēch
n. sand on the shore

BEECH
n. a kind of tree

BEACHCOMBER bēch'kō mer
n. one who lives off items found near the sea
n. a long, rolling wave

BEAD bēd
n. a round object, as used for necklaces
n. part of a gun

BEAM bēm
n. a support in a house
n. a ray of light
v. to smile happily

BEAN bēn
n. a kind of seed

BEEN bēn, bin
v. part of the verb to be

BIN bin
n. a storage box

BEARD bērd
n. hair on a man's face
n. a tuft, as of wheat
v. to defy

BEARING bair'ing
n. posture
n. a crop
n. reference

BEAT bēt
v. to thrash, win
BEET
n. a vegetable

BEATEN bēt'ən
adj. whipped
adj. very tired

BEAVER bē'vər
n. a dam-building animal
n. a kind of hat

BECOMING bi kum'ing
v. changing
adj. attractive

BED bed
n. a place to sleep
n. the bottom of a body of water
n. a place to grow flowers

BEEF bēf
n. cattle
v. to complain

BEER bēr
n. a drink
BIER
n. a stand for a coffin

BEETLE bēt'əl
n. a kind of insect
adj. prominent and overhanging
n. a hammering instrument

BEGUM be'gəm
n. a high-ranking Muslim woman
BEGUM bi gum'
v. to smear or clog as with gum

BELL bel
n. something that rings
v. to bellow like a deer
BELLE
n. a girl with many friends

BELLOWS bel'ōz
n. something that blows air
v. cries like a bull or cow

BELT belt
n. a band for the waist
n. region, zone
v. to flog
v. to rush

BENCH bench
n. a long seat
v. to keep a player out of a game

BEND bend
n. curve, crook
v. to influence

BENT bent
adj. curved
adj. determined

BERG berg
n. an iceberg
BURG
n. a city or town

BERRY be'rē
n. a small fruit
BURY
v. to place in the earth

BERTH berth
n. a place to sleep
BIRTH
n. the fact of being born

BESET bi set'
v. to attack on all sides
v. to decorate

BEST best
adj. of the highest quality
v. to defeat

BETTER bet'ər
adj. more worthy
BETTOR
n. one who bets

BEVY bev'ē
n. a group of girls
n. a flock of larks or quails
n. a group of roebucks

BIAS bī'əs
n. a preconceived idea
n. an oblique line across a woven fabric

BID bid
v. to order
v. to invite

BIDET bē dā'
n. a low, basinlike bath
n. a small saddle horse

BIGGIN big'in
n. a kind of close-fitting cap
n. a kind of coffee pot

BILE bīl
n. a secretion of the liver
n. ill temper

BILGE bilj
n. part of a boat
n. foolish talk

BILL bil
n. notice of a debt
n. a bird's beak

BILLET bil'it
n. lodging for a soldier
n. part of a log cut for fuel

BIMONTHLY bī munth'lē
adj. occurring every two months
adj. occurring twice a month

BINDING bīn'ding
n. the outside of a book
adj. duty-bound

BIRCH berch
n. a kind of tree
v. to beat, punish

BIRDS-EYE berdz'ī
adj. seen from above
adj. lacking in details, hasty
n. a kind of fabric

BIRR ber
n. force, energy, vigor

BUR
n. the rough outer part of some plants

BURR
n. a whirring noise or sound

BIS bis
n. a sheer linen fabric
adv. twice, encore

BISCUIT bis'kit
n. a kind of bread
n. unglazed earthenware

BISHOP bish'əp
n. the highest ranking clergyman
n. a chess piece
n. a kind of hot drink

BISQUE bisk
n. a thick soup
n. pinkish-tan
n. a point in tennis

BIT bit
n. a small amount
n. part of a harness
n. a boring tool
v. began to eat

BITE bīt
v. to grip or cut with teeth

BIGHT
n. the middle of a rope
n. a bay or gulf

BITING bī'ting
v. cutting with teeth
adj. keen
adj. unkind

BITTER bit'ər
adj. harsh, acrid in taste
adj. distressing

BITTERSWEET bit'ər swēt
n. a kind of plant
adj. both pleasant and painful

BLACK blak
adj. lacking hue
adj. gloomy, sad

BLACKGUARD blag'ard
n. a scoundrel
v. to vilify

BLACKHEAD blak'hed
n. a mass in a skin follicle
n. any of several herds
n. a disease of birds

BLACKHEART blak'härt
n. a disease of plants
n. a kind of cherry

BLACKJACK blak'jak
n. a short, leather-covered club
n. a card game
n. a large cup
n. a small oak

BLACKLEG blak'leg
n. a disease of animals or plants
n. a swindler

12

BLACKLETTER blak′let′ər
n. dark type
BLACK-LETTER
adj. tragic

BLACKOUT blak′out′
n. the concealment of visible lights
n. stoppage of a communications medium
n. unconsciousness

BLACKTHORN blak′thorn
n. a kind of shrub
n. a kind of walking stick

BLADE blād
n. a flat, cutting edge
n. a dashing young man

BLANCH blanch
v. to bleach
v. to scald
v. to force back or to one side

BLANK blank
adj. free from marks
adj. complete, utter

BLANKET blank′ət
n. a kind of cover
v. to interfere with

BLAST blast
n. a sudden gust of wind
n. a loud noise
v. to ruin, destroy

BLAZE blāz
n. a bright flame
n. a mark on a tree to show the way
n. a mark on an animal's face
v. to shoot steadily
v. to proclaim, publish

BLAZER blāz′ər
n. a sports jacket
n. a kind of cooking vessel

BLEACHERS blē′chers
n. area for watching games in
n. those who make things white

BLEAK blēk
adj. bare, dreary
n. a kind of fish

BLEED blēd
v. to lose blood
v. to feel pity

BLENCH blench
v. to shrink, quail
v. to blanch, make white

BLESSED bles′id, blest
adj. holy
adj. fortunate

BLEST
v. was blessed

BLIND blīnd
adj. unable to see
n. a place where hunters hide

BLINK blink
n. a rapid wink
v. to ignore, evade

BLISTER blis′tər
n. a watery skin sore
v. to punish
v. to criticize

BLOCK blok
n. a mass of wood or stone
n. a tool used with ropes
v. to stop someone in a game

BLOC
n. people who unite in order to vote for a cause

BLOCKHEAD blok′hed
n. a dunce
n. a fire block in a mine

BLOOD blud
n. fluid in the veins
n. kinship

BLOOM bloom
v. to yield flowers
v. to cause a cloudy area on a shiny object

BLOOMERS bloom′ərz
n. flowers
n. an article of clothing

BLOT blot
n. a kind of spot
v. to remove

BLOTTER blot'ər
n. a kind of paper that drinks up ink
n. a book of records

BLOW blō
n. a blast of air or wind
n. a hard stroke, as with a fist
n. a shock
v. to breathe upon

BLOWN blōn
adj. out of breath
adj. opened, as a flower

BLUBBER blub'ər
n. fat of whales
v. to weep noisily

BLUE bloo
n. a color
adj. sad
adj. blasphemous
adj. stemming from rigid morals

BLEW
v. did blow

BLUE CHIP bloo chip
n. a disk used in some games
n. a secure item of property

BLUE-CHIP
adj. leading, exemplary

BLUES blooz
n. melancholy
n. a form of jazz
n. a kind of military uniform

BLUFF bluf
v. mislead
n. a steep cliff
adj. open, frank

BLUNT blunt
adj. not sharp
adj. impolite

BOA bō'ə
n. a kind of snake
n. a scarf of feathers

BOARD bōrd
n. a plank
n. a group of directors
v. to take one's meals at a fixed price
v. to get onto a train, plane, or ship

BORED
adj. not interested

BOAST bōst
v. to brag
v. to dress stone roughly

BOATER bōt'ər
n. one riding in a boat
n. a kind of straw hat

BOB bob
n. a jerky motion
n. a short haircut
n. a polishing wheel

BOBBER bob'ər
n. a float for a fishing line
n. a member of a bobsled team

BODY bod'ē
n. the structure of an animal or plant
n. a collective group
n. the main part, as of a book, speech, or car

BOGEY bō'gē
n. a score in golf

BOGIE
n. a rear-wheel assembly for trucks

BOGY
n. an evil spirit

BOIL boil
v. to make bubbles by heating
n. a kind of sore

BOLD bōld
adj. fearless
adj. shameless, immodest
adj. steep, abrupt

BOWLED
v. rolled a ball in a game

BOLSTER bōl'stər
n. a long pillow
v. to support, add to

BOLT bōlt
n. a rod used to fasten
v. to run
v. to sift through a cloth

BOMB bom
n. an explosive device

BOMBE bom, bomb
n. a kind of dessert

BOMBAY bom'bā'
n. (u.c.) a city in India

BOMB BAY
n. part of an airplane

BOMBÉ
adj. curving outward (of furniture)

BOND bond
n. something that holds or binds together
n. a sealed written agreement

BONE bōn
n. part of the skeleton
v. to study, cram

BONER bōn'ər
n. a foolish mistake
n. one who or that which bones

BONGO bong'gō
n. one of a pair of small drums
n. a kind of antelope

BOOBY boo'bē
n. a silly person
n. a kind of sea bird

BOOK boͦok
n. a bound written work
v. to list, engage

BUKH
n. small talk, bragging

BOOM boom
n. a long, movable pole
n. a part of some snails
v. to make a deep sound
v. to flourish

BOON boon
n. a blessing
n. waste of flax
adj. friendly, jolly

BOOT boot
n. a high shoe
n. a Navy or Marine recruit
v. to kick

BORDER bor'dər
n. an eage
n. a flower bed

BORE bōr
n. a tiresome person
n. a rise of tidal water
v. carried
v. to make a hole

BOAR
n. a male swine

BOER
n. (u.c.) South African of Dutch descent

BOWER
n. a maker of bows and arrows

BORER bōr'ər
n. a tool for making holes
n. a kind of insect

BORNE bōrn
v. p.p. of *to bear* (give birth)
n. a circular sofa

BOROUGH bur'ō
n. a small municipality

BURRO
n. a small donkey

BURROW
v. to tunnel

BOSS bos, baus
n. one in charge
n. name for a cow
n. a piece of metal, often with a design

BOTTOM bot'əm
n. the lowest or deepest part
n. the rump
n. cause, origin

BOUGH bou
n. a limb of a tree

BOW
n. the front of a ship
v. to bend

BOULDER bōl'dər
n. a large, detached rock

BOLDER
adj. braver

BOUND bound
n. limit, boundary
v. to leap
adj. on the way to
adj. tied

BOUQUET boo kā'
n. nosegay
n. a group of pheasants

BOW bou
v. to bend

BOW bō
n. a looped knot
n. a bent piece of wood used in archery

BEAU
n. a male suitor

BOWED bōd
v. played with a bow, as the violin or cello

BODE
v. to portend

BOWER bou'ər
n. an arbor
n. a cottage

BOWER bō'ər
n. a musician with a stringed instrument

BOWL bōl
n. a deep dish
v. to play tenpins

BOLE
n. a tree trunk or stem
n. a red-brown color

BOLL
n. a seed vessel, as of cotton

BOWLER bō'lər
n. one who bowls
n. a kind of hat

BOX boks
n. a case with a lid
n. a green shrub
v. to fight in a match

BOXER bok'sər
n. a prizefighter
n. a breed of dog

BRACE brās
v. to support, prop
n. a pair, couple

BRACER brā'sər
n. one who makes firm
n. a wrist guard used in archery

BRACING brā'sing
adj. invigorating
n. a brace

BRACKET brak'it
n. a support
n. a class, grouping
n. a mark used in writing

BRAID brād
n. a kind of trimming on clothes
n. a plait, pigtail

BRAYED
v. cried like a donkey

BRAILLE brāl
n. (u.c.) a system of writing for the blind

BRAIL
v. to bind a bird's wings
v. to transfer fish from a net to the ship

BRAIN brān
n. the area of the mind
v. to hit on the head

BRAISE brāz
v. to cook food in a small amount of water

BRAYS
v. cries like a donkey

BRAZE
v. to make of brass

BRAKE brāk
n. a device to make a vehicle stop
n. a thicket
n. a kind of fern

BREAK
v. to shatter
n. a lucky event

BRANCH branch
n. part of a tree
n. a stream
v. to divide

BRAND brand
n. a kind, grade, or make
v. to mark with a hot iron

BRASH brash
n. a pile of debris
adj. hasty, impetuous, tactless

BRASS bras
n. a metal
n. an officer
n. nerve, crust
n. class of musical instruments

BRASSY bras'ē
adj. made of brass
adj. loud, bold

BRASSIE
n. a golf club

BRAVE brāv
adj. bold
n. a native American Indian warrior

BRAY brā
v. to cry like a donkey
v. to pound, as in a mortar

BRAZE brāz
v. to make of brass
v. to unite metals by solder

BRAZEN brā'zən
adj. made of brass
adj. impudent

BRAZIER brā'zhər
n. something to hold coals
n. one who makes brass objects

BREACH brēch
n. break, gap

BREECH
n. part of a gun

BREAD bred
n. a kind of food

BRED ˙
v. brought up

BREAK brāk
v. to shatter
n. a lucky event

BREAKER brāk'ər
n. one who shatters
n. a wave
n. a small water cask

BREAST brest
n. bosom, chest
n. part of a chimney
v. to climb over an obstacle

BREATHE brēʍ
v. to take air into the lungs
v. to whisper
v. to rest

BREECHES brich'əz
n. short pants for boys

BREECHES brēch'əs
n. gun bores

BREEDING brē'ding
n. good manners
v. producing offspring

BREEZE brēz
n. a light current of air
n. a gadfly

BRIDAL brid'əl
adj. of a wedding

BRIDLE
n. part of a harness
v. to control
v. to show disdain

BRIDE brīd
n. a newly married woman
n. a thread or threads used in lacemaking

BRIEF brēf
adj. short
n. an outline of something written

BRIER brī'ər
n. a pipe to smoke
n. a thorn

BRIG brig
n. a place of confinement, guardhouse
n. a kind of sailing ship

BRIGHT brīt
adj. clever
adj. shiny

BRIM brim
n. the edge of something hollow
n. a kind of fish

BRISTLE bris'el
n. a coarse, stiff hair
v. to show anger

BROACH brōch
v. to suggest
n. one of several kinds of tools
v. to break the surface of water

BROOCH
n. a kind of pin

BROAD braud
adj. wide
adj. indecent

BROADCAST braud'kast
v. to send a radio or TV program
v. to scatter seed

BROGUE brōg
n. an Irish accent
n. a heavy shoe

BROIL broil
v. to cook by direct heat
v. to quarrel

BROKE brōk
v. did break
adj. without money

BRONZE bronz
n. a kind of metal
v. to make or get tan on the skin

BROOD brood
n. a number of fowl, as of chickens, of the same age
v. to ponder

BROOK brŏŏk
n. a small stream
v. to tolerate

BROOM broom, brŏŏm
n. a brush for sweeping
n. a kind of plant

BROW brou
n. the forehead
n. the eyebrow

BROWN broun
n. a color
v. to fry or scorch in cooking

BROWNIE broun'ē
n. a kind of cookie
n. (u.c.) a junior Girl Scout
n. a friendly goblin

BROWSE brouz
v. to graze (of cattle)
v. to glance at casually

BROWS
n. eyebrows

BRUISE brooz
n. a discolored spot on the skin

BREWS
v. makes beer

BRUSH brush
n. bushes
v. to make one's hair neat

BRUTE broot
n. a beast
n. an early English chronicle
v. to shape a diamond

BRUIT
v. to rumor

BUBBLE bub'əl
n. a body of air in liquid
n. a dishonest sale

BUCK buk
n. a male animal
n. a dollar bill
n. a sawhorse
v. to leap, as a horse, in order to throw off a rider

BUCKLE buk'əl
n. a clasp
v. to bend, warp, or collapse
v. to prepare oneself for action

BUD bud
n. the start of a flower or leaf
n. brother

BUDGE buj
v. to shove slightly
v. to change opinion, yield
n. a kind of fur

BUFF buf
n. a tannish color
n. a kind of leather
v. to clean or polish
v. to stop the force of a blow

BUFFER buf'ər
n. something that acts as a shield
n. a device for polishing

BUFFET boo fā'
n. a piece of furniture
n. a meal

BUFFET buf'it
n. a blow with the fist or hand

BUG bug
n. an insect
n. a virus
v. to annoy
v. to place a microphone in order to hear secrets

BUGGY bug'ē
n. a kind of horse-drawn carriage
adj. full of insects

BUILD bild
v. to erect

BILLED
v. received or sent a bill

BUILDING bil'ding
n. an edifice
n. a group of rooks

BULB bulb
n. a kind of flower bud
n. something to go in a lamp

BULK bulk
n. the greater part
n. food fiber
n. a structure projecting from a building

BULL bool
n. a male animal
n. nonsense
n. a kind of buyer of stocks
n. a paper by the Pope

BULLDOG bool'dog
n. a kind of dog
n. a short-barreled revolver

BULLDOZE bool'dōz
v. to clear land
v. to frighten

BULLFINCH bool'finch
n. a kind of bird
n. a high hedge

BULLISH bool'əsh
adj. stupid, stubborn
adj. hopeful

BULLY bool'ē
n. an overbearing person
adj. fine, excellent

BUM bum
n. a tramp
v. to get for nothing
adj. false

BUMBLE bum'bəl
v. to blunder
v. to buzz
v. to mumble

BUMP bump
n. a swelling or rise
v. to knock into

BUMPER bum'pər
n. something to absorb shocks
n. one who bumps
n. a glass filled to the brim
adj. abundant

BUN bun
n. a sweet bread
n. a coil of hair

BUNCH bunch
n. a cluster or group
n. a knob, lump

BUNDLE bun'dəl
n. a package
v. to leave in a hurry

BUNK bunk
n. a built-in bed
n. nonsense, falsehood

BUNKER bunk'ər
n. a kind of fort
n. a large bin

BUNT bunt
v. to butt
n. part of a square sail
n. a disease of wheat

BUNTING bun'ting
n. a kind of cotton for flags
n. a baby's sleeping robe

BURDEN ber'dən
n. a load
n. the main idea

BUREAU būr'ō
n. a chest of drawers
n. an office

BURLY ber'lē
adj. sturdy

BURLEY
n. a type of tobacco

BURN bern
v. to be on fire
n. a brook

BURNT bernt
v. scorched
adj. (of colors) changed to a deeper hue

BURR ber
n. a cutting tool
n. a washer for a rivet
n. rough speech

BURST berst
v. to fly apart
n. a sudden show of emotion

BUS bus
n. a large motor vehicle for passengers

BUSS
n. a kiss

BUSHED boosht
adj. overgrown with bushes
adj. tired

BUST bust
n. the chest or breast
n. a portrait of the head and shoulders

BUSSED
v. went by bus
v. kissed

BUSTLE bus'əl
n. a show of energy
n. a fullness below the waist of a dress

BUT but
conj. yet, except

BUTT
n. a larger end of something

BUTCHER booch'ər
n. a meat dealer
v. to botch

BUTT but
n. the object of unkind wit
n. a large cask
n. a kind of fish

BUTTER but'ər
n. a solid food made from milk
n. an animal that pushes with its horns

BUTTERY but'ə rē
adj. full of butter
adj. flattering
n. pantry, larder

BUTTONHOLE but'ən hōl
n. a slit for a button
v. to detain in conversation

BUY bī
v. to purchase

BI-
pref. twice

BY
prep. near

BYE
n. something secondary or out of the way

BAI
n. a yellow mist of the Orient

C

C sē
n. third letter of the English alphabet

SEA
n. ocean

SEE
v. to look at
v. to understand
n. office of a bishop

SI
n. a note in the musical scale

CABBAGE kab′ij
n. a kind of vegetable
v. to steal (cloth)

CABINET kab′i nət
n. a piece of furniture
n. a group of advisors

CABLE kā′bəl
n. a strong rope
v. to send a message overseas

CACKLE kak′əl
n. the sound made by a hen
n. idle talk

CADDIE kad′ē
n. one who carries golf clubs for another

CADDY
n. a box for tea

CADDIS kad′is
n. a kind of yarn or braid
n. larva of a kind of insect; caddis fly

CADRE kä′drɔ
n. a group trained to lead
n. an outline or scheme

CAGE kāj
n. enclosure for birds or animals

CADGE kaj
v. to borrow, bum

CAKE kāk
n. a baked sweet
v. to lump

CALCAR kal′kär
n. a growth, spur
n. a kind of furnace used in glassmaking

CALENDAR kal′ən dər
n. a list of days or months

CALENDER
n. a machine for glazing cloth, paper, etc.

CALF kaf
n. a young cow or bull
n. the fleshy part of a leg

CALK kauk
v. to make watertight; caulk
n. a projection on a horseshoe

CALL kaul
v. to cry out
v. to visit

CAUL
n. a membrane sometimes seen at birth
n. a cap or hat
n. a plate used in pressing veneers together

CALLING kau′ling
n. a trade
v. crying out

CALLOUS kal′əs
adj. hard-hearted

CALLUS
n. a thickened piece of skin

CALVE kav
v. to give birth to a calf
v. (of an iceberg) to break off and detach

CALVOUS kal′vəs
adj. bald

CALVUS
adj. having certain changes in cloud formations

CAME kăm
v. did come
n. a bar of lead for holding glass in windows

CAMEL kam′əl
n. a kind of animal
n. a float serving as a fender

CAMEO kam′ē ō
n. an engraved gem or stone
n. a literary sketch

CAMERA kam′ər ə
n. a picture-taking device that holds film
n. a judge's private office

CAMP kamp
n. a place for temporary shelter
n. irony, delight in artificiality

CAMPER kamp'ər
n. one who goes to camp
n. a kind of trailer

CAN kan
n. a metal container
v. to be able

CANAL kə nal'
n. a narrow waterway
n. a duct in an animal or plant
n. a line on the surface of Mars

CANDLE kan'dəl
n. a wax taper
v. to grade eggs

CANE kān
n. a walking stick
v. to weave a chair seat

CAIN
n. (u.c.) a son of Adam and Eve

CANINE kā'nīn
adj. of a dog
n. a pointed tooth

CANNON kan'ən
n. a mounted gun

CANON
n. a rule of the church
n. a clergyman of a cathedral

CANT kant
n. pious speech
n. a sudden pitch or toss

CAN'T
v. cannot

CANTEEN kan tēn'
n. a flask to hold water
n. a place where enlisted men are
entertained

CANTER kan'tər
n. an easy gallop
n. one who uses pious speech

CANTOR
n. an official in a synagogue

CANTON kan'ton
n. a district, esp. in Switzerland
n. a pilaster

CANVAS kan'vəs
n. a heavy cloth used for sailing or
painting

CANVASS
v. to try to get votes

CAP kap
n. a small hat
n. a capital letter
v. to do better than another

CAPE kāp
n. a sleeveless coat
n. a piece of land jutting into the sea

CAPER kāp'ər
n. a prank
n. a bud used in cooking

CAPITAL kap'i təl
n. the city where the seat of
government is located
n. wealth
n. the top of a pillar or column
n. upper case
adj. involving loss of life

CAPITOL
n. a statehouse

CAPSULE kap'sool
n. a small container that holds
medicine
n. a small cabin used in space flights

CAR kär
n. a vehicle
n. a box made to hold live oysters in
the water

CARAT ka'rət
n. a unit of weight of gem stones

CARET
n. a mark used in printing

CARROT
n. a kind of vegetable

CARBONADO kär'bən ā dō
n. a broiled piece of meat or fish
n. a kind of diamond

CARBUNCLE kar'bung kəl
n. a sore like a boil
n. a kind of gem stone

CARCASS kär′kəs
n. the dead body of an animal
n. the unfinished framework of a building or ship

CARD kärd
n. a piece of stiff paper
n. a machine used in weaving
n. a funny person

CARDINAL kär′di nəl
n. a kind of bird
n. a high Catholic Church official
adj. main, chief

CAREER kə rē′ər
n. profession
n. full speed

CARKING kär′king
adj. troubled
adj. stingy

CARNAL kär′nəl
adj. animal, lustful
adj. natural, human

CAROL ka′rəl
n. a joyful song
n. a seat in a bay window

CARREL
n. an area in a library stack

CARP kärp
n. a kind of fish
v. to find fault

CARPET kär′pit
n. a kind of rug
n. a system for jamming radar

CARRIAGE ka′rij
n. a horse-drawn vehicle
n. posture

CARRIER ka′ri ər
n. one who or that which carries
n. one who spreads a disease without being afflicted by it

CARRYALL kar′ē ol
n. a kind of vehicle
n. a large basket or bag

CART kärt
n. a wagon

CARTE
n. a menu

CARTEL kär təl′
n. a monopoly
n. an agreement for the exchange of prisoners

CARTON kär′tən
n. a large cardboard box
n. a shot that hits the bull's-eye of a target

CASE kās
n. the state of things
n. a box, container

CASH kash
n. coins or paper money

CACHE
n. something hidden

CASHIER ka sheer′
n. a bank clerk
v. to dismiss in disgrace

CASK kask
n. a kind of container

CASQUE
n. a kind of helmet

CAST kast
n. people in a play
n. a plaster bandage
v. to throw

CASTE
n. social rank

CASTER kas′tər
n. one who throws
n. a salt or pepper shaker

CASTOR
n. a beaver
n. an oil used for medicine

CASUAL kas′ū əl
adj. happening by chance
n. a soldier temporarily at a station

CASUIST kazh′ū ist
n. one who studies specific moral problems
n. an oversubtle reasoner

CAT kat
n. a kind of animal
n. a kind of boat
n. a kind of fish

CATAPHRACT kat′ə frakt
n. a gallery of ancient Greece
n. an armored Roman soldier

CATARACT kat′ə rakt
n. a waterfall
n. an abnormality of the eye

CATER kāt′ər
v. to provide food
v. to flatter, amuse

CATER kat′ər
adv. near

CATERPILLAR kat′ər pil ər
n. the wormlike larva of a butterfly or moth
n. a tank or power shovel on endless tracks

CATHOLIC kath′ə lik
adj. (u.c.) of the church of Rome
adj. of interest to all

CATTY kat′ē
adj. like a cat
adj. spiteful

CAUDAL kaud′əl
n. a warm drink for the sick
adj. at or near the tail

CAUSE kauz
v. to bring about

CAWS
v. makes the sound of a crow

CAVIL kav′əl
v. to find fault, complain
n. a hammer for the rough dressing of stone

CEDAR sē′dər
n. a kind of tree

SEEDER
n. a device for sowing seed
n. a device that removes seeds

CEILING sēl′ing
n. the overhead part of a room
n. the maximum amount of money that can be charged

SEALING
v. closing

CELL sel
n. a small room
n. the unit of plant and animal life
n. an electrical device

SELL
v. to trade for money

CELLAR sel′ər
n. basement

SELLER
n. one who offers something for sale

CEMENT si ment′
n. a mixture of clay and limestone
v. to join together, unite

CENSOR sens′ər
n. one who examines writings for their morals

SENSOR
n. device that responds to physical stimulus

CENSER
n. a container for incense

CENT sent
n. penny

SCENT
n. odor, smell

SENT
v. did send

CENTRAL sen′trəl
adj. at, in, or near the middle
adj. chief, principal

CENTUM sen′təm
n. one hundred

CENTUM ken′təm
adj. of some Indo-European language groups

CEREAL sēr′ē əl
n. a breakfast food

SERIAL
n. a story that develops in separate units

CESSION sesh′ən
n. act of yielding

SESSION
n. a meeting

CHAFE chāf
v. to warm by rubbing
v. to irritate, annoy

CHAFF chaf
n. the husks of grain or grasses
v. to tease

CHAIN chān
n. a series of connected objects
n. a mountain range

CHAIR chair
n. a seat
n. a position of authority

CHAMP champ
n. champion
v. to bite

CHAMPAGNE sham pān'
n. a kind of wine

CHAMPAIGN
n. level, open country

CHANCE chans
n. luck or fortune
n. risk or hazard

CHANTS
v. sings

CHANGE chānj
n. coins
v. to make something different

CHANNEL chan'əl
n. the bed of a stream
n. a band for TV or radio
communication

CHANTER chant'ər
n. a singer
n. the pipe of a bagpipe

CHAPEL chap'əl
n. a room for worship
n. a print shop

CHAPERON shap'ə rōn
n. a guardian
n. an old-fashioned headdress

CHAPLET chap'lət
n. a wreath or garland for the head
n. a string of beads

CHAPS chaps
v. reddens the skin
n. cowboy leggings
n. boys

CHAR chär
v. to burn, scorch
n. a kind of fish

CHARACTER ka'rik tər
n. honesty
n. a person in fiction

CHARGE chärj
v. to fill or supply
v. to arrange to pay later
v. to rush

CHARGER chär'jər
n. one who charges
n. a horse

CHARM chärm
v. to delight
n. a small object for a bracelet
n. a magic spell

CHARTER chär'tər
n. a treaty
v. to rent a boat, plane, or vehicle

CHASE chās
v. to pursue, hunt
n. a trench
v. to decorate metal

CHASTE chāst
adj. decent

CHASED
v. hunted

CHAT chat
v. to talk in a familiar way
n. a kind of bird
n. a kind of seed

CHATTER chat'ər
v. to talk rapidly
v. to have one's teeth click, as from
the cold

CHAUFFEUR shō'fər
n. one who drives another's car

SHOFAR
n. a ram's horn used as a musical
instrument

CHEAP chēp
adj. not costly
CHEEP
n. a chirp
CHECK chek
n. a mark
n. a written payment
v. to halt
v. to inspect
CZECH
n. (u.c.) Czechoslovakian

CHECKERS chek'ərs
n. a game for two
n. inspectors
n. persons who guard coats and hats temporarily

CHEEK chēk
n. part of the face
n. impudence

CHEESE chēz
n. a food made from milk
n. one who is important
v. to stop

CHEESY chēz'ē
adj. of cheese
adj. of poor quality

CHESS ches
n. a game for two
n. a kind of plank
n. a kind of pie

CHEST chest
n. part of the body
n. a box

CHESTERFIELD ches'tər fēld
n. an overcoat
n. a sofa

CHESTNUT ches'nut
n. a kind of tree
n. a stale joke

CHEWS chooz
v. grinds with teeth
CHOOSE
v. opt

CHIC shēk
adj. in style

SHEIK
n. an Arab chief

CHICKEN chik'ən
n. a fowl
adj. cowardly

CHILI chil'ē
n. a hot pepper
CHILE
n. (u.c.) country in South America
CHILLY
adj. cool

CHIME chīm
v. to ring bells
n. the edge of a cask

CHIN chin
n. part of a face
v. to pull one's self up by the arms

CHINA chī'nə
n. ceramic dishes
n. (u.c.) a country in East Asia

CHINK chink
n. a crack or cleft
v. to make a sharp ringing sound

CHIP chip
n. a broken-off piece
v. to cheep

CHIPPER chip'ər
adj. lively
v. to chirp
n. one who chips or cuts

CHISEL chiz'əl
n. a tool
v. to cheat

CHIT chit
n. notice of money owed
n. a child

CHOIR kwīr
n. a company of singers
QUIRE
n. a set of 24 sheets of paper

CHOKE chōk
v. to stop the breath of
n. part of a carburetor
v. to fill chock-full

CHOLER kol′ər
n. anger

COLLAR
n. something worn around the neck

CHOPPER cho′pər
n. a short ax
n. a helicopter

CHOPS chops
n. ribs of meat
n. the jaw
v. cuts

CHORD kaurd
n. two or more tones in music

CORD
n. a thin rope or string
n. 8 feet of fuel wood

CHORUS kōr′əs
n. a singing group
n. a repeated verse in a poem

CHOW chou
n. a kind of dog
n. food

CHUCK chuk
n. a cut of beef
v. to toss

CHUFF chuf
n. a rustic
n. the sound of a steam engine

CHUM chum
n. a friend
n. ground bait

CHUMP chump
n. a short piece of wood
n. blockhead
v. to munch

CINCH sinch
n. part of a saddle
n. something easy

CIRCLE ser′kəl
n. a closed curve
n. a group of people with common ties

CIRRHOSIS sə rō′sis
n. a disease of the liver

SOROSIS
n. a type of fruit
n. a women's society

CIVIL siv′əl
adj. polite
adj. of citizens

CLACK klak
n. a quick, sharp sound

CLAQUE
n. a group hired to clap at a performance

CLAD klad
v. was dressed
v. to bond metals

CLAM klam
n. a kind of seafood
n. a silent person

CLAMOR klam′ər
n. uproar

CLAMMER
n. one who digs for clams

CLAMP klamp
n. a kind of tool
n. a stack of raw bricks
v. to tread heavily

CLAPPER klap′ər
n. one who strikes his hands together
n. the tongue of a bell

CLASH klash
n. a collision
v. to make a loud noise

CLAUSE klauz
n. a part of many sentences

CLAWS
n. sharp nails of some animals

CLAY klā
n. earth, mud
n. the human body
n. a kind of fabric

CLEAR klēr
adj. free from darkness; plain
v. to remove
v. to declare innocent

CLEAVE klēv
v. to cling
v. to split

CLERICAL kle'ri kəl
adj. of clerks
adj. of the clergy

CLIMB clīm
v. to mount, rise

CLIME
n. climate, region

CLINK klink
n. a light, sharp sound
n. jail

CLIP klip
n. a metal clasp
n. rate, pace
v. to cut off or out

CLIPPER klip'ər
n. one who clips
n. a sailing vessel

CLOBBER klob'ər
v. to strike, defeat
v. to paint over a ceramic piece

CLOCK klok
n. a timepiece
n. a design in a sock or stocking

CLOD klod
n. a lump of earth
n. a stupid person

CLOSE klōs
adv. near

CLOSE klōz
v. to shut

CLOTHES
n. attire

CLOVE klōv
n. a spice
n. an outgrowth of a plant's bulb
v. did cleave

CLUB klub
n. a heavy stick
n. an organized group

CLUE kloo
n. a guide in problem solving

CLEW
n. a ball of yarn

CLUTCH kluch
v. to snatch
n. a hatch of eggs
n. part of a car

COACH kōch
n. a carriage or bus
v. to train

COACTION kō ak'shun
n. force or compulsion
n. joint action

COAL kōl
n. black fuel

COLE
n. cabbage

COARSE kōrs
adj. inferior, rough

COURSE
n. direction, way

COARSER kōrs'ər
adj. rougher

COURSER
n. a swift horse
n. one who chases
n. a kind of desert bird

COAST kōst
n. land next to the sea
v. to slide

COASTER kōst'ər
n. a sled
n. a ship engaged in coastwise trade
n. a small tray or mat

COAT kōt
n. a garment
n. a layer

COTE
n. a shelter for pigeons

COATING kō'ting
n. a layer
n. a fabric for making coats

COB kob
n. corncob
n. a male swan
n. a horse with a high gait

COBBLE kob'əl
v. to mend shoes
n. a round stone

COCK kok
n. a rooster
n. part of a firearm
n. a pile of hay
v. to turn up or to one side

COCKER kok'ər
n. a kind of dog
v. to pamper

COCK-EYED kok'īd
adj. cross-eyed
adj. foolish, wrong

COCKLE kok'əl
n. a kind of shellfish
n. a small boat
n. a pucker
n. a kind of candy

COCKSCOMB koks'kōm
n. comb of a cock
n. a kind of flower
n. a hat worn by professional fools

COCKTAIL kok'tāl
n. a drink or portion of food
n. a horse with a docked tail
n. a person of little breeding who passes for a gentleman

COCKY kok'ē
adj. conceited

KHAKI kok'ē, kä'kē
n. a kind of cloth

COCOA kō'kō
n. a chocolate drink

COCO
n. coconut

COD kod
n. a kind of fish
n. a bag or sack

COFFIN kof'in
n. a box or case for a corpse
n. a bone in a horse's foot

COG kog
n. a gear tooth
n. a tongue in a timber
n. a kind of medieval ship
v. to cheat in dice

COIF kwaf
n. a hair-do

COIF koif
n. a hood-shaped hat

COIL koil
v. to wind in rings
n. tumult, trouble

COIN koin
n. a piece of money
v. to invent

COIGN
n. a cornerstone

COLD kōld
adj. chilly
n. a virus infection

COALED
v. took in coal for fuel

COLLARD kol'ərd
n. a kind of vegetable

COLLARED
v. seized by the collar

COLLECT kol ekt'
v. to gather

COLLECT kol'ekt
n. a short prayer

COLON kō'lən
n. a punctuation mark (:)
n. part of the intestine

COLON ko lon'
n. (u.c.) a city in Panama

COLONEL ker'nəl
n. an officer in the army

KERNEL
n. the soft part of a nut or seed

COLOSSUS kol o'sus
n. anything huge
n. (u.c.) a bronze statue of Apollo

COLUMBINE kol'um bīn
n. a kind of flower
adj. like a dove
n. (u.c.) an actress in a special play

COLUMN kol'um
n. an upright pillar
n. a list, as of numbers
n. a part of a newspaper
n. a line of soldiers

COMA kō'mə
n. a state of unconsciousness
n. part of a comet
n. a tuft at the end of a seed

COMBER kōm'ər
n. one who combs
n. a wave

COMBINE kom'bīn
n. a machine for cutting grain
COMBINE kum bīn'
v. to unite

COMFORTER kum'tər tər
n. one who consoles
n. a long woolen scarf

COMMANDING kə man'ding
adj. dignified
v. ordering
adj. overlooking, as in a location

COMMEND kə mend'
v. to praise
v. to entrust

COMMIT kə mit'
v. to give in trust or charge
v. to consign to custody
v. to pledge

COMMODE kə mōd'
n. a low cabinet
n. a toilet

COMMON kom'ən
n. the body of people
n. a park
adj. coarse, vulgar

COMMUNE kom ūn'
v. to talk together
v. to take part in a church ritual
COMMUNE kom'ūn
n. a small division in a state or country

COMMUTE kom ūt'
v. to change, give and take
v. to travel between home and office

COMPACT kəm pakt'
adj. dense
COMPACT kom'pakt
n. a contract
n. a small car
n. a box for pressed powder

COMPANION kom pan'yən
n. an associate
n. a handbook, guide

COMPANY kum'pə nē
n. a group of people
n. a small group of soldiers
n. a business

COMPASS kum'pəs
n. an instrument for finding directions
v. to comprehend, grasp with the mind

COMPENSATE kom'pen sāt
v. to offset, be equivalent to
v. to pay

COMPETENT kom'pi tənt
adj. able
adj. fairly good

COMPLACENT kəm plā'sənt
adj. self-satisfied

COMPLAISANT
adj. obliging

COMPLEMENT kom'plə mənt
n. something that makes perfect

COMPLIMENT
n. praise

COMPLEX kom'pleks
n. a group of like things, as buildings
COMPLEX kom'pleks, kom pleks'
adj. difficult
COMPLEX kom pleks'
adj. made of various parts

COMPLEXION kəm plek'shən
n. the color of skin
n. a viewpoint, attitude

COMPORT kəm pōrt'
v. to behave
COMPORT kom'pōrt
n. a glass dish

COMPOSE kom pōs'
v. to make by putting together, to create
v. to make calm, quiet

COMPOSITION kom pō zish'ən
n. the act of combining to form a whole
n. a written essay

COMPOUND kom'pound
n. an enclosure
v. to pay interest
adj. made of two or more parts

COMPRESS kəm pres'
v. to force into less space
COMPRESS kom'pres
n. a kind of bandage

CON kon
adv. against an idea
n. a convict
v. to study
v. to trick

CONCEIT kon sēt'
n. high self-pride
n. a fancy, whim

CONCEIVE kon sēv'
v. to imagine
v. to beget, bring into being

CONCENTRATE kon'sen trāt
v. to think hard
v. to make stronger by reducing the content

CONCERN kən sern'
v. to be of interest, to worry
n. a company

CONCERT kon'sert
n. a musical recital
n. combined action
CONCERT kon sert'
v. to plan

CONCLUDE kon klood'
v. to bring to an end
v. to decide

CONCRETE kon'krēt
adj. real, actual
n. a stonelike material

CONDITION kon dish'ən
n. state of health
n. social position
n. stipulation
v. to prepare for a result

CONDUCT kon'dukt
n. way of acting

CONDUCT kən dukt'
v. to behave
v. to lead, guide

CONDUCTOR kon duk'tər
n. a leader
n. material that carries heat or electricity

CONE kōn
n. an oval-topped shape
n. part of the eye

CONFER kən fer'
v. to give a gift or honor
v. to consult together

CONFIDE kən fīd'
v. to have faith
v. to tell secrets trustfully

CONFINED kən fīnd'
adj. enclosed
adj. being in childbirth

CONFIRM kon ferm'
v. to verify
v. to make someone a church member

CONJUNCTION kən junk'shən
n. a part of speech
n. a joining together

CONJURE kon'jūr
v. to invoke by magic
CONJURE kən jūr'
v. to appeal to earnestly

CONNECTION kən ek'shən
n. link, association
n. kinsman

CONSERVE kən serv'
v. to keep from loss
v. to cook fruit

CONSOLE kon'sōl
n. a piece of furniture to hold a radio or TV
CONSOLE kon sōl'
v. to comfort

CONSONANT kon'sə nant
n. a letter not a vowel
adj. in agreement

CONSORT kon'saurt
n. spouse

CONSORT kən saurt'
v. to keep company

CONSTITUTIONAL kon sti too'shə nəl
adj. essential; of or pertaining to official papers
n. a walk

CONSTRICTOR kən strik'tər
n. a kind of snake
n. a kind of muscle

CONSUMPTION kən sump'shun
n. the act of using up
n. a kind of illness

CONTENT kən tent'
n. satisfied
CONTENT kon'tent
n. something that is included

CONTIGUOUS kən tig'ū əs
adj. touching, in contact
adj. near but not touching

CONTINENCE kon'ti nens
n. self-restraint

CONTINENTS
n. large bodies of land

CONTINGENT kən tin'jənt
adj. accidental or conditional
n. a quota

CONTRACT kon'trakt
n. an agreement
CONTRACT kən trakt'
v. to shrink, draw together

CONTRACTION kən trak'shən
n. a shortened form, as of a word
n. the act of getting, as a disease or debt
n. the shortening of a muscle

CONTRACTOR kən trak'tər
n. one who agrees to furnish supplies
n. something that draws together, as a muscle

CONTRAST kən trast'
v. to compare opposites
CONTRAST kon'trast
n. a striking difference

CONTROL kən trōl'
v. to command, dominate
n. a standard of comparison

CONVENTIONAL kən vensh'i nəl
adj. conforming, traditional
adj. of or pertaining to an assembly

CONVERSE kən vers'
v. to talk together
CONVERSE kon'vers
adj. opposite

COO koo
v. to murmur like a dove

COUP
n. a clever action

COOL kool
adj. not warm
adj. calm, distant

COOP koop
n. a cage or pen for small animals

COUPE
n. ice cream with fruit

COUPE koop, koop ā'
n. a kind of car

COP kop
n. a policeman
v. to steal

COPE kōp
v. to contend, with some success
n. a kind of mantle
n. the sky

COPPER kop'ər
n. a kind of metal
n. a policeman
n. a kind of butterfly

COPS kops
n. policemen

COPSE
n. a thicket of small trees

CORDIAL kaurd'yəl
adj. friendly
n. a sweet drink

CORDON kaurd'dən
n. a braid or ribbon
n. a line of police

CORE kōr
n. the central, essential part
CORPS
n. a group of persons acting together

CORK kaurk
n. a stopper for a bottle
n. a kind of tree

CORN kaurn
n. a plant or its edible parts
n. a hard place on the skin
v. to preserve in salt

CORNER kaur'nər
n. an angle
v. to keep someone from escaping

CORNFLOWER kaurn flou'ər
n. a certain blue flower

CORN FLOUR
n. flour made from corn

CORONA kə rō'nə
n. a circle of light
n. the tonsure of a cleric

CORONAL kor'ə nəl
n. a crown

CORONAL kə rōn'əl
adj. of or pertaining to the tip of the
tongue

CORONARY kor ə nā'rē
adj. of or pertaining to the human
heart
adj. of or like a crown

CORPORAL kor'pə rəl
n. a noncommissioned officer
n. a communion cloth
adj. of the human body

CORRECTION kə rek'shən
n. repair of error
n. punishment

CORRESPOND ko rəs pond'
v. to write to
v. to agree

CORSAGE kaur säzh'
n. a bunch of flowers
n. the waist of a dress

COSMOS koz'məs
n. the universe
n. a kind of flower

COT kot
n. a small bed
n. a small house, cottage

COTTON kot'ən
n. part of a kind of plant
v. to begin to like

COUCH kouch
n. a sofa
v. to put into words

COUNCIL koun'səl
n. a group of advisors

COUNSEL
n. advice
n. a lawyer

COUNT kount
v. to check one by one
n. a nobleman
v. to have merit, importance

COUNTENANCE kount'ə nens
n. the face
v. to permit or approve

COUNTER kount'ər
n. one who or that which counts
n. a table or shelf in a store
adv. against

COUNTERPOINT kount'ər point
n. the art of combining melodies
v. to clarify by contrast

COUNTRY kun'trē
n. nation
n. land not in urban areas

COURSE kōrs
n. a path, route
n. part of a meal
n. a natural order of events
n. a series of classes

COARSE
adj. inferior, rough

COURT kōrt
n. an area open to the sky
n. people in a king's palace
n. a place where a judge rules
v. to woo

COURTESY ker'tə sē
n. polite behavior

CURTESY
n. life tenure of land by a widower

COUSIN kuz'ən
n. a son or daughter of an uncle or aunt

COZEN
v. to cheat

COW kou
n. a kind of animal
v. to intimidate

COWARD kou'ərd
n. one who is not brave

COWERED
v. crouched in fear or shame

COWL koul
n. a hooded garment
n. part of an automobile

COZY ko'zē
adj. snug
n. a cover for a teapot

CRAB krab
n. a kind of shellfish
n. a disagreeable person
n. a crabapple

CRACK krak
n. a slight opening
v. to make a sudden sharp sound
v. to fail, give way

CRACKER krak'ər
n. a thin, crisp biscuit
n. a firecracker

CRAFT kraft
n. skill
n. a ship or plane
n. members of a working group

CRAM kram
v. to overfeed
v. to study intensively
n. a dense crowd

CRAMP kramp
n. a painful spasm in the muscles
n. a clamp

CRANE krān
n. a machine that lifts
n. a wading bird

CRANK krank
n. a kind of lever
n. a cross person
adj. of a tendency to roll easily, as a ship

CRAP krap
n. a losing throw of dice
n. nonsense, a lie
n. junk

CRASH krash
v. to shatter
n. a kind of fabric

CRATER krā'tər
n. a hole or pit in the ground

KRATER
n. an antique mixing bowl

CRAWL kraul
v. to creep
v. to swim with a certain stroke
n. an enclosure of shallow water

CRAZE krāz
v. to make insane
v. to make small cracks, as on glaze or paint

CREAK krēk
v. to squeak

CREEK
n. a small stream of water

CREAM krēm
n. the fatty part of milk

CREME krēm, krām
n. a kind of thick, sweet drink

CREDIT kred'ət
n. trustworthiness
n. time allowed for payment

CREEP krēp
v. to crawl
v. to sneak up behind

CREEPERS krēp'ərs
n. something worn by an infant
n. some vines
n. some birds

CREPE krāp
n. a kind of fabric
n. a black band or veil for mourning
n. a pancake

CREW kroo
n. a group of persons working
together
v. crowed

CRICKET krik'ət
n. a kind of insect
n. a kind of game
n. a small stool
n. a small roof

CRIMP krimp
n. an agent who recruits seamen or
soldiers by coercion
v. to make wavy

CRISP krisp
adj. brittle
adj. clean, neat, well-pressed
adj. crinkled, wrinkled

CRITIC kri'tik
n. a person skilled in judging
literature or arts
n. a person who tends to make
unpleasant judgments

CROCK krok
n. an earthen pot or jar
n. an old ewe or horse

CROOK kro͝ok
n. a hook
n. a thief, dishonest person

CROP krop
n. harvest
n. a short stick
v. to cut short
n. a digestive organ in birds

CROSS kros, kraus
n. an upright piece with another
athwart
adj. disagreeable

CROUP kroop
n. a kind of illness
n. part of a horse's rump

CROW krō
n. a kind of bird
v. to cry like a rooster
v. to boast

CROWD kroud
n. a large number
n. an ancient musical instrument

CROWN kroun
n. symbolic or ornamental headgear
n. the top or highest part of anything

CRUEL kroo'əl
adj. unkind, severe

CREWEL
n. a worsted yarn used in embroidery

CRUISE krooz
n. a trip by sea

CREWS
n. sailors

CRUST krust
n. the outer part of bread
n. nerve, gall

CRY krī
v. to weep
v. to call out, shout

CUBE kūb
n. a solid with six equal sides
v. to tenderize meat

CUE kū
n. a hint
n. a pool or billiards stick

Q
n. seventeenth letter of the English
alphabet

QUEUE
n. a line of people
n. a pigtail

CUFF kuf
n. the edge of a sleeve
v. to strike

CULTIVATE kul'ti vāt
v. to prepare land, till
v. to seek friendship of a person

CULTURE kul'tūr
n. a stage of civilization
n. a group of tissues or cells for
laboratory study

CURB kerb
n. a raised paving
n. part of a bit for a horse
v. to restrain

CURIOUS kū'rē əs
adj. inquiring
adj. odd, strange

CURL kerl
n. a ringlet
v. to play the game of curling

CURRENCY ku'rən sē
n. money
n. fashion

CURRENT ku'rənt
n. flow, as of a stream
adj. prevalent

CURRANT
n. a kind of berry

CURRY ku'rē
n. a spiced food
v. to rub a horse
v. to beat, thrash

CURSED kerst
v. swore at

CURSED ker'sid
adj. damned, hateful

CURTAIL ker tāl'
v. to cut short
n. a spiral at the lower end of some stair railings

CUSSED kust
v. swore

CUSSED kus'əd
adj. stubborn

CUSTOM kus'təm
n. habit
n. business support
n. duties imposed on imports
adj. made specially

CUT kut
v. to make an incision
v. to snub
n. a straight path
n. a printed picture

CUTTER kut'er
n. one who or that which cuts
n. a kind of sailing vessel

CUTTLE kut'əl
n. cuttlefish or cuttlebone
v. to fold cloth face to face

CYCLE sī'kəl
n. a period of years
n. a bicycle
n. a circle, wheel

CYST sist
n. a sac on the body containing fluid

CIST
n. a tomb or casket

D

DAB dab
n. a small quantity
n. a kind of fish
v. to pat gently

DABBLE dab'əl
v. to work at something from time to time
v. to wet slightly

DACTYL dak'təl
n. a kind of meter in verse
n. a finger or toe

DAILY dā'lē
adj. each day
n. a newspaper

DAINTY dān'tē
adj. of delicate beauty
n. a delicious food

DAISY dā'zē
n. a kind of flower
n. part of a pork shoulder

DALLY dal'ē
v. to waste time
v. to pet

DAM dam
n. a barrier across water
n. an animal mother

DAMN
v. to condemn

DAMASK dam'əsk
n. a kind of fabric
n. pink

DAMMED damd
adj. stopped up
DAMNED
adj. doomed

DAMP damp
adj. moist
v. to discourage

DAMPER dam′pər
n. part of a furnace or stove
adj. more moist

DANE dān
n. a kind of dog
n. (u.c.) a person of Denmark
DEIGN
v. to stoop so far as to grant

DARN därn
n. to mend
interj. expression of a mild curse

DART därt
n. a small pointed stick
v. to move swiftly

DASH dash
v. to strike or throw
v. to make hopeless
n. a small quantity
n. a short race

DATE dāt
n. a period in time
n. a social engagement
n. a kind of fruit

DATED dā′tid
adj. out of date
adj. having or showing a date

DATELINE dāt′līn
n. an imaginary line for computing
the day
DATE-LINE
n. a printed line giving the place of
origin of a news story

DAYS dāz
n. period of time between nights
DAZE
n. confusion, bewilderment

DEACON dē′kən
n. a cleric or church officer
v. to falsify
v. to pack fruit or vegetables with the
best sides up

DEAD ded
adj. no longer living
adj. direct, accurate

DEADBEAT ded′bēt
n. a person who does not pay his
debts
DEAD BEAT
adj. very tired

DEADHEAD ded′hed
n. a person who uses a ticket without
having paid for it
n. a dullard
v. to move an empty car or train

DEADLY ded′lē
adj. fatal
adj. boring
adj. accurate

DEADWOOD ded′wood
n. dead branches or trees
n. something or someone useless

DEAL dēl
v. to act, trade
n. a quantity
n. an agreement
n. a fir or pine wood

DEALER dēl′ər
n. a trader
n. a player who gives out the cards

DEAN dēn
n. a college official
n. a church official
n. a senior member

DEAR dēr
adj. loved
adj. costly
DEER
n. a kind of animal

DECK dek
n. the floor of a ship
n. a set of 52 playing cards
v. to dress or ornament

DECLENSION de klen'shən
n. case and number in grammar
n. a moving downward
n. a deviation
n. a refusal

DECLINE də clīn'
v. to refuse
n. a failing or loss
n. a downward slope

DECORATE dek'ə rāt
v. to furnish or adorn
v. to honor with a badge or medal

DEDICATE ded'ə kāt
v. to set apart for sacred use
v. to inscribe to someone, as a book

DEED dēd
n. an action
n. a kind of legal paper

DEEM dēm
v. to judge, think

DEME
n. a township in Greece

DEFECT dē'fect
n. a flaw

DEFECT de fekt'
v. to desert one's country

DEFER di fer'
v. to put off until later
v. to yield in judgment

DEFERENT def'ər ənt
adj. respectful
adj. flowing away

DEFIANCE di fī'əns
n. bold resistance
n. contempt

DEFILE di fīl'
v. to make dirty
v. to march in line
n. a narrow passage between mountains

DEFLATE di flāt'
v. to release air from something
v. to put down someone's spirits

DEFLOWER di flour'
v. to strip of flowers
v. to ravage, rape

DEGREE di grē'
n. a point in any scale
n. a title from a college or university

DELIVER di liv'ər
v. to carry and give to, surrender
v. to give birth

DEMEAN di mēn'
v. to lower in dignity
v. to behave in a certain manner

DEMESNE
n. an estate, land

DEMON dē'mən
n. a devil

DAEMON
n. a spirit

DEMONSTRATIVE di mon'strə tiv
adj. showing openly
adj. of some pronouns

DEN den
n. an animal's cave
n. a small, quiet room

DENIER di nī'ər
n. one who says that something true is false

DENIER den'yər
n. a unit of weight for fibers

DENS denz
n. caves
n. a tooth or toothlike part

DENSE dens
adj. stupid
adj. crowded

DENT dent
n. a hollow, as from a blow
n. a projection, as a tooth of a gear wheel

DENTAL den'təl
adj. of the teeth

DENTIL
n. a small block under a cornice

DEPEND di pend'
v. to rely upon
v. to hang down
v. to be undetermined

DEPORT di pōrt′
v. to banish
v. to behave one's self in a particular way
DEPOSE di pōs′
v. to remove from office
v. to bear witness
DEPOSIT di poz′ət
v. to set down carefully
n. a heap or mass
v. to place for safekeeping or in payment
DEPRESS di pres′
v. to make gloomy
v. to press down
DEPRESSION di presh′ən
n. a low area
n. gloom
n. a time of inactivity in trade and money markets
DERMA derm′ə
n. skin
n. beef or fowl intestine
DESCANT des′kant
n. a melody
n. a comment
DESCENDANT di send′ənt
n. an offspring
DESCENDENT
adj. going or coming down
DESCENT di sent′
n. the act of going to a lower place
n. lineage
DISSENT
n. disagreement
DESERT dez′ərt
n. an arid region
DESERT di zert′
v. to abandon
n. reward or punishment that is deserved
DESSERT
n. a sweet at the end of a meal
DESIGNS di zīns′
n. sketches
n. an evil scheme

DESTROYER di stroi′ər
n. one who or that which destroys
n. a fast warship
DETACHED di tacht′
adj. separate
adj. aloof, not concerned
DEUCE doos
n. a card with two spots
n. the devil
DEVICE di vīs′
n. an invention
n. a motto
n. a trick
DEVISE di vīz′
v. to plan
v. to transmit property
DEW doo
n. small drops of water
DO
v. to act
DUE
adj. owed
DEXTEROUS dek′stər əs
adj. skillful
adj. right-handed
DIAMOND dī′ə mənd
n. a precious stone
n. a certain shape
n. a baseball field
DIAPER dī′ə per
n. underpants for babies
n. a fabric pattern
DICING dī′sing
v. cubing food
v. playing with certain small cubes
n. a kind of ornamentation
DICKER dik′ər
v. to bargain
n. the number or quantity 10, esp. of hides or skins
DICKEY dik′ē
n. a garment like a bib
n. a small bird

DICTATE dik'tāt
v. to speak aloud something to be written down
n. a rule of action

DICTATOR dik tā'tər
n. a person with great power
n. one who has his words written down

DIE dī
n. a carved metal plate used in engraving
v. to stop living

DYE
v. to color another hue

DIET dī'ət
n. food and drink
n. a national or provincial assembly

DIFFUSE di fūz'
v. to spread out, pour

DIFFUSE di fūs'
adj. wordy

DIG dig
v. to make a hole
n. in archaeology, a site being uncovered

DIGEST di jest'
v. to absorb food

DIGEST dī'jest
n. a shortened written work

DIGIT dij'it
n. a finger or toe
n. any number between one and nine

DILIGENCE dil'i jəns
n. persistence
n. a stage coach

DINK dink
n. a dinghy
n. a small cap, beanie

DIP dip
v. to lower and raise
n. a soft food to go with crackers or chips

DIPPER dip'ər
n. a cuplike container
n. a certain group of stars

DIRE dī'ər
adj. dreadful

DYER
n. one who changes a color

DIRECT di rekt'
v. to guide, address
adj. straight

DIRECTLY di rekt'lē
adv. without delay, at once
adv. soon, shortly

DIRT dert
n. earth
n. filth

DISARM dis arm'
v. to deprive of a weapon
v. to make friendly

DISCHARGE dis charj'
n. performance
v. to get rid of

DISCOUNT dis'kount
n. a sum taken off a price
v. to disregard

DISCREET dis crēt'
adj. prudent

DISCRETE
adj. separate, distinct

DISPOSAL dis pō'səl
n. arrangement
n. a machine that grinds garbage

DISPOSITION dis pō zish'ən
n. mood
n. bestowal, control

DISTAFF dis'taf
n. a tool used in spinning
n. the female sex

DISTEMPER dis temp'ər
n. a disease of dogs
n. a method of painting

DITTY dit'ē
n. a short song
n. a bag that holds thread and needles

DIVAN dī'van
n. a sofa
n. a committee in the Middle East
n. a collection of certain poems

DIVE dīv
n. a plunge into water
n. a sordid place

DIVERS dī'verz
n. plungers
adj. several

DIVIDE di vīd'
v. to separate into parts
n. high land where water spills on
both sides

DIVIDEND div'i dend
n. a number used in arithmetic
n. an extra award
n. a sum of money paid from earnings

DIVINE di vīn'
v. to find a source of underground
water
adj. holy, sacred

DIVISION di vi'zhun
n. separation
n. a military or naval unit

DO doo
v. to act, perform

DO dō
n. the first note in the musical scale

DOE
n. a female deer or rabbit

DOUGH
n. a paste for bread or cake

DOCK dok
n. a wharf
n. a kind of weed

n. in British courtrooms, the place
where the prisoner sits
v. to cut off the end of an animal's tail

DOCTOR dok'tər
n. a physician
v. to falsify

DODDER dod'ər
v. to shake, tremble
n. the love vine

DODGER doj'ər
n. a shifty person
n. a handbill

DOES duz
v. acts, finishes

DOES dōz
n. female deer or rabbits

DOZE
v. to nap
v. to move earth with a bulldozer

DOG dog
n. a kind of animal
n. a kind of tool
v. to follow with persistence

DOGGY dog'ē
n. a puppy
adj. showy

DOLLY dol'ē
n. a kind of toy
n. a small locomotive
n. a platform for a camera

DOLMAN dol'mən
n. a kind of sleeve

DOLMEN
n. a kind of old gravesite

DOLPHIN dol'fin
n. a kind of marine animal
n. a fender on a tugboat

DOMINO dom'i nō
n. a flat, dotted piece used in a game
n. a kind of mask

DON don
v. to dress in
n. a man of great importance

DONE dun
adj. finished

DUN
n. a dull, grayish-brown color
n. a demand for payment

DOPE dōp
n. a fixative
n. a narcotic
n. a foolish person

DORY dōr'ē
n. a kind of boat
n. a kind of fish

DOT dot
n. a speck
n. a dowry

DOTTY dot'ē
adj. dotted
adj. crazy, eccentric

DOUBLE dub'əl
adj. twice as much
adj. insincere
n. a counterpart
v. to fold

DOUBLET dub'let
n. a kind of jacket
n. a pair of like things, couple

DOUBTER dout'ər
n. one who is not sure

DOUTER
n. a kind of candle snuffer

DOVE duv
n. a kind of bird

DOVE dōv
v. did dive

DOWDY dou'dē
adj. shabby
n. a kind of pudding: *pandowdy*

DOWN doun
adv. not up
n. soft feathers
n. open, rolling grassy country

DOWNCAST doun'kast
adj. sad
n. a downward look
v. to ruin

DOWNFALL doun'faul
n. ruin
n. a sudden rain or snow fall

DOWNGRADE doun'grād
n. a downward slope
v. to denigrate

DOWRY dou'rē
n. the money a woman brings to her marriage
n. a natural gift or talent

DRAB drab
n. a dull gray
n. an untidy woman

DRAFT draft
n. a current of air
n. a sketch
n. a way of choosing people for military service
v. to pull

DRAUGHT
n. a drink, dose

DRAG drag
v. to pull
v. to level and smooth land

DRAIN drān
n. a pipe that lets water run off
v. to exhaust

DRAKE drāk
n. a male duck
n. a small cannon of the 17th century

DRAPE drāp
v. to adorn with cloth
v. to let fall carelessly

DRAW drau
v. to sketch
v. to pull
v. to suck in

DRAWERS drau'ərz
n. underpants
n. those who pull or sketch
n. topless, sliding containers in furniture

DRAWING drau'ing
n. a sketch, design
n. a lottery

DRAWN draun
v. was sketched
adj. tense, haggard

DREAM drēm
n. a vision during sleep
n. hope, aim

DREARY drē'rē
adj. sad
adj. tiresome, boring

DREDGE drej
n. a machine that scoops up earth
v. to sprinkle food with flour

DRESS dres
v. to put on clothing
v. to prepare meat for cooking
DRESSER dres′ər
n. one who helps someone dress
n. a kind of cabinet, bureau
DRESSING dres′ing
n. stuffing for meat, poultry, or fish
n. a sauce
n. a bandage
v. becoming clad
DRIFT drift
n. pressure
n. a snowdrift
n. meaning, intent
n. course along which something moves
DRILL dril
n. a tool for boring holes
n. a small furrow for seeds
n. a kind of fabric
n. a kind of baboon
n. strict training, as in school
DRIVE drīv
n. force
v. to direct, as a car
DRIVER drī′vər
n. one who forces or conducts
n. a kind of golf club
n. a chauffeur
DRONE drōn
n. a male bee
n. a monotonous sound
DROP drop
n. a small quantity of liquid
v. to let fall
DROPPER drop′ər
n. a kind of glass tube for medicine
n. a kind of dog
DROVE drōv
v. did drive
n. a herd, flock
DRUG drug
n. a medicine
n. a narcotic
n. a surfeit

DRUM drum
n. a hollow musical instrument
n. part of the ear
v. to dismiss in disgrace
DRY drī
adj. not wet
adj. dull
adj. matter-of-fact
DUAL doo′əl
adj. of two
DUEL
n. a contest between two
DUB dub
v. to name
v. to add sound to film
DUCK duk
n. a kind of fabric
n. a kind of bird
v. to avoid
v. to stoop momentarily
DUCT dukt
n. a tube
DUCKED
v. avoided
DUE dū
adj. owed
adj. expected to arrive
n. regular payment to a group; debt
DUFF duf
n. organic matter on the floor of a forest
n. a stiff flour pudding
DUG dug
v. did dig
n. the nipple of a female mammal
DULL dul
adj. not shiny
adj. not sharp
adj. not clever
DUMMY dum′ē
n. a copy
n. one who has nothing to say
DUMP dump
n. a place for garbage or trash
n. a place where ammunition is stored
v. to let fall in a mass

43

DUMPY dum'pē
adj. sulky, dejected
adj. short and squat

DUSK dusk
n. late afternoon
adj. dark

E

E'S ēz
n. more than one of the fifth letter of the English alphabet

EASE
n. comfort

EAR ēr
n. the organ of hearing
n. part of some plants that bear fruit

EARLY er'lē
adj. back in time
adj. ahead of time

EARN ern
v. to get in return for service
URN
n. a large vase
n. part of a moss

EARNEST ern'əst
adj. serious
n. a pledge

EARTHBOUND erth'bound
adj. attached to the earth
adj. headed for the earth

EARTHLY erth'lē
adj. of a certain planet
adj. of worldly, not spiritual matters

EASTER ēst'ər
n. a wind from the East
n. (u.c.) a Christian festival

EAT ēt
v. to chew and swallow food
v. to corrode

EBONY eb'ə nē
n. a deep black
n. a kind of wood

ECCENTRIC ek sen'trək
adj. odd, unusual
adj. not in the center

ECLIPSE i klips'
n. the loss of light of the sun from the moon's shadow
v. to surpass

ECONOMY i kon'ə mē
n. thrift
n. wealth

EFFECTS i feks'
n. personal property, goods
v. brings about, makes happen

EGG eg
n. a round body produced by females
v. to urge

ELDER el'dər
n. an older person
adj. older
n. a kind of tree or shrub

ELECTRIC i lek'trik
adj. pertaining to electricity
adj. exciting

ELEVATOR el'ə vā'tər
n. a machine that lifts up and down
n. a place for storage of grain

ELICIT i lis'it
v. to evoke
ILLICIT
adj. unlawful

EMBALM em baum'
v. to treat a corpse so as to preserve it
v. to impart a balmy fragrance

EMBARK em bärk'
v. to board a ship
v. to invest in an enterprise

EMBRACE em brās'
v. to circle with one's arms
v. to attempt to influence a judge or jury

EMERGE i merj'
v. to come forth

IMMERGE
v. to plunge

EMERGENT i mer'jent
adj. coming into view
adj. urgent, needing action

EMPIRE em'pīr
n. vast regions under one sovereign or government

EMPIRE om'pēr
adj. of the furniture or art of France, 1804–15

EMPTY em'tē
adj. containing nothing
adj. delusive, vain

ENGAGED en gājd'
adj. busy
adj. pledged to be married

ENOUGH i nuf'
adv. adequately
adv. tolerably
adv. fully

ENROLL en rōl'
v. to place upon a list
v. to wrap up

ENTAIL en tāl'
v. to cause or involve by necessity
v. to impose as a burden
v. to limit inheritance to specified heirs

ENTER en'tər
v. to come or go in
v. to record

ENTERPRISE en'tər prīz'
adj. boldness, energy
n. a business firm

ENTERTAIN en'tər tān'
v. to amuse
v. to consider

ENTRANCE en'trans
n. a doorway

ENTRANCE en trans'
v. to fill with delight

ENTREE än trā'
n. access
n. a dinner dish served before the main course

ENTRY en'trē
n. a place of ingress, as a vestibule
n. a written record

ENVOY en'voi
n. a diplomatic agent
n. a part of some poems

EPIC ep'ək
n. a certain form of poetry

EPOCH
n. a particular period of time

EQUITY ek'wi tē
n. fairness
n. the interest of the owner of common stock in a corporation

ERECT i rekt'
v. to establish, found
adj. upright

ERUPT i rupt'
v. to burst forth

IRRUPT
v. to intrude with force

ESSAY es'ā
n. a short prose writing
v. to try, attempt

ESSENCE es'ens
n. the basic nature of things
n. a perfume

ESTABLISH es tab'lish
v. to build, found
v. to prove

ESTATE es tāt'
n. landed property
n. a period of life

EVE ēv
n. the day before a holiday
n. (u.c.) wife of Adam

EAVE
n. the lower edge of a roof

EVEN ē'ven
adj. level, flat
adv. still, yet

EVER ev'ər
adv. always
adv. at any time: *Did you ever ski?*

EVERY ev'rē
adj. each
adv. all possible: *every prospect of success*

EWE ū
n. a female sheep

U
n. twenty-first letter of the English alphabet

YEW
n. a kind of tree or shrub

YOU
pro. second-person singular or plural

EWER ū'ər
n. a pitcher for liquids

YOU'RE
v. you are

EXACT eg zakt'
adj. correct
v. to demand

EXCHANGE eks chānj'
v. to trade one object for another
n. a central office, as a telephone exchange

EXCISE ek'sīz
n. a kind of tax
v. to cut out or off

EXCRETION eks krē'shən
n. waste matter, as sweat or urine
n. an abnormal growth

EXCUSE eks kūs'
n. an explanation

EXCUSE eks kūz'
v. to pardon

EXECUTE eks'ē kūt
v. to accomplish
v. to put to death according to law

EXHAUST ek zaust'
v. to drain of strength or energy
n. the escape of steam or gas

EXPLOIT ek'sploit
n. a notable deed, feat

EXPLOIT ek sploit'
v. to use selfishly

EXPRESS ek spres'
v. to put a thought into words
adj. quick
adj. special, definite

EXTEND ek stend'
v. to stretch out
v. to offer, give

EXTRACT eks trakt'
v. to pull out
v. to reduce written matter
v. to distill

EYE ī
n. the organ of sight

I
pro. myself

EYED īd
v. looked at

I'D
v. I did or I had

F

FABLE fā'bəl
n. a short story, often about animals, with a moral
n. a falsehood, lie

FABRIC fab'rik
n. a cloth
n. a building

FABRICATE fab′ri kāt
v. to make
v. to tell a lie

FACE fās
n. the front part of the head
n. good reputation

FACET fas′it
n. a surface of a gem
n. an aspect, phase

FACILE fas′il
adj. moving with ease
adj. agreeable

FACING fās′ing
v. looking at
n. an outer layer

FACTOR fak′tər
n. an element
n. a gene
n. a steward

FACULTY fak′əl tē
n. ability
n. the teaching body of a school

FADE fād
v. to lose brightness of color
v. to lose strength or health

FAG fag
v. to tire by labor
n. the last part of something

FAIL fāl
v. to fall short of success
v. to disappoint
v. to lose strength, die away

FAINT fānt
adj. not strong

FEINT
n. a trick to deceive

FAIR fair
adj. free from bias
adj. not dark
n. a carnival

FARE
n. the price of a ticket
n. food

FAKE fāk
n. fraud, imposter
v. to coil a rope

FAKER fā′kər
n. one who deceives

FAKIR
n. a Muslim or Hindu monk

FALL faul
n. autumn
v. to drop down

FALLOW fa′lō
adj. unplowed
n. light brown

FAN fan
n. an admirer
v. to force an air current

FANCY fan′sē
n. gay imagination
n. the breeding of animals to develop points of excellence

FANTAIL fan′tāl
n. a kind of pigeon
n. the rounded stern of some ships

FARROW fa′rō
n. a litter of pigs
adj. (of a cow) not pregnant

FARO
n. a gambling game

FASCINATOR fas′in ā tər
n. one who charms or delights
n. a kind of scarf

FASHION fash′ən
n. style, fad
v. to make

FAST fast
adj. quick
adj. held in place
v. to stop eating
n. a chain or rope for a vessel

FAT fat
n. grease, oil
adj. not thin

FATE fāt
n. one's future
n. destiny

FETE
n. a holiday
n. a party

FATED fā'təd
adj. doomed
FETED fā'təd, fe'təd
v. entertained with a feast
FETID fē'təd
adj. stinking

FATHOM fath'um
n. a unit of length equal to six feet
v. to understand thoroughly

FATIGUES fa tēgz'
v. exhausts, tires
n. an informal military uniform

FAULT fault
n. a defect, flaw, mistake
n. a break in a long mass of rock

FAVOR fā'vər
n. a kind act, good will
n. a gift

FAWN faun
n. a young deer
v. to seek notice by servile demeanor
FAUN
n. an ancient rural deity

FAY fā
n. a fairy
v. to fit, as timbers in shipbuilding

FAZE fāz
v. to daunt
PHASE
n. form, shape
n. a stage in development

FEAT fēt
n. a bold act
FEET
n. parts of the body
FEATHER feth'ər
n. part of a bird's body
n. species, character
v. a kind of oar stroke in rowing

FEATURE fē'chər
n. a part of the face
n. a special attraction

FEDERAL fed'ər əl
adj. of a union of states
adj. of U.S. arts and crafts, 1790–1830

FEIGN fān
v. to pretend
FAIN
adv. willing
FANE
n. a church

FELL fel
v. did fall
v. to cut down
adj. fierce, cruel
n. the skin or hide of an animal

FELLOW fel'ō
n. a man or boy
n. one of a pair; a mate

FELON fel'ən
n. one who has committed a crime
n. a kind of soreness of the finger or toe

FELT felt
n. a kind of fabric
v. touched, experienced

FENCE fens
n. a barrier around a field or yard
v. to act the sport of dueling with swords

FENDER fen'dər
n. part of an automobile
n. a guard in front of a fireplace

FERAL fe'rəl
adj. existing in a natural state; wild
adj. causing death, gloomy

FERMENT fer'ment
n. state of unrest
FERMENT fer ment'
v. to excite
v. to change so as to give off gas, as by yeast

FERN fern
n. a kind of plant
FIRN
n. glacial ice

FERRET fe'rit
v. to search out, torment
n. a kind of animal
n. a narrow tape or ribbon

FERRULE fe'rool
n. a metal sleeve for too...
FERULE
n. a piece of wood used to slap children

FESTOON fe stoon'
n. a garland
n. part of the gums

FETCH fech
v. to get
n. a ghost of a living person

FEUD fūd
n. a bitter quarrel between families
n. an estate in inheritance, fee simple

FEUDAL fūd'əl
adj. of a bitter quarrel between families
adj. of the Middle Ages

FEW fū
adj. not many
PHEW
interj. expression of disgust or surprise

FIANCÉ fē än sā'
n. an engaged man
FIANCÉE
n. an engaged woman

FIDDLE fid'əl
n. a violin
v. to waste time

FIELD fēld
n. a piece of open land
n. an area of special interest or activity

FIGURE fig'ūr
n. a number
n. form or shape
n. an important person

FILE fīl
n. a kind of cabinet
n. a tool for smoothing surfaces
FILE fi lā'
n. sassafras leaves used in soups or gumbos
FILLET
n. a boneless cut of meat or fish

FILM film
n. a thin layer or sheet
n. material used in photography

FILTER fil'tər
n. something that separates solids and liquids
PHILTER
n. a magic drink

FIN fin
n. part of a fish
FINN
n. (u.c.) a native of Finland

FIND fīnd
v. to come upon by chance
FINED
v. assessed a penalty

FINE fīn
n. a levy
adj. of high quality
FINE fēn
n. ordinary French brandy
FINE fē'nä
n. the end of a repeated section of music

FINERY fī'nər ē
n. showy dress
n. hearth used in metalwork; refinery

FINING fīn'ing
n. a process used in glassmaking
n. a process used in clarifying wine

FINISH fin'ish
n. the surface coating of wood or metal
v. to complete, end

FINISHED fin'isht
adj. ended
adj. skilled

FIR fer
n. a kind of tree
FUR
n. bodily covering of some animals

FIRE fīr
n. a burning mass
v. to shoot at
v. to dismiss from a job

FIRM ferm
n. a business organization
adj. not soft

FISH fish
n. a water animal
v. to try to find out indirectly

FISHER fish'ər
n. one who or that which tries to catch fish

FISSURE
n. a narrow opening, cleft

FISHY fish'ē
adj. like a fish
adj. not likely

FIST fist
n. the doubled up hand
n. cur, mutt, feist

FIT fit
v. to adjust to the right shape
adj. proper
n. a sudden attack of a disease

FIX fiks
v. to make firm or stable
v. to set, plant
v. to establish
n. dilemma, plight

FLAG flag
n. cloth used as a symbol
n. a kind of flower
n. a flagstone
v. to droop
v. to wave vigorously

FLAIR flair
n. talent, smartness

FLARE
n. a kind of light

FLAME flām
n. a burning gas or vapor
n. strong emotion
n. red-orange

FLAPPER flap'ər
n. a flap
n. a young woman of the 1920s
n. a young bird

FLASH flash
n. a brief burst of light
n. a brief moment

FLASHING flash'ing
n. pieces of protective metal
n. act of creating an artificial flood
adj. blinking

FLAT flat
adj. level
adj. downright, positive
n. an apartment

FLATTER flat'ər
v. to praise too much
adj. more level
n. a kind of tool

FLAVOR flā'vər
n. a taste in the mouth
n. a special quality, essence

FLAW flau
n. defect, fault
n. a short spell of rough weather

FLAXEN flaks'ən
adj. made of a flax
adj. of a yellowish color

FLEA flē
n. a kind of insect

FLEE
v. to run away

FLEET flēt
n. a number of ships
adj. quick

FLESH flesh
n. skin

FLÈCHE
n. a steeple
n. an attack in fencing

FLICK flik
n. a sudden light blow
n. a movie

FLICKER flik'ər
n. a brief occurrence
v. to wave to and fro
n. a kind of bird

FLIER flī'ər
n. an aviator
n. a handbill

FLYER
n. a machine used in textile making

GARDNER-WEBB COLLEGE LIBRARY
P. O. Box 836
Boiling Springs, N.C. 28017

FLIGHT flīt
n. act of flying
n. act of fleeing

FLINCH flinch
v. to draw back, wince
v. to strip off blubber

FLIP flip
v. to turn over with a rapid gesture
adj. pert, smart
n. a kind of drink

FLIRT flert
v. to trifle or toy
v. to move with a jerk

FLITCH flich
n. the side of a hog, salted and cured
n. a thin piece of wood
n. a halibut steak

FLITTER flit'ər
v. to flutter
n. fine metallic fragments

FLOAT flōt
v. to suspend on the surface of liquid
n. a flat truck decorated for a parade

FLOCK flok
n. a group of like animals
n. a lock or tuft of wool, cotton, or hair

FLOC
n. a tuftlike mass, as in chemistry

FLOCKS floks
n. groups of like animals

PHLOX
n. a kind of flower

FLOOR flōr
n. the base of a room

FLOWER
n. one who or that which flows

FLORID flo'rəd
adj. reddish
adj. flowery, showy

FLOUNCE flouns
n. an impatient body movement
n. a wide ruffle on a skirt

FLOUNDER floun'dər
v. to struggle helplessly
n. a kind of fish

FLOUR flour
n. the ground meal of grain, esp. wheat

FLOWER
n. a blossom

FLOWER flō'ər
n. one who or that which flows

FLOURISH flur'ish
v. to thrive, prosper
n. a trumpet call

FLOW flō
v. to move in a stream

FLOE
n. a sheet of floating ice

FLOWN flōn
v. did fly
adj. decorated with colors fluidly blended

FLU floo
n. a kind of sickness

FLEW
v. did fly

FLUE
n. a duct for smoke
n. fluff
n. a fishing net
v. to splay

FLUFF fluf
n. a light, downy mass
v. to make a mistake in giving a speech

FLUKE flook
n. a stroke of good luck
n. a kind of fish
n. part of an anchor
n. part of a whale

FLUSH flush
n. a rosy glow
v. to flood with water
n. a set of cards of one suit
adj. even or level
v. to cause birds to fly up

FLUTE floot
n. a kind of musical instrument
n. a groove or furrow in decoration

FLY flī
n. a kind of insect
v. to move through the air
n. material over a zipper
n. part of a tent

FOB fob
n. a chain on a watch
v. to cheat

FODDER fod'ər
n. plants used to feed farm animals
n. people thought to be of little value

FOG fog
n. a kind of cloud
n. long grass left over the winter

FOIL foil
n. a thin strip of metal
n. a fencing weapon
v. to defeat

FOLD fōld
n. a flock of sheep
v. to bend something upon itself

FOALED
v. gave birth to a colt

FOLLOW fol'ō
v. to come after
v. to obey

FOLLY fol'ē
n. a foolish action or thought
n. a whimsical building

FOND fond
adj. loving, tender
n. a background, esp. of lace

FONT font
n. article that holds water for baptism
n. an assortment of type of one size

FOOL fool
n. a silly or stupid person
v. to trick, deceive

FOOT fŏŏt
n. a part of the body
n. 12 inches

FOR fōr
prep. with the purpose of

FORE
adj. first in place or time

FOUR
n. a number

FOREARM fōr'arm
n. part of the arm
v. to equip with weapons beforehand

FOREBEAR fōr'bair
n. an ancestor

FORBEAR fōr bair'
v. to keep back

FOREGO fōr'gō
v. to go before
v. to do without

FORELOCK fōr'lok
n. a tuft of hair above the forehead
n. a pin for a bolt

FORGE fōrj
n. a hearth in which metal is heated
v. to go ahead with difficulty

FORK fork
n. a tool for lifting
n. a branch of a stream or road

FORM form
n. the shape of a thing or person
v. to teach

FORMER for'mər
adj. earlier
n. one who or that which forms

FORNICATE for'ni kāt'
v. to commit illegal sexual congress
adj. (in biology) arched or vaulted in form

FORT fōrt
n. a strong place for troops

FORTE
n. activity in which one excels

FORTE for'tā
n. a loud passage in music

FORTH fōrth
adv. out, away

FOURTH
adj. next after third

FORWARD for'wərd
adj. ahead
n. a member of a basketball team

FOREWORD
n. preface

FOUL foul
adj. dirty, horrid
adj. unfair

FOWL
n. a domesticated bird

FOUND found
v. did find
v. to set up, begin something
v. to melt and pour into a mold

FOUNDER found'ər
n. one who starts something, as a company
v. to wreck, fail, sink

FOX foks
n. a kind of animal
v. to deceive, cheat

FRACTION frak'shən
n. part of a whole number
n. act of breaking; a break

FRAIL frāl
adj. weak, feeble
n. a kind of basket

FRAME frām
n. an enclosure
n. the human body
v. to make, plan

FRANK frank
adj. open, sincere
v. to mail free of charge

FRANC
n. a coin of France or Switzerland

FRAYS frāz
n. noisy battles
v. ravels

PHRASE
n. a unit in a sentence

FREAK frēk
n. abnormal person or thing; a monster
n. a sudden, apparently causeless change of events
v. to fleck or streak

FREEZE frēz
v. to make icy

FREES
v. sets at liberty

FRIEZE
n. a long wall decoration
n. a heavy woolen cloth

FRESH fresh
adj. newly made or obtained
adj. rude, sassy

FRET fret
v. to worry
n. a kind of design
n. part of a stringed musical instrument

FRIAR frī'ər
n. a monk

FRYER
n. a young chicken

FRITTER frit'ər
v. to waste
n. a small, fried piece of food

FRIZZLE friz'əl
n. a short curl of hair
v. to make a noise in frying

FROG frog
n. a kind of animal
n. a button and loop for clothing
n. a holder used in flower arrangements

FRONT frunt
n. the foremost part
n. a group of people with a special idea

FROST frost, fraust
v. to begin to freeze
v. to cover a cake with a sweet icing

FRUITION froo ish'ən
n. enjoyment
n. state of bearing fruit

FRY frī
v. to cook in fat
n. the young offspring of some animals

FUDGE fuj
n. a kind of candy
v. to talk nonsense

FULL fŏŏl
adj. complete, filled
v. to cleanse and thicken cloth

FUMES fūmz
n. odors from smoke or gas
v. shows irritation

FUNNY fun'ē
adj. comic, amusing
n. a kind of light skiff

FURS ferz
n. animal coats

FURZE
n. a kind of plant

FUSE fūz
n. a circuit breaker
v. to blend
n. a device to detonate an explosive charge

FUSIL fū'zəl
n. a light musket
adj. fused

G

G jē
n. seventh letter of the English alphabet

GEE
interj. (to a horse): *get up!*
interj. gosh!

GAD gad
v. to move aimlessly
n. a goad for cattle

GAFF gaf
n. a hook used in fishing

GAFFE
n. a social error

GAG gag
n. a joke
n. a kind of bandage over the mouth
n. a kind of fish

GAIN gān
v. to win, get
n. a notch in wood

GAINE
n. a kind of tapering pillar

GAIT gāt
n. a way of walking

GATE
n. a doorlike opening

GALL gaul
n. nerve
n. something bitter
n. a sick growth of plants
v. to chafe, rub

GAUL
n. (u.c.) part of the old Roman empire

GALLANT gal'ənt
adj. brave
adj. polite and attentive to women

GALLERY gal'ər ē
n. a long room or porch
n. a railing on a table

GALLEY gal'ē
n. a kitchen on a boat
n. a long rowed boat

GAMBLE gam'bəl
v. to bet

GAMBOL
v. to skip about

GAME gām
n. an amusement or pastime
n. some wild animals hunted for food

GAMMON gam'ən
n. the game of backgammon
n. a smoked ham
v. to fasten a bowsprit to the stern of a ship

GAPES gāps
v. stares with open mouth
n. a disease of some birds

GARNET gär'nət
n. a kind of gem
n. a gun tackle

GARNISH gär'nish
v. to adorn, decorate
v. to attach, as money due

GAS gas
n. a substance that is neither solid nor liquid
n. gasoline
n. empty talk

GASH gash
n. a long, deep cut
adj. wise
adj. neat

GAT gat
n. a pistol or revolver
n. a passage that goes inland from the shore

GATHER gath'ər
v. to bring together, pluck
v. to increase, as speed in a car

GAUGE gāj
v. to estimate

GAGE
n. a pledge or challenge
n. a kind of plum

GAUNTLET gaunt'lət
n. a kind of glove
n. an attack from two sides

GAVEL gav'el
n. a small mallet
n. feudal rent

GEAR gēr
n. part of a machine
n. possessions, as the clothing or equipment of sailors, huntsmen

GEMS jemz
n. precious stones
n. a chamois, gemsbok

GENERAL jen'ər əl
n. a military rank
adj. common to most
adj. not specific

GENES jēnz
n. units of heredity

JEANS
n. sturdy slacks

GENET jen'it
n. a kind of animal like the civet
n. a female donkey

GENIAL jē'nyəl
adj. friendly, cheerful

GENIAL je nī'əl
adj. of the chin

GERMAN jer'mən
adj. having the same mother and father
adj. (u.c.) of Germany

GET get
v. to receive, acquire
v. to cause to do, move
v. to beget (of animals)

GIB gib
n. a kind of metal strip
n. a male cat

GIBBET jib'it
v. to put to death by hanging
v. to hold up to public scorn

GIBE jīb
v. to mock

JIBE
v. to shift, as a boat before the wind
v. to agree

GIFT gift
n. a present
n. a talent

GIG gig
n. a light rowboat
n. a kind of fishhook
n. a demerit
n. a kind of one-horse carriage

GIGOT jig'ət
n. a kind of sleeve
n. a leg of lamb or mutton

GILD gild
v. to coat with gold

GUILD
n. an organization of persons with like interests

GILL gil
n. a breathing organ of fish

GILL jill
n. one-fourth of a pint

GILT gilt
adj. golden
n. a young female swine

GUILT
n. remorse

GIN jin
n. a kind of liquor
n. a card game
n. a machine used in seeding cotton
JINN
n. a magical spirit

GINGER jin'jər
n. a kind of spice
n. pep
n. a reddish brown

GIRD gerd
v. to bind with a belt
v. to jeer

GIRT gert
n. a heavy beam supporting rafters
adj. tightly moored

GIVE giv
v. to present, bestow
v. to yield

GLANCE glans
v. to look at or away from quickly
v. to bounce off at an angle
n. a shine on metal

GLANDS glanz
n. secreting organs or cells
n. lantern rings
GLANS
n. the head of the penis or clitoris

GLARE glair
n. a bright light
n. an angry stare
n. a smooth surface, as of ice
GLAIR
n. an egg white

GLAZE glāz
v. to fill or furnish with glass
v. to cover food with sugar

GLEE glē
n. joy, gaiety
n. a kind of song

GLIDE glīd
v. to move along smoothly
n. a semivowel

GLOBE glōb
n. a sphere
n. the earth

GLOOM gloom
n. darkness, shade
n. sadness, despondency
v. to scowl
GLUME
n. a bract of grass

GLOSS glos
n. a surface shine
v. to explain away

GLOZE glōz
v. to explain away
v. to shine

GLUTEN gloot'ən
n. an elastic protein substance in flour
n. flour low in starch

GLUTTON glut'ən
n. one who eats a lot
n. a kind of weasel

GNARL narl
n. a knot on a tree
v. to twist
v. to growl

GNOME nōm
n. an imaginary elf
n. an aphorism
NOME
n. (u.c.) a city in Alaska

GO gō
v. to move to or from something
v. to have a place

GOB gob
n. a mass or lump
n. a sailor

GOBBLE gob'əl
n. the cry of a male turkey
v. to eat hastily

GONDOLA gon'dəl ə
n. a boat used mostly in Venice
n. the basket under a balloon

GOOSE goos
n. a kind of bird
n. a silly person
n. a tailor's iron

GORE gōr
n. blood that is shed
v. to pierce with the horns
n. a triangular piece of cloth

GORGE gōrj
n. a small canyon
v. to stuff with food

GORILLA gə ril′ə
n. a large ape

GUERRILLA
n. a soldier who goes on surprise raids

GOTHIC goth′ək
adj. of art and architecture, from 12th to 16th centuries
adj. rude, gloomy

GOURD gōrd
n. the fruit of certain plants

GORED
v. was pierced, as by a bull

GOUT gout
n. a kind of disease
n. a drop or splash

GOÛT goo
n. taste, style

GOVERNOR guv′ər nər
n. the head of a state
n. a machine to maintain speed

GRAB grab
v. to seize, snatch
n. a kind of oriental ship

GRACE grās
n. beauty of motion
n. God's favor and love
n. a short prayer

GRADE grād
n. a class in school
n. a slope

GRAYED
v. became gray, as hair or skin

GRADUS grā′dəs
n. a work of musical exercises
n. a book about poetic meters

GRAFT graft
n. a transplant
n. dishonesty

GRAIN grān
n. a small, hard seed
n. a pattern in wood surfaces

GRAM gram
n. a metric unit of mass
n. the chickpea

GRAND grand
adj. large, stately
n. a kind of piano
pref. one generation more remote

GRANT grant
n. an award
v. to give, bestow
v. to admit, concede

GRAPES grāps
n. some fruits that grow in clusters
n. a disease of cattle and horses

GRAPHIC gra′fik
adj. vivid, clear
adj. written or drawn

GRASP grasp
v. to clutch, hold firmly
n. power to understand

GRATE grāt
n. a basket that holds wood or coal
v. to rub together, irritate

GREAT
adj. large

GRATING grāt′ing
n. a frame of bars that admits air
adj. irritating, rasping

GRAVE grāv
n. a place for a dead body
adj. solemn
v. to clean the bottom of a vessel
v. to engrave, impress

GRAVEL grav′əl
n. small stones
adj. harsh and grating

GRAVITY grav′i tē
n. a force that pulls objects down to the earth
n. seriousness

GRAY grā
n. a color between black and white
adj. old, ancient

GRAZE grāz
v. to feed on grass
v. to rub lightly, scrape the skin

GRAYS
v. becomes old

GREASE grēs
n. melted fat

GREASE grēz
v. to smear with fat or oil

GREECE grēs
n. (u.c.) a Balkan country

GREEN grēn
n. a color
n. one of several vegetables
adj. not ripe
adj. inexperienced

GRENADINE gren′ə dēn
n. a kind of fabric
n. a kind of syrup

GRIFFIN grif′ən
n. an eagle-lion mythical beast

GRIFFON
n. a kind of dog

GRILL gril
n. a utensil for broiling
v. to torment with heat

GRILLE
n. a grating or openwork barrier

GRIN grin
n. a broad smile
v. to separate or part

GRIND grīnd
v. to sharpen, whet
v. to crush
v. to persecute
v. to abrade

GRIP grip
n. a firm grasp
n. a small suitcase
n. a handle

GRIPPE
n. the flu

GRIPE grīp
n. a complaint
n. a kind of pain
v. to seize and hold firmly

GRISLY griz′lē
adj. horrible, grim

GRIZZLY
adj. grayish, as a grizzly bear
n. a device for screening ore

GRIT grit
n. small, sharp dust particles
n. courage, pluck

GROAN grōn
n. a low cry of pain

GROWN
adj. adult

GROOM groom
n. one who tends horses
n. a bridegroom

GRUME
n. viscous blood

GROOVE groov
n. a long, narrow cut
n. a fixed routine

GROSS grōs
adj. bad-mannered
adj. huge
adj. without deductions
n. 12 dozen things

GROUND ground
n. dry land
n. foundation, reason
v. reduced to dust by grinding

GROUSE grous
n. a kind of bird
v. to grumble, complain

GRUB grub
n. larva of some insects
v. to dig, clear land
n. food

GUARANTEE ga′rən tē
v. to promise to make good
GUARANTY
n. a pledge of security

GUEST gest
n. a visitor
GUESSED
v. answered by chance

GUIDE gīd
n. a pilot, escort
GUYED
v. made fun of

GUISE gīz
n. appearance
GUYS
n. boys, men

GULL gul
n. a kind of bird
v. to cheat, trick

GULLET gul′ət
n. the throat
n. a ravine

GUM gum
n. rubber
n. glue
n. a part of the mouth
n. a kind of tree

GUN gun
n. rifle or pistol
v. to increase speed

GUNNEL gun′əl
n. a kind of fish
GUNWALE
n. part of a vessel

GUT gut
n. part of the body
v. to plunder
v. to destroy the interior of

GUTTER gut′ər
n. a channel
n. a place of dirt and immorality

GUY gī
n. boy, man
n. a guide rope
v. to make fun of

H

HABIT hab′it
n. customary use
n. a kind of uniform

HACK hak
v. to cut, chop
v. to cough
n. a taxi
n. artist or writer who works to make money quickly

HACKLE hak′əl
n. a neck feather of some birds
n. a comb for dressing flax
v. to cut roughly

HAG hag
n. an ugly old woman
n. a hagfish

HAGGARD hag′ərd
adj. wild-looking
adj. exhausted-looking
n. an untamed adult hawk

HA-HA hä′hä
interj. expression of laughter
n. a sunken fence

HAIL hāl
n. rain of icy balls
v. to welcome
HALE
adj. free from disease
v. to pull, drag

HAIR hair
n. part of the head or skin
HARE
n. a kind of animal

HALCYON hal′sē ən
n. a mythical bird
adj. calm, joyful
adj. rich

HALL haul
n. a passageway

HAUL
v. to pull, carry

HALT hault
v. to stop
v. to falter, as in speech

HALTER hault'ər
n. part of a harness
n. one who hesitates

HALVE hav
v. to divide into two parts

HAVE
v. to own

HAM ham
n. a kind of meat
n. one who overacts

HAMLET ham'lit
n. a small village
n. a kind of sea bass
n. (u.c.) a Shakespearean character

HAMMER ham'ər
n. a kind of tool
n. part of the middle ear

HAMMOCK ham'ək
n. a kind of hanging bed
n. a knoll; hummock

HAMPER ham'pər
v. to hinder
n. a large basket

HAND hand
n. part of the body
n. a worker

HANDLE hand'dəl
n. a part of something made to be held
v. to manage

HANDMADE hand'mād
adj. not made by a machine

HANDMAID
n. a female attendant

HANDSOME han'səm
adj. good-looking

HANSOM
n. a two-wheeled one-horse carriage

HANG hang
v. to suspend
v. to exhibit pictures
v. to lynch

HANGER hang'ər
n. a frame that holds clothes

HANGAR
n. a shelter for planes

HARBOR här'bər
n. a place of protection for ships
v. to keep in mind

HARD härd
adj. not soft
adj. not easy

HARDY här'dē
adj. sturdy, strong
n. a kind of chisel

HARMONY härm'ə nē
n. agreement
n. pleasing musical tones

HARRIER ha'ri ər
n. one who annoys
n. a kind of hunting dog
n. a kind of hawk
n. a cross-country runner

HARROW ha'rō
n. a kind of farm tool
v. to violate

HARVEST här'vest
v. to gather crops
v. to gain, as a prize

HATCH hach
v. to bring forth young from eggs
n. part of a boat
v. to mark with lines in an engraving

HAUNTING haun'ting
n. visitation
adj. not quickly forgotten

HAW hau
n. a command to a horse
n. the fruit of the hawthorn
v. to hesitate in speech

HAWK hauk
n. a kind of bird
v. to peddle
v. to clear the throat

HAY hā
n. dried forage
n. a kind of country dance

HEY
interj. expression of greeting

HAZARD haz'ərd
n. danger
n. chance

HAZE hāz
n. a smoky mist
v. to play unkind tricks

HAYS
n. various dried plants

HEADWAY hed'wā
n. progress in space
n. headroom

HEAL hēl
v. to make whole or sound

HEEL
n. part of the foot
v. to tilt

HE'LL
v. he will or shall

HEAR hēr
v. to listen

HERE
adv. in this place

HEART härt
n. part of the body

HART
n. a male deer

HEAT hēt
n. hotness
n. a race or contest

HEDGE hej
n. a row of small bushes
v. to stave off making a pledge

HEED hēd
v. to give careful attention to

HE'D
v. he had, he would

HELM helm
n. a wheel or tiller
n. a wind in parts of England
n. a medieval helmet

HELP help
v. to encourage, befriend
v. to serve food

HEM hem
n. a folded edge of cloth
v. to hesitate in speaking

HERD herd
n. a group of animals

HEARD
v. listened

HERMIT her'mət
n. one who lives in seclusion
n. a kind of cookie

HEROIN he'rō in
n. a narcotic

HEROINE
n. a female protagonist

HEW hū
v. to strike with an ax; chop

HUE
n. a tint
n. an outcry

HIDE hīd
n. the pelt of an animal
v. to conceal

HIED
v. sped

HIGH hī
adj. up

HI
interj. hello

HIE
v. to speed

HIM him
pro. that man or boy

HYMN
n. a song of praise

HIND hīnd
n. a female deer
adj. at the back

HINDER hind'ər
v. to delay
HINDER hĭnd'ər
adj. at the rear

HIP hip
n. part of the body
n. the fruit of the rose
interj. hurray!

HIRE hī'ər
v. to employ
HIGHER
adj. further up

HIT hit
v. to deal a blow
v. to collide
v. to agree with
n. a success

HITCH hich
v. to fasten, tie, tether
n. a kind of minnow

HIVES hīvz
n. nests for bees
n. a kind of skin disease

HOAR hôr
n. frost
HOER
n. one who hoes
WHORE
n. a harlot

HOARD hôrd
n. a hidden supply
HORDE
n. a large group
WHORED
v. was a prostitute

HOB hob
n. a shelf in a fireplace
n. an elf

HOBBY hob'ē
n. an interest
n. a toy horse

HOCK hok
n. a joint on the leg of some animals
n. a kind of wine
v. to pawn

HOE hō
n. a kind of tool
HO
interj. expression of laughter

HOG hog
n. a kind of animal
v. to take more than one's share

HOGSHEAD hogz'hed
n. a large cask
HOG'S HEAD
n. head of a hog

HOLD hōld
v. to keep fast
n. cargo space in a ship

HOLE hōl
n. an opening
WHOLE
adj. complete

HOLLOW hol'ō
adj. empty
n. a valley

HOLY hōl'ē
adj. sacred
HOLEY
adj. full of holes
WHOLLY
adv. altogether

HOMELY hōm'lē
adj. not pretty
adj. homelike

HOMER hōm'ər
n. a home run
n. (u.c.) a Greek poet

HOMESPUN hōm'spun
adj. of cloth made at home
adj. simple, rustic

HONEST on'ist
adj. just, truthful
adj. plain, humble

HONESTY on'i stē
n. justice
n. a kind of flower

HONOR on'ər
n. fame, glory
n. integrity

HOOD ho͞od
n. a soft head-cover
n. a gangster

HOOK ho͝ok
n. a curved piece of metal, as a fishhook
n. a punch in boxing

HOOP hoop
n. a large ring

WHOOP hoop, hwoop
n. a cry or shout

HOOT hoot
v. to cry aloud like an owl
n. a trifle

HOP hop
v. to leap on one foot
n. a kind of flowering plant

HOPPER hop'ər
n. one who hops
n. a bin for storage

HORN haurn
n. a growth on the head of some animals
n. a kind of musical instrument

HORROR ho'rər
n. dread, fear
n. hatred

HOSE hōz
n. a tube carrying liquid
n. stocking or sock

HOES
v. works with a hoe

HOST hōst
n. one who has a guest
n. a great number

HOSTEL host'təl
n. a lodging place for young people

HOSTILE
adj. antagonistic

HOT hot
adj. not cold
adj. angry, violent

HOUND hound
n. a kind of dog
v. to harass without respite
n. a kind of brace

HOUR our
n. 60 minutes

OUR
adj. belonging to us

HOUSING hou'zing
n. shelter, dwelling place
n. a cloth covering for a horse

HOWL houl
n. the cry of a dog
n. a joke

HUFF huf
n. temper
v. to puff

HULL hul
n. the husk of a seed
n. the hollow part of a vessel

HUMERUS hū'mər əs
n. a long bone in the arm

HUMOROUS
adj. comic, funny

HUMOR hū'mər
n. a comic quality, wit
n. mood

HUNCH hunch
n. an idea
v. to arch

HURL herl
v. to throw

HERL
n. barbs of a feather

HURTER her'tər
n. a person or thing that causes pain
n. a piece on an axle

HUSBAND huz'bənd
n. a married man
v. to economize

HUSKY hus'kē
adj. big and strong
adj. hoarse, semiwhispered
n. a kind of dog

HYDRA hī'drə
n. a tiny water animal
n. a many-sided problem
n. a mythological serpent

I

I ī
n. the ninth letter of the English alphabet
pro. myself

AY
adv. yes

AYE
adv. yes
adv. ever

EYE
n. organ of sight

ICING ī'sing
n. a sweet covering, as on cakes
n. frozen air or moisture on an aircraft

ID id
n. source of energy of the mind

I'D īd
v. I had, I would

I.D. ī'dē
n. identification

IDIOM id'i əm
n. dialect
n. a colorful phrase

IDLE īd'əl
adj. not active; lazy

IDOL
n. an image worshipped by some

ILIAC il'ē ak
adj. of or pertaining to the small intestine
adj. of or pertaining to an intestinal cramp

ILL il
adj. sick

I'LL īl
v. I will, I shall

ISLE
n. a small island

ILLUMINATE i loo'mə nāt
v. to light up
v. to paint a manuscript

ILLUSION i loo'zhən
n. something that deceives
n. a thin tulle

IMAGE im'ij
n. a likeness
n. an idol

IMPART im pärt'
v. to tell
v. to give

IMPASSABLE im pas'ə bəl
adj. not allowing passage

IMPASSIBLE
adj. incapable of emotion

IMPERIAL im pēr'ē əl
adj. of an empire or emperor
n. a small, pointed beard

IMPERIOUS im pēr'ē əs
adj. arrogant
adj. urgent

IMPORT im pōrt'
v. to bring in goods from abroad

IMPORT im'pōrt
v. to be of importance; matter

IMPOSE im pōz'
v. to demand
v. to intrude

IMPRESS im pres'
v. to affect the mind or feelings
v. to force into public office

IMPRINT im'print
n. a mark made by pressure

IMPRINT im print'
v. to fix firmly in the mind

IN in
adv. within

INN
n. a small hotel

INCARNADINE in kär'nə dīn
adj. pale pink
adj. blood red

INCENSE in'sens
n. perfumed smoke

INCENSE in sens'
v. to make angry

INCITE in sīt'
v. to urge
INSIGHT in'sīt
n. perception

INCLINE in klīn'
v. to slope
v. to have a mental tendency

INCUBOUS in'kū bəs
adj. (of leaves) overlapping
INCUBUS
n. an imaginary evil spirit

INDENT in dent'
v. to set back from a margin
v. to make a dent

INDEX in'deks
n. a list of the contents of a book
n. the forefinger

INDIAN in'di ən
n. (u.c.) an early native of America
n. (u.c.) a native of India

INDICT in dīt'
v. to accuse of wrongdoing
INDITE
v. to compose or write

INDISPOSED in dis pōzd'
adj. slightly ill
adj. unwilling

INDRAWN in'drawn
adj. quiet, thoughtful
adj. with the breath drawn in

INFECT in fekt'
v. to spread germs, poison
v. to influence

INFER in fer'
v. to decide through reason
v. to hint

INFLECT in flekt'
v. to turn from a direct line
v. to modulate the voice or a word

INFUSE in fūz'
v. to inspire
v. to soak (leaves) in a fluid

INFUSIBLE in fū'zə bəl
adj. incapable of being fused
adj. capable of being infused

INNING in'ing
n. a division of a baseball game
n. land reclaimed from the sea

INSPIRE in spīr'
v. to influence, arouse
v. to take in air, inhale

INSTALLMENT in staul'ment
n. a division of a debt or story
n. act of placing in position

INSTANCE in'stəns
n. an example
INSTANTS
n. moments

INSTINCT in'stinkt
n. a natural impulse
INSTINCT in stinkt'
adj. filled with some animating principle

INSTITUTE in'sti tūt
v. to set up, establish
n. part of a university

INTEGRAL in'tə grəl
adj. of a necessary part of the whole
n. entire, the whole

INTENSE in tens'
adj. acute, strong
INTENTS
n. purposes

INTENSION in ten'shən
n. high degree
INTENTION
n. purpose

INTENT in tent'
n. purpose
adj. earnest

INTERCESSION in tər sesh'ən
n. a plea, prayer
INTERSESSION
n. a period between two academic terms

INTEREST in'tər əst
n. concern, curiosity
n. money paid back on a loan

INTERN in'tern
n. a young doctor in a hospital

INTERN in tern'
v. to confine, imprison

INTERSTICE in ter'stis
n. an intervening space
n. an interval of time

INTIMATE in'ti mit
n. a close friend

INTIMATE in'ti māt
v. to hint

INVADE in vād'
v. to enter forcefully as an enemy

INVEIGHED
v. protested strongly

INVALID in'va lid
n. a weak, sick person

INVALID in val'id
adj. without force, void

INVEST in vest'
v. to put money to use
v. to furnish with power or rank

IRIS ī'ris
n. a kind of flower
n. part of the eye

IRON ī'ərn
n. a kind of metal
v. to press clothes

ISSUE is'ū
n. a point in question
n. offspring
v. to distribute

ITS its
pro. belonging to it

IT'S
v. it is

J

J jā
n. tenth letter of the English alphabet

JAY
n. a kind of bird

JACK jak
n. a kind of tool
n. one of the cards in a deck

JACKSTRAWS jak'straus
n. scarecrows
n. a kind of game

JADE jād
n. a variety of stone
n. an old, broken-down horse

JAG jag
n. a state of intoxication
v. to form notches or ragged points

JAM jam
n. fruit preserve
v. to press or squeeze

JAMB
n. part of a frame of an opening

JAPAN jə pan'
n. a kind of black varnish
n. (u.c.) a country

JAR jär
n. a wide-mouthed container
v. to shake
v. to produce a harsh sound

JARGON jär'gən
n. language peculiar to a trade or
discipline
n. a kind of gem, zircon

JAUNDICE jaun'dis
n. a form of illness
v. to distort or prejudice

JAW jau
n. part of the face
n. a machine part or parts that grasp

JEER jēr
v. to sneer, jest
n. a nautical tackle

JELLIED jel'id
adj. of jelly

GELID
adj. cold, icy

JERK jerk
v. to pull quickly
v. to preserve meat in the sun

JERSEY jer'zē
n. a knitted sweater or shirt
n. (u.c.) a British island
n. a breed of cattle

JEST jest
n. a joke
GEST
n. a story or tale
n. deportment, conduct
JET jet
n. a forceful stream of air or liquid
n. a kind of aircraft
n. a deep, glossy black
JETTY jet′ē
n. a pier or wharf
adj. of the color of jet
JIB jib
n. a kind of sail
n. an arm of a mechanical crane
JIBE jīb
v. to alter the course of a sailboat
v. to agree
JIG jig
n. a rapid dance
n. a kind of fish lure
JIGGER ji′gər
n. a small glass
n. a light tackle
n. one who dances a jig
JINGLE jing′əl
n. a light clinking sound
n. a kind of informal poetry
JINX jinks
n. something or someone supposed to bring bad luck
JINKS
n. pranks
JIVE jīv
n. jazz music
GYVE
n. a leg shackle
JOB job
n. a piece of work
JOB jōb
n. (u.c.) a book of the Bible
JOCKEY jok′ē
n. one who rides a horse in a race
v. to cheat or trick

JOG jog
v. to run at a steady trot
n. a notch
JOKER jōk′ər
n. one who does something funny
n. a kind of playing card
JOT jot
v. to write quickly or briefly
n. the least part of something
JOURNAL jer′nəl
n. a diary or publication
n. part of a shaft or axle
JOWL joul
n. the lower jaw
n. a cut of pork
JUBILEE joo′bi lē
n. a celebration
adj. of fruit served in flaming brandy
JUDGES juj′iz
v. decides
n. (u.c.) a book of the Bible
JUG jug
n. a kind of container for liquids
n. a sound made by some birds
JUMPER jum′pər
n. one who springs up
n. a sleeveless dress
JUNIOR joon′yər
adj. younger
n. a grade in high school or college
JUNK junk
n. old, worthless articles, as rags
n. a kind of Chinese ship
JUNKET junk′it
n. a kind of pudding
n. a pleasure excursion
n. a recreational trip by a government official paid for with public funds
JUST just
adj. upright, fair
adv. exactly
adv. nearly
JUSTICE jus′tis
n. moral rightness
n. a judge

K

K kā
n. eleventh letter of the English alphabet

CAY
n. a small, low island

KEEL kēl
n. part of a boat
v. to upset, turn, or fall over
n. a disease of ducks

KEEN kēn
adj. sharp, clever
v. to wail for the dead

KEEP kēp
v. to maintain, reserve
n. part of a castle

KEEPING kēp'ing
n. logical conformity
n. custody

KEG keg
n. a small cask
n. a unit of weight for nails

KENNEL ken'əl
n. a house for a dog
n. an open gutter

KETTLE ket'əl
n. a kind of pot
n. a kind of drum

KEY kē
n. a lock opener
n. musical pitch

QUAY
n. a landing place by water

KICK kik
v. to strike with the foot
n. a thrill

KID kid
n. a young goat
n. a young person
n. a kind of leather
v. to tease

KILL kil
v. to cause death, destroy, veto

KILN kil, kiln
n. a kind of oven

KIND kīnd
n. a class or group with like characteristics
adj. gentle, good

KINDLE kin'dəl
v. to start a fire
n. a litter of rabbits

KING king
n. one who rules
n. a piece in chess or checkers
n. one of the playing cards

KIP kip
n. the hide of a young beast
n. a unit of weight equal to 1,000 pounds

KISS kis
n. a kind of demonstration of affection
n. a kind of cookie

KIT kit
n. a case for special tools or supplies
n. a small violin

KITE kīt
n. a flying toy
n. a kind of bird

KITTY kit'ē
n. a small cat
n. a pool of money in a game

KNACK nak
n. a talent
n. a sharp, cracking sound

KNAVE nāv
n. a dishonest person
n. a jack, in playing-cards

NAVE
n. part of a church

KNICKERS nik'ərz
n. short breeches

NICKERS
v. neighs like a horse

KNIT nit
v. to make something with yarn
v. (of bones) to grow back together

NIT
n. a kind of young insect

KNOB nob
n. a handle, as for a door or drawer

NOB
n. the jack in some card games

KNOCK nok
v. to rap, as on a door
v. to criticize

NOCK
n. a notch in an arrow

KNOLL nōl
n. a rounded hill
v. to ring a bell, toll

KNOT not
n. a looped cord or ribbon
n. a kind of sandpiper

NOT
adv. a form of denial

KNUCKLE nuk'əl
n. part of the hand
v. become serious

L

L el
n. twelfth letter of the English alphabet

ELL
n. an extension on a house
n. an old unit of measure

LABEL lā'bəl
n. a piece of paper affixed to an object indicating identification or ownership
n. a form of molding

LABOR lā'bər
n. toil
n. childbirth

LACE lās
n. a cord
n. filmy cloth
v. to lash, beat, thrash

LACERATED las'ə rā tid
adj. mangled, tortured
adj. (of a leaf) having the edge cut

LACK lak
n. scarcity

LAC
n. a kind of resin

LACQUER lak'ər
n. a shiny surface for wood
v. to gloss over faults with words

LADE lād
v. to burden, load
v. to move liquid, as with a ladle

LAID
v. did lay

LAG lag
v. to fall behind
n. a stave or strip on a drum

LAGGING lag'ing
adj. slow and dragging
n. a heat-insulating cover for a boiler or oil tank

LAKE lāk
n. a body of water surrounded by land
n. a red pigment

LAMA lä'mə
n. a priest in some countries

LLAMA lä'mə, yä'mə
n. a kind of animal

LAMB lam
n. a young sheep
n. a gentle, innocent person

LAM
n. hurried flight

LAMENT lə ment'
v. to mourn
n. a kind of song or poem

LANCE lans
n. a kind of weapon
n. a hose used to clean furnaces

LAND land
n. the dry parts of the earth
v. to arrive

LANE lān
n. a path or narrow passage

LAIN
v. p.p. of *to lie*, rest

LAP lap
n. part of the seated human body
n. completion of circuit of a race course
v. to fold
v. to wash against

LAPPET lap'it
n. a small flap of fabric on a garment
n. a wattle on a bird's head

LAPSE laps
n. a temporary decline; error

LAPS
n. parts of seated human bodies

LAPPS
n. (u.c.) people of Lapland

LARD lärd
n. the rendered fat of hogs
v. to ornament

LARK lärk
n. a kind of bird
n. prank, frolic

LASH lash
n. part of a whip
v. to attack with words

LAST last
adv. final, at the end
v. to go on in time
n. a model of the human foot
n. 4,000 pounds in weight

LATE lāt
adj. tardy
adj. recently deceased; former

LATHER lath'ər
n. foam made of soap and water
n. sweat, as of a horse

LAUNCH launch
n. a kind of boat
v. to set off on a course

LAVER lā'vər
n. a basin or font
n. an edible seaweed

LAWN laun
n. grass-covered land
n. a kind of sheer cloth

LAX lax
adj. careless, negligent

LACKS
v. is without, is deficient in

LAY lā
v. to set down (an object)
v. did lie, rest
adj. of church members not of the clergy
n. a kind of song or poem

LEI
n. a wreath of flowers

LAYER lā'ər
n. a thickness on a surface
n. a hen

LAZE lāz
v. to be idle

LAYS
v. sets down

LEAD lēd
v. to show the way

LEAD led
n. a kind of metal

LED
v. went first

LEAF lēf
n. part of a growing plant
n. a page in a book

LIEF
adv. gladly

LEAGUE lēg
n. a group with like interests
n. about three miles

LEAK lēk
n. an unintended hole or crack

LEEK
n. a kind of onion

LEAN lēn
v. to bend
adj. thin

LIEN lēn, lē'ən
n. right to hold property

LIEN lī'ən
n. the spleen

LEANT lent
v. did lean against

LENT
v. did lend
n. (u.c.) a period of the Christian year

LEAST lēst
adj. smallest

LEASED
v. rented

LEAVE lēv
v. to go away
n. permission
v. to put forth leaves, as a plant

LEE lē
n. shelter
n. sediment, as of wine

LEA
n. open grassland
n. a measure of yarn

LEECH lēch
n. one who depends upon another for profit
n. a kind of blood-sucking worm

LEACH
v. to percolate

LEFT left
v. went away
adj. opposite of right side

LEG leg
n. part of the body
n. part of a trip

LEMMA lem'ə
n. a theme or subject
n. a bract in a grass spikelet

LESSON les'ən
n. part of a course of study

LESSEN
v. to reduce

LET let
v. to allow
v. to rent
n. a play in tennis

LETTER let'ər
n. one of the 26 units of the English alphabet
n. a missive written and mailed

LEVEE lev'ē
n. a dike raised to hold back water
n. a formal reception

LEVY
v. to impose a tax

LIAR līr
n. teller of falsehood

LIER
n. one who lies in wait

LYRE
n. kind of musical instrument

LIBERAL lib'ər əl
adj. open-minded
adj. generous

LICENSE lī'sens
n. a permit
n. lawlessness, excessive freedom

LICK lik
v. to pass the tongue over
v. to beat, thrash

LIE lī
n. an untruth
v. to rest, as on a bed

LYE
n. a caustic material

LIED līd
v. told an untruth

LIED lēd
n. a kind of German song

LIGHT līt
v. to get down
adj. not dark
adj. not heavy

LIGHTER lī'tər
n. one who or that which makes a flame
adj. less heavy
n. a kind of barge

LIGHTSOME līt'səm
adj. airy, nimble
adj. well-lighted

LIKE līk
adj. similar
v. to find agreeable

LIMA lī′mə
n. a kind of bean

LIMA lē′mə
n. (u.c.) a city in Peru

LIMB lim
n. a leg or arm
n. part of a tree
n. the edge of a planet

LIMN
v. to describe

LIMBER lim′bər
adj. flexible
n. bilge on a boat
n. a vehicle that tows a field gun

LIMBO lim′bō
n. the state of being between two extremes
n. a West Indian dance

LIME līm
n. a solid used in making cement and for crops
n. a kind of fruit
n. a linden tree

LIMP limp
v. to walk with a jerky motion
adj. relaxed, tired

LINE līn
n. something long and narrow
n. a business
v. to cover the inner side of

LINER lī′nər
n. a ship or plane
n. an inner cover

LING ling
n. a kind of fish
n. a kind of heather

LINKS links
n. rings on a chain
n. some torches
n. a golf course

LYNX
n. a kind of animal

LIP lip
n. part of the mouth
v. to speak softly

LIQUID lik′wid
adj. fluid. not dry
adj. clear, graceful

LIST list
n. a series of names or numbers
v. to lean to one side
n. a stripe or band

LISTER lis′tər
n. a kind of plow
n. an assessor

LITERAL lit′ər əl
adj. true to fact

LITTORAL
adj. pertaining to the shore of a body of water

LITTER lit′ər
n. rubbish
n. a number of animals born at same time
n. a stretcher for sick people

LIVE liv
v. to exist

LIVE līv
adv. being in life

LIVER liv′ər
n. part of the body
n. a resident

LIVER līv′ər
adj. more active, alert

LIVERY liv′ər ē
n. a uniform
adj. having a liver out of order
n. a stable for horses

LIVID liv′əd
adj. dark like a bruise
adj. furious, angry
adj. pale, ashen

LOAD lōd
n. a burden

LODE
n. a body of ore in the earth

LOWED
v. made the sound of cattle

LOAF lōf
n. a shaped mass of bread
v. to idle

LOAFER lōf'ər
n. an idle person
n. a kind of shoe

LOAN lōn
n. the act of lending

LONE
adj. separate

LOATH lōth
adj. unwilling

LOATHE lōth
v. to despise

LOB lob
n. a stroke in tennis
n. a kind of worm

LOBBY lob'ē
n. an entrance hall
v. to try for votes of legislators

LOCAL lō'kəl
adj. of a special place
n. an often-stopping train

LOCK lok
n. something that keeps a door closed
n. part of a canal
n. a portion of hair

LOCKS loks
n. things that keep doors closed

LOX
n. smoked salmon

LOCUST lō'kust
n. a kind of grasshopper
n. a kind of tree

LODGE loj
n. a cabin or hut
n. members of a secret society

LOG log
n. part of a felled tree
n. a written record of a trip or job

LONG long
adj. not short
v. to yearn

LOOM loom
n. a machine for weaving
v. to come into view

LOOP loop
n. a cord doubled so as to form a hole

LOUPE
n. a kind of magnifying glass

LOOT loot
n. plunder

LUTE
n. a kind of musical instrument

LOP lop
v. to cut off from a tree
v. to droop

LORE lōr
n. folk knowledge
n. the space between the eye and bill of a bird

LOWER
adj. under

LOWER lou'ər
v. to frown, be dark

LOT lot
n. a share
n. a plot of ground

LOUNGE lounj
v. to pass time idly
n. a sofa
n. a public room

LOW lō
adj. not high
v. to moo

LO
interj. behold

LUG lug
v. to pull with effort
n. a kind of supporting piece

LUMBAR lum'bər
adj. of the loin

LUMBER
n. sawed boards
v. to move clumsily

LUMPY lum'pē
adj. full of or covered with bumps
adj. clumsy, crude

LUPINE loo'pin
n. a kind of flower

LUPINE loo'pīn
adj. savage, wolflike

LURCH lerch
v. to sway or roll
n. the position of a loser in a game

LUSTER lus'tər
n. glitter
n. a person who yearns

M

M em
n. thirteenth letter of the English alphabet

EM
n. a measure used in printing

MACE mās
n. a club used in war
n. a kind of spice
n. a spray used to quell riots

MAD mad
adj. insane
adj. cross
adj. merry

MADDER mad'ər
adj. angrier
n. a kind of dye

MAGAZINE mag'ə zēn
n. a publication
n. a storeroom for gun powder
n. part of a gun

MAGGOT mag'ət
n. larva of some insects
n. a whim

MAID mād
n. a girl

MADE
v. did make

MAIL māl
n. letters or packages
n. armor

MALE
adj. masculine

MAIN mān
adj. chief, most important
n. physical strength

MAINE
n. (u.c.) one of the states

MANE
n. hair on a horse's neck

MAJOR mā'jər
n. an army officer
adj. greater in size, importance

MAKE māk
v. to produce, cause to exist
v. to arrive at

MALL maul
n. a public walkway

MAUL
v. to use roughly
n. a heavy hammer

MAMMA mä'mə
n. mother

MAMMA mam'ə
n. breast or udder

MAN man
n. an adult male person
v. to take one's place for service

MANDARIN man'də rin
n. an official in old China
n. a kind of orange

MANGLE mang'əl
v. to mar badly
n. a machine that presses cloth

MANGY mān'jē
adj. having a kind of skin disease
adj. shabby, mean

MANIFOLD man'i fōld
adj. numerous and varied
n. part of a car's engine

MANIKIN man'ə kin
n. a little man, drawf
n. a clothes model

MANNER man'ər
n. custom, style

MANOR
n. the main house of an estate

MANSE mans
n. the house of a minister or priest

MAN'S manz
adj. of a man

MANTEL man'təl
n. a shelf over a fireplace

MANTLE
n. a loose cloak or cape

MARBLE mär'bəl
n. a kind of limestone
n. a small ball of stone, glass, etc.,
  used in a game

MARCH märch
v. to walk with a measured tread
n. a frontier
n. (u.c.) the third month of the year

MARE mair
n. a female horse

MARE mär'ā
n. a dark plain on the moon

MARGIN mär'jin
n. a border or edge
n. leeway

MARINE mə rēn'
adj. of the sea
n. one of a class of soldiers serving
  on ships

MARK märk
n. a trace on something, as a spot
  or line
n. a characteristic

MARC
n. a residue of the grape

MARL märl
n. a kind of fertilizer
v. to wind a rope a certain way

MAROON mə roon'
n. brownish-red
v. to put ashore and abandon

MARQUEE mär kē'
n. a roof over an entrance

MARQUIS
n. a nobleman

MARRY ma'rē
v. to wed
v. to splice two ropes

MARS märz
n. (u.c.) a planet
n. (u.c.) a god of ancient Greece
v. damages, spoils

MARSHAL märsh'əl
n. a kind of officer
v. to arrange in order

MARTIAL
adj. warlike, brave

MARTEN mär'tən
n. a kind of animal

MARTIN
n. a kind of bird

MASH mash
n. a kind of fodder
v. to reduce to a pulpy mass

MASK mask
n. a cover for the face

MASQUE
n. a kind of dance and play

MASS mas
n. a large number of like elements
n. (u.c.) a religious celebration

MAST mast
n. the spar that holds sails of a vessel
n. the fruit of some forest trees

MASSED
v. gathered together

MASTER mas'tər
n. an expert
v. to overcome

MAT mat
n. a piece of fabric to go under
something
n. cardboard used in framing

MATTE
adj. lusterless

MATCH mach
n. something that provides fire
v. to be equal or alike

MATE māt
n. one of a pair
n. an officer on a ship
n. a move in chess

MATERIAL ma tē'rē əl
n. matter, substance
n. fabric
adj. vital, important

MATTED mat'əd
adj. covered with a dense growth or
mass
adj. having a dull finish

MATTER mat'ər
n. substance, anything occupying
space
v. to be of importance

MATTING mat'ing
n. a fabric of grass or straw
n. a dull surface

MATURE ma tūr'
adj. grown, adult
adj. ripe, ready

MAY mā
v. is able
n. (u.c.) the fifth month

MAZE māze
n. a confusing network

MAIZE
n. corn

ME mē
pro. myself

MI
n. a note in the musical scale

MEAD mēd
n. a kind of drink
n. a meadow

MEAL mēl
n. breakfast, lunch, or dinner
n. part of some grains

MEAN mēn
v. to intend
v. to signify
adj. unkind
adj. inferior
n. the average

MIEN
n. air, bearing

MEASURE mezh'ūr
v. to find the limits of something
n. a legal bill
n. a short rhythm

MEAT mēt
n. flesh of animals

MEET
v. to come upon

METE
v. to allot
n. a boundary

MEDAL med'əl
n. a small piece of metal worn as an
honor

MEDDLE
v. to interfere, pry

MEDIATE mē'dē āt
v. to settle a dispute
v. to be in the middle

MEDIUM mē'dē əm
n. agency or instrument
n. a person who talks with the dead
adj. halfway, average

MEDUSA mə doo'sə
n. a jellyfish
n. (u.c.) in Greek mythology, a
Gorgon with snakes for hair

MEET mēt
v. to come upon
adj. suitable, proper
n. an assembly

MELEE mā′lā
n. confusion, jumble
n. a group of diamonds
MALAY
n. (u.c.) a peninsula in India

MEMBER mem′bər
n. one of a group
n. a part or organ of an animal's body

MENSAL men′səl
adj. monthly
adj. of or used at the table

MENTAL men′təl
adj. of the mind
adj. of the chin

MERCURY mer′kū rē
n. quicksilver
n. (u.c.) a planet
n. (u.c.) a Greek god

MERE mēr
adj. just enough
n. a lake or pond

MESH mesh
n. an open space in a net
v. to engage, as gear teeth

MESON mē′zən
n. an element between an electron and a proton
MESON mes′on
n. a plane that divides a body into two equal parts

MESS mes
n. a dirty, untidy state
n. a kind of meal

MESSENGER mes′en jər
n. one who carries news
n. a kind of rope or chain

METAL met′əl
n. a solid, such as gold or copper
METTLE
n. spirit, courage

METEOR mēt′ē ər
n. a shooting star
MEATIER
adj. more pithy

METER mē′tər
n. 39.37 inches
n. a pattern or rhythm in verse
n. an instrument that measures time, gas, etc.

METRIC me′trik
adj. pertaining to a meter
adj. pertaining to distance

MEW mū
v. to cry like a cat
n. a kind of sea gull
v. to molt, shed feathers

MID mid
adj. near the middle
prep. amid, among

MIDST midst
n. the state of being in the center
prep. amidst

MIGHT mīt
n. power
v. part of the verb *may*

MITE
n. a tiny insect
n. a small sum of money

MIKE mīk
n. a microphone
n. a support for a light cannon

MILESTONE mīl′stōn
n. a measuring post
n. an event in one's life

MILL mil
n. a building fitted with machinery
v. to wander aimlessly
MIL
n. .001 of an inch

MILLINERY mil′ə ne rē
n. women's hats
MILLENARY
adj. pertaining to the millenium

MILLING mil′ing
n. the act of making something in a mill
n. the act of raising the edge of a coin

MINCE mins
v. to cut or chop
v. to soften one's words

MINTS
n. certain candies

MIND mīnd
n. the thinking part of the brain
v. to obey

MINED
v. dug for ore

MINE mīn
v. to dig in the earth for ore
pro. of me

MINER mīn'ər
n. one who digs for ore

MINOR
n. a musical key or tone
adj. under legal age
adj. lesser in importance

MINISTER min'is tər
n. a clergyman
n. a diplomat

MINT mint
n. a kind of herb
n. a kind of candy
n. a place where money is coined or printed

MINUTE min'it
n. 60 seconds

MINUTE mī nūt'
adj. tiny

MINX minkz
n. a pert girl

MINKS
n. certain animals

MISCUE mis'kū
n. a stroke in a game of pool
v. to fail to answer a cue on stage

MISPRISION mis prizh'ən
n. a wrongful action of commission
n. scorn or contempt

MISS mis
n. a girl
v. to fail to meet or hit

MISSILE mis'əl
n. an object or weapon for throwing, hurling, or shooting

MISSAL
n. a prayer book

MIST mist
n. a wet cloud

MISSED
v. did miss

MITER mīt'ər
n. a joint in carpentry
n. headdress of a priest or bishop

MOAN mōn
n. a prolonged, low sound of grief

MOWN
v. was cut down, as grass or wheat

MOAT mōt
n. a trench filled with water

MOTE
n. a speck

MOCHA mō'kə
n. a mixture of coffee and chocolate
n. a kind of glove leather

MODE mōd
n. style, fashion
n. a method, way of acting

MOWED
v. cut down, as grass or wheat

MOLAR mōl'ər
n. a kind of tooth
adj. pertaining to a body of matter as a whole

MOLD mōld
n. a hollow frame or form
n. small fungi
n. rich earth

MOLDER mōl'dər
n. one who molds, as ceramics
v. to turn to dust

MOLE mōl
n. a skin blemish
n. a kind of animal
n. a pier, wharf

MOMENT mō'mənt
n. an instant
n. importance, gravity

MONARCH mon'ark
n. a king or queen
n. a kind of butterfly

MONITOR mon'i tər
n. something or someone that warns
n. a kind of lizard

MONKEY munk'ē
n. a kind of animal
n. a mimic, copycat

MONSTER mon'stər
n. a creature part human, part animal
n. a cruel, wicked person

MOOD mood
n. frame of mind, feelings
n. a term used in grammer

MOOED
v. cried like a cow

MOOR mōr
n. a tract of open land
v. to fasten a boat
n. (u.c.) a native of Africa

MORE
adj. in greater quantity

MOOSE moos
n. a kind of animal

MOUSSE
n. a kind of dessert

MOOT moot
adj. doubtful
n. a ring gauge for checking treenails

MOP mop
v. to wash or wipe up
n. a mass of hair
n. an unhappy face, grimace

MORDANT mor'dənt
adj. sarcastic
n. a melodic embellishment
n. an acid used in dyeing

MORGUE morg
n. a place for dead bodies
n. a library of a newspaper

MORTAL mort'əl
n. a human being
adj. deadly or implacable
adj. of or pertaining to death

MORTAR mort'ər
n. a kind of bowl
n. a kind of cannon
n. a mixture of lime and cement

MORTIFY mort'i fī
v. to hurt someone's feelings
v. to become gangrened

MOTHER muth'ər
n. a female parent
n. a solid film that appears on some liquids

MOUND mound
n. a heap or raised mass
n. a golden globe of the English king or queen

MOUNT mount
v. to climb up
n. a horse
n. a hill or mountain

MOUSE mous
n. a small rodent
n. a black eye
v. to prowl

MOVE moov
v. to go or send from one place to another
v. to influence, guide

MOW mō
v. to cut grass, grain, etc.

MOW mou
n. a place in a barn for storage

MUDDLE mud'əl
v. to mix up, confuse
v. to smooth clay

MUFF muf
n. a round hand warmer
v. to fail, bungle

MUG mug
n. a cup with a handle
n. a thug
n. a photograph of the head and face only

MUGGER mug'ər
n. one who assaults in order to rob
n. a kind of crocodile

MULE mūl
n. a kind of animal
n. a bedroom slipper
MEWL
v. to cry like a baby
MULL mul
v. to study over
v. to heat and spice
n. a thin muslin
MULLER mul'ər
n. a thinker
n. an instrument for grinding
n. a kind of pot
MULTIPLY mult'i plī
v. to make many, increase in number
MULTIPLY mult'i plē
adv. in a varied manner
MUM mum
adj. silent
v. to act in a mask
MUMMY mum'ē
n. a preserved dead body
n. mother
MURMUR mer'mər
n. a low continuous sound
v. to complain
MUSCLE mus'əl
n. a tissue of the body
MUSSEL
n. a water animal like a clam
MUSE mūz
n. (u.c.) one of several Greek goddesses
v. to think in silence
MEWS
v. cries like a cat
n. an alley, park
MUSH mush
n. soft-boiled corn meal
v. to travel over snow with a dog team
MUST must
v. ought to, should
n. new wine
n. moldiness

MUSSED
adj. messed up
MUSTARD mus'tərd
n. a kind of seasoning
MUSTERED
v. called together, as for battle
MUSTY mus'tē
adj. old-smelling
adj. dull, apathetic
MUTE mūt
adj. speechless
v. to reduce the intensity of a color
MUTUAL mū'tū əl
adj. having in common
n. a kind of insurance
MUZZLE muz'əl
n. part of a gun
n. parts of an animal's face
MYSTERY mis'tər ē
n. something kept secret
n. a kind of story
n. a religious rite

N

N en
n. fourteenth letter of the English alphabet
EN
n. a measure used in printing
NAG nag
v. to tease, torment without cease
n. an old horse
NAIL nāl
n. metal used in carpentry
n. hard end of a finger or toe
NAP nap
n. a short sleep
n. the fuzzy surface of some fabrics
NAPPE
n. a large mass or rock
NATURAL nach'ər əl
adj. pertaining to nature
adj. illegitimate

NAVAL nāv'əl
adj. of warships or the navy
NAVEL
n. the umbilicus

NAVE nāv
n. part of a church
n. part of a wheel; hub
KNAVE
n. a dishonest person
n. a jack in playing cards

NAVY nā'vē
n. warships and sailors
n. a dark blue

NAY nā
adv. no

NEIGH
v. to whinny like a horse
NÉE
adj. born

NEAR nēr
adv. close, not far off
adj. stingy

NEAT nēt
adj. orderly, pleasant
adj. clever, apt

NECESSARY nes'es er'ē
adj. required, needed
n. a bathroom

NECK nek
n. part of the body
v. to kiss

NEED nēd
v. to require
KNEAD
v. to work dough
KNEED
v. struck with the knee

NEEDS nēds
v. does require
adv. of necessity

NEGATIVE neg'ə tiv
n. denial, refusal
n. a type of photographic image

NERVE nerv
n. part of the body that sends messages to the brain
n. courage

NET net
n. a lacy fabric; mesh
adj. remaining after deductions

NETTLE net'əl
n. a plant with stinging hairs
n. a jellyfish

NEUTER nū'tər
n. a kind of verb
n. a kind of noun
adj. neither male nor female

NEW nū
adj. not old
GNU
n. a kind of antelope
KNEW
v. did know

NIB nib
n. bill or beak of a bird
n. a pen point

NICE nīs
adj. pleasing, agreeable
NICE nēs
n. (u.c.) a city in France
NIECE
n. daughter of one's sister or brother

NICK nik
v. to chip, notch
v. to cheat

NICKER nik'ər
n. one who or that which nicks
v. to snicker, laugh

NIGHT nīt
n. the dark part of the 24-hour day
KNIGHT
n. a man of noble birth
n. a chess piece

NIP nip
n. a sip
v. to pinch, bite, snip

NO nō
n. a refusal
adv. not at all
adv. not any
KNOW
v. to understand

NOBLE nō'bəl
adj. of high birth
adj. moral, splendid

NOG nog
n. a drink made with eggs
n. a wooden peg or block

NOISE noiz
n. a loud sound
v. to gossip

NOSE nōz
n. part of the face
KNOWS
v. understands
NOES
n. negative votes

NOTE nōt
n. a brief letter or jotting
n. a tone in music

NOTED nōt'əd
v. took notes
adj. famous

NOTICE nōt'is
n. a warning
v. to treat with favor

NOVEL nov'əl
n. a book of fiction
adj. new, different

NUMBER num'bər
n. a numeral
NUMBER num'ər
adj. more numb

NUN nun
n. a woman who has vowed to serve in the church
NONE
pro. not one
NONE nōn
n. the fifth hour for prayers

NURSE ners
n. one who cares for a child or sick person
v. to suckle

NURSERY nèrs'ər ē
n. a place for young children
n. a place for trees and plants

NUT nut
n. a kind of edible fruit
n. part of a violin

NUZZLE nuz'əl
v. to root with the nose
v. to cuddle up

O

O ō
n. fifteenth letter of the English alphabet
OH
interj. expression of surprise
OWE
v. to be in debt to

OAK ōk
n. a kind of tree
OKE
adj. okay

OBJECT ob'jekt
n. something visible; a goal
OBJECT ob jekt'
v. to dislike, express disapproval

OBLATE ob'lāt
n. one who lives in a monastery but not under vows
adj. flattened at the poles

OBNOXIOUS ob nok'shəs
adj. offensive, odious
adj. exposed or liable to attack or injury

ODD od
adj. unusual, strange
adj. not even
OD
n. a hypothetical force in nature

ODE ōd
n. a kind of poem

OH'D
v. said *"Oh"*

OWED
v. was in debt

OFFENSIVE ə fen'siv
n. an attack, as in war
adj. disagreeable to the senses

OIL oil
n. a kind of liquid
v. to flatter

OLEO ō'lē ō
n. margarine

OLIO
n. a dish of many ingredients

ONAGER on'ə jer
n. a wild ass of Asia
n. an ancient engine of war

ONE wun
n. the first number

WON
v. did win

OOZE ooz
n. soft mud or slime
v. to flow slowly

OPERA op'ə rə
n. a musical play
n. literary or musical compositions

OPERATE op'ər āt
v. to make a machine, etc., work
v. to perform surgery

OPPONENTS ə pō'nenz
n. rivals

OPPONENS
n. a kind of muscle

OR ōr, aur
conj. used as a connective
n. gold

OAR ōr
n. a paddle for rowing

O'ER
prep. over

ORE
n. a mineral

OWER
n. one who owes

ORACLE aur'i kəl, o'ri kəl
n. one who spoke for the gods

AURICLE
n. part of the ear

ORAL ō'rəl
adj. spoken, vocal

AURAL
adj. of the ear
adj. of an aura

ORANGE o'rinj
n. a kind of fruit
n. a red-yellow color

ORATORY o'rə tō rē
n. the art of public speaking
n. a small chapel

ORDER aur'der
n. command
n. regularity
n. a division of plants or animals

ORDINAL aur'də nəl
adj. of a class of plants or animals
n. a kind of religious book

ORDINANCE aur'də nens
n. decree, command

ORDONNANCE
n. arrangement, as of a building or picture

ORDINARY aur'də nār'ē
adj. of the usual kind
n. an inn or dining room of Colonial America

ORGAN aur'gen
n. a musical instrument
n. a part of a plant or animal with a special function
n. periodical with a viewpoint

ORGANIC aur'gan'ək
adj. of living organisms
adj. essential

ORIENT ō'rə ent
v. to adjust, familiarize
n. (u.c.) the East
n. the iridescence of a pearl

ORIOLE ōr'ē ōl
n. a kind of bird

AUREOLE
n. a halo

ORRIS o'ris
n. a kind of flowering iris
n. a lace of silver or gold

OSMUND oz'mənd
n. a kind of fern
n. a kind of iron

OTTER ot'ər
n. a kind of animal

OTTAR
n. a perfume oil: *attar*

OUGHT aut
v. should
n. anything at all
v. zero, cipher

AUGHT
n. anything
n. zero

OUNCE ouns
n. one-sixteenth of a pound or pint
n. a kind of leopard

OUTCAST out'kast
n. one who is kept out

OUTCASTE
n. one who has no social group

OUTGOING out gō'ing
adj. responsive to others
adj. going out

OVER ō'vər
prep. above
adv. finished

OVERAGE ō'vər āj'
adj. beyond the necessary age
OVERAGE ō'vər ij
n. too much merchandise

OVERBLOWN ō'vər blōn'
adj. unusually large
adj. more than full blown (of a flower)

OVERCAST ō'vər kast'
adj. cloudy
n. a way of sewing

OVERDO ō'vər doo'
v. to do to excess
OVERDUE ō'vər doo', dū
adj. late

OVERDONE ō'vər dun'
adj. exhausted
adj. cooked too much

OVERDRAW ō'vər drau'
v. to withdraw more money from the bank than is deposited
v. to exaggerate
v. to have too much draft in a fireplace

OVERDRIVE ō'vər drīv'
n. a kind of gear
v. to push or carry to excess

OVERHAND ō'vər hand'
adj. overarm, as in a certain toss of a ball
n. a way of sewing

OVERHEAD ō'vər hed'
n. the cost of running a business
adv. up in the air

OVERLAY ō'vər lā'
v. to finish with an added decoration
v. smothered

OVERLOOK ō'vər look'
v. to fail to notice
v. to look from a high position
v. to disregard or ignore

OVERREACH ō'vər rēch'
v. to go beyond an aim
v. to outwit, cheat

OVERRIDE ō'vər rīd'
v. to crush by riding over
v. to set a bone
n. a commission
v. to ride (a horse) too much

OVERRUN ō'vər run'
v. to invade
v. to print more copies than were needed

OVERSEAS ō'vər sēs'
adj. beyond or across the sea
OVERSEES
v. manages, directs

OVERSET ō'vər set'
v. to upset, overthrow
v. to set too much type

OVERSHOT ō'vər shot'
adj. driven beyond
adj. having an upper jaw projecting

OVERSIGHT ō'vər sīt'
n. failure to notice
n. watchful care

OVERTURE ō'vər tūr'
n. an opening offer
n. a musical piece

OWN ōn
v. to possess
v. to admit, confess

OXFORD oks'ford
n. a kind of shoe
n. a kind of fabric
n. (u.c.) a university in England

OXIDE oks'īd
n. a chemical compound

OX-EYED
adj. having large, round eyes

OYSTER oi'stər
n. a kind of sea mollusk
n. a noncommunicative person

P

P pē
n. sixteenth letter of the English alphabet

PEA
n. a seed of some plants

PEE
v. to urinate

PACE pās
n. a rate of movement

PACE pā'sē
prep. with the permission of

PACK pak
v. to bundle
n. a group of like persons or things
v. to choose so as to serve one's purpose

PACKET pak'it
n. a small pack
n. a kind of boat

PACIFIC pə sif'ik
adj. peaceable, mild
n. (u.c.) one of the oceans

PACIFIER pa'si fī'ər
n. one who or that which makes peace
n. a teething ring

PACT pakt
n. an agreement, covenant

PACKED
v. filled suitcases or the like

PAD pad
n. a cushion
n. a water-lily leaf
n. a rocket platform
n. a dull sound
n. a highwayman
n. a writing tablet

PADDLE pad'əl
n. a kind of oar
v. to spank
v. to dabble in water

PAEAN pē'ən
n. a song of praise

PAEON
n. one long and three short syllables

PEON
n. a laborer

PAGE pāj
n. a leaf of a book, manuscript, etc.
n. a boy attendant

PAGEBOY pāj boi
n. a kind of hair style

PAGE BOY
n. a boy or man who works as a page in a hotel

PAIL pāl
n. a bucket

PALE
adj. lacking color
n. a picket of a fence
n. a boundary

PAIN pān
n. suffering, hurt

PANE
n. a plate of glass in a window

PANÉ pa nā'
n. food prepared with bread crumbs

PAINFUL pān'fəl
adj. distressing
adj. laborious

PAINTER pān'tər
n. an artist or other who works with paint
n. a rope on a boat

PAIR pair
n. a group of two

PARE
v. to peel

PEAR
n. a kind of fruit

PALATE pal'it
n. part of the mouth
n. taste

PALLET
n. a bed of straw

PALLETTE
n. an artist's board for paint

PALISADE pal'i sād
n. a fence of pales
n. a line of cliffs

PALL paul
n. a cloth over a coffin
v. to become tired of something

PAWL
n. a bar for a ratchet wheel

PALM paum
n. part of the hand
n. a kind of tree
v. to cheat at cards

PALMER pau'mər
n. one who cheats at cards
n. a pilgrim

PALMY paum'ē
adj. covered with palm trees
adj. prosperous, flourishing

PALPATE pal'pāt
v. to examine (for illness) by touch
adj. having a kind of sense organ in insects

PALSY paul'sē
n. tremblings of the body

PALSY pal'sē
adj. friendly

PAN pan
n. a metal container
n. (u.c.) a Greek god
v. to move a camera
v. to wash for gold
v. to criticize severely

PANNE
n. a light-weight velvet

PANACHE pə nosh'
n. an ornamental plume
n. verve, style, flair

PANEL pan'əl
n. a division of a wall
n. a group of persons gathered to judge or advise

PANHANDLE pan'han dəl
n. the handle of a pan
n. a narrow strip of land
v. to beg

PANIC pan'ik
n. sudden fear
n. an edible grass

PANNIER pan'yer
n. a kind of basket
n. drapery over the hips of a dress

PANTS pants
n. trousers
v. breathes hard

PAP pap
n. soft food
n. an idea or writings with little value
n. a nipple

PAPIER-MÂCHÉ pap yā'mosh ā'
n. objects made from wet paper
adj. false, illusory

PAR pär
n. equality in value

PARR
n. the young of some fish

PARABOLIC pa rə bol'ik
adj. having the form of a kind of curve
adj. of or pertaining to a kind of short story

PARAGON pa'ra gən
n. a model of excellence
n. a large, round pearl

PAIN pān
n. suffering, hurt

PANE
n. a plate of glass in a window

PANÉ pa nā'
n. food prepared with bread crumbs

PAINFUL pān'fəl
adj. distressing
adj. laborious

PAINTER pān'tər
n. an artist or other who works with paint
n. a rope on a boat

PAIR pair
n. a group of two

PARE
v. to peel

PEAR
n. a kind of fruit

PALATE pal'it
n. part of the mouth
n. taste

PALLET
n. a bed of straw

PALLETTE
n. an artist's board for paint

PALISADE pal'i sād
n. a fence of pales
n. a line of cliffs

PALL paul
n. a cloth over a coffin
v. to become tired of something

PAWL
n. a bar for a ratchet wheel

PALM paum
n. part of the hand
n. a kind of tree
v. to cheat at cards

PALMER pau'mər
n. one who cheats at cards
n. a pilgrim

PALMY paum'ē
adj. covered with palm trees
adj. prosperous, flourishing

PALPATE pal'pāt
v. to examine (for illness) by touch
adj. having a kind of sense organ in insects

PALSY paul'sē
n. tremblings of the body
PALSY pal'sē
adj. friendly

PAN pan
n. a metal container
n. (u.c.) a Greek god
v. to move a camera
v. to wash for gold
v. to criticize severely

PANNE
n. a light-weight velvet

PANACHE pə nosh'
n. an ornamental plume
n. verve, style, flair

PANEL pan'əl
n. a division of a wall
n. a group of persons gathered to judge or advise

PANHANDLE pan'han dəl
n. the handle of a pan
n. a narrow strip of land
v. to beg

PANIC pan'ik
n. sudden fear
n. an edible grass

PANNIER pan'yer
n. a kind of basket
n. drapery over the hips of a dress

PANTS pants
n. trousers
v. breathes hard

PAP pap
n. soft food
n. an idea or writings with little value
n. a nipple

PAPIER-MÂCHÉ pap yā'mosh ā'
n. objects made from wet paper
adj. false, illusory

PAR pär
n. equality in value
PARR
n. the young of some fish

PARABOLIC pa rə bol'ik
adj. having the form of a kind of curve
adj. of or pertaining to a kind of short story

PARAGON pa'ra gən
n. a model of excellence
n. a large, round pearl

PARALLEL pa'ra lel
adj. equidistant
adj. similar

PARCEL pär'sel
n. a package
n. a group of persons or things distinct from others
v. to apportion

PARCH pärch
v. to make dry, as by heat
v. to dry or shrivel from cold

PARIETAL pə rī'i təl
adj. of a kind of bone in the skull
adj. of authority over residence in a school or college

PARITY pa'ri tē
n. equality
n. the fact of having borne offspring

PARK pärk
n. an area of land for recreation
v. to halt a vehicle for a period of time

PARLAY pär'lā
n. a kind of bet
PARLEY
n. a conference

PAROLE pə rōl'
n. conditional release from prison
PAROL
adj. oral

PARQUET pär'kā
n. a floor with a design
n. part of a theater

PARROT pa'rət
n. a kind of bird
v. to imitate

PARSE pärs
v. to describe a word in grammar
PARS pärz
n. a part of a prescription

PART pärt
n. a fraction of a whole
n. a role in a play
v. to separate
v. to take leave

PARTIAL pär'shəl
adj. incomplete
adj. fond, devoted

PARTICULAR pär tik'ū lar
adj. specific, special
adj. scrupulous
adj. discriminating
n. a witch's friend

PARTISAN pär'ti sən
n. a supporter
n. a kind of spear

PARTNERS pärt'nerz
n. associates, sharers
n. a frame around a ship's deckhole

PARTY pär'tē
n. a social gathering
n. a group of persons with like ideas or causes

PASCHAL pas'kəl
adj. of the Passover
adj. of Easter

PASS pas
n. a narrow route
n. a permission to enter
v. to go by
v. to disregard

PASSABLE pas'ə bəl
adj. fit to be traversed

PASSIBLE
adj. capable of feeling

PASSAGE pas'ij
n. part of a written or musical work
n. a route
n. a hall
n. a trip
n. a slow trot

PASSÉ pas'ā
adj. out-of-date
n. a kind of ballet step

PASSE-PARTOUT pas'pär too'
n. a mat for a picture
n. a skeleton key

PAST past
adj. previous in time

PASSED
v. went by

PASTE pāst
n. flour and water mixture
v. to smack, hit

PACED
v. stepped off

PASTEL pas'tel
n. a soft color
n. a kind of chalk used in drawing
n. a kind of plant: *woad*
n. blue from the woad

PASTOR pas'tər
n. a minister or priest
n. a kind of bird

PAT pat
v. to hit gently
adj. to the point; apt

PATCH pach
n. a cover over a hole or tear
n. a plot of ground

PATE pāt
n. the head

PÂTE pät
n. a paste used in ceramics

PÂTÉ pä tä'
n. meat paste

PATENT pat'ent
n. a government grant to an inventor
adj. clear, not hidden

PATHETIC pə thet'ik
adj. causing sadness or sympathy
adj. inadequate

PATIENCE pā'shens
n. act of not complaining in sorrow

PATIENTS
n. people under a doctor's care

PATIENT pā'shent
n. someone under a doctor's care
adj. long-suffering, quiet

PATRONIZE pā'trə nīz
v. to trade, do business with
v. to condescend

PATTER pat'ər
n. rapid speech
v. to make light tapping sounds

PATTERN pat'ərn
n. design
v. to imitate

PAUSE pauz
n. a short rest

PAWS
n. feet of some animals

PAVE pāv
v. to cover a road or walk

PAVÉ pav ā'
n. a way of setting jewelry

PAWN paun
v. to pledge, borrow
n. a piece used in chess

PAY pā
n. salary
v. to cover part of a ship with tar

PEACE pēs
n. freedom from war

PIECE
n. a part of something

PEEP pēp
v. to look through a small opening
v. to cheep, squeak

PEEPER pē'pər
n. a kind of frog
n. one who looks

PEER pēr
v. to look narrowly or searchingly
n. a person who is equal to another
n. a nobleman

PIER
n. a dock or wharf

PELT pelt
n. the hide or skin of an animal
v. to attack with repeated blows

PEN pen
n. a writing tool that uses ink
n. an enclosure for animals

PENANCE pen'əns
n. punishment

PENNANTS
n. long flags

PENCIL pen'səl
n. a writing tool that uses lead

PENCEL
n. a small flag on a lance

PENSILE
adj. hanging, as nests of some birds

PEND pend
v. to remain undecided

PENNED
v. wrote with a pen
p.p. caged

PENDANT pen'dənt
n. a hanging ornament, as an earring

PENDENT
adj. undecided
adj. suspended

PENETRATE pen'ə trāt
v. to pierce or pass into
v. to understand

PENT pent
adj. shut in
n. a shed with a sloping roof

PEPPER pep'ər
n. a kind of spice
v. to pelt with shot

PERCH perch
n. a roost for birds
n. a square rod of land
n. a kind of fish

PERFECT per'fekt
adj. without flaw
n. a tense in grammar

PERIOD per'ē əd
n. a length of time
n. the mark put at the end of a
sentence

PERIWINKLE pe'ri wink əl
n. a sea snail
n. a kind of flower

PERK perk
v. to become lively
v. to make coffee

PERMIT per mit'
v. to allow

PERMIT per'mit
n. a license

PERSONAL per'sə nəl
adj. of or pertaining to an individual
human
n. a kind of newspaper short notice

PERSONATE per'sən āt
v. to act, as in a play
adj. masklike

PERVADE per vād'
v. to go, pass, or spread through

PURVEYED
v. provided food

PEST pest
n. a nuisance
n. a deadly disease

PET pet
n. a tamed animal favorite
v. to stroke

PETTY pet'ē
adj. of secondary importance or rank

PETIT
adj. small, minor

PEAK pēk
n. the top of a mountain
v. to become sickly
PEEK
n. a brief look
PIQUE
n. a feeling of anger
PIQUÉ pē'kā'
n. a kind of fabric

PEAKED pēkt
adj. having a quick look
PEAKED pē'kid
adj. pale, sickly

PEAL pēl
n. a ringing of bells
PEEL
n. the skin or rind of fruits
n. a baker's tool
n. an ancient tower

PEARL perl
n. a kind of gem
PURL
n. a stitch used in knitting
v. to flow with a murmuring sound

PECK pek
n. eight dry quarts
v. to strike with the beak like a bird

PEDAL pēd'əl
adj. of the foot
PEDAL ped'əl
n. a lever, as on a bicycle
PEDDLE
v. to sell in small quantities

PEDESTRIAN pə des'tri ən
n. one who walks
adj. commonplace, dull

PHLEGM flem
n. mucus
n. calm, apathy

PHONE fōn
n. telephone
n. a speech sound

PI pī
n. a symbol (π) used in mathematics
n. mixed type

PIE
n. a kind of dessert

PIANO pē ä'nō
n. a kind of musical instrument
adj. soft, low

PIAZZA pē ät'zə, pē ä'zə
n. an open square in a city
n. a porch

PICA pī'kə
n. printers' measurement: 12 points
n. craving for unnatural food
PIKA
n. a kind of rabbit

PICK pik
v. to choose, select
n. a kind of tool

PICKER pik'ər
n. one who picks or gathers
n. one who works a weaving device

PICKET pik'it
n. a post, stake in a fence
n. one who tries to keep customers away during a strike

PICKLOCK pik'lok
n. a thief
n. high-grade wool

PICKS piks
v. chooses
PYX
n. a box or chest used in Communion services

PICTURE pik'tūr
n. a painting, drawing, or photograph
v. to imagine

PIED pīd
adj. with patches of colors
adj. mixed, scrambled, as of type

PIG pig
n. a young swine
n. a mass of metal

PIGEON pi'jin
n. a kind of bird
PIDGIN
n. a substandard English language

PIGEONHOLE pij'ən hōl
n. a part of some desks
v. to postpone

PIKE pīk
n. a kind of fish
n. a toll road
n. a kind of weapon
n. a kind of dive
n. the pointed end of a spear or arrow

PILE pīl
n. a heap, mass
n. a strong cylinder used to shore up a wall
n. hair
n. a kind of fabric

PILOT pī'lət
n. one who steers or guides

PILATE
n. (u.c.) a Roman of the Bible

PIN pin
n. a fastener, brooch
n. a move in chess

PINCH pinch
v. to squeeze painfully
v. to economize
n. an emergency

PINE pīn
n. a kind of tree
v. to long for, yearn
v. to fail in health

PINION pin'yən
n. a kind of gear
n. a bird's wing
v. to shackle

PINK pink
n. a color
n. a kind of flower
n. excellence
v. to stab, notch
adj. left-wing

PIP pip
n. a spot on dice or dominoes
n. a disease of birds
n. a small seed
v. to peep or chirp

PIPE pīp
n. a cylinder used to convey liquids
n. a kind of musical instrument
n. a large cask
n. an object used for smoking tobacco

PIPING pīp'ing
n. the sound of musical pipes
n. a kind of trimming for clothes
adj. shrill

PIRATE pī'rət
n. a thief at sea
v. to publish someone's work without legal rights

PISTOL pis'təl
n. a kind of firearm

PISTIL
n. part of a flower

PIT pit
n. a cave
n. a scar
n. part of a theater
n. the stone of a fruit

PITCH pich
n. musical tone
n. a paving material
n. pine-tree sap
v. to throw
v. to erect

PITCHER pich'ər
n. a container for liquids
n. a baseball player

PITH pith
n. the essential part; heart
v. to destroy the spinal cord of

PITIFUL pit'i fəl
adj. pathetic
adj. mean, low, base
adj. full of pity

PLACE plās
n. a space or spot
n. responsibility
v. to hire
n. second-place winner in a horse race

PLAICE
n. a kind of fish

PLACEBO plə sē'bō
n. nonmedicine given to satisfy or test a patient
n. vespers for the dead

PLACER pla'sər
n. gravel with bits of gold

PLACER plā'sər
n. a person or animal that is among the winners of a race

PLAGUE plāg
n. an epidemic disease
n. vexation

PLAIN plān
n. flat land
adj. clear, distinct
adj. not fancy

PLANE
n. a level surface
n. a kind of tool
n. an airplane
v. to glide

PLAN plan
n. a scheme of action
n. a kind of drawing

PLANK plank
n. a piece of timber
n. a political opinion

PLANT plant
n. a tree or flower
n. a factory
v. to insert

PLANTAIN plan'tin
n. a kind of fruit
n. a kind of weed

PLANTER plant'ər
n. one who or that which plants
n. a container for plants

PLAQUE plak
n. an ornamental plate
n. a deposit on teeth

PLASH plash
n. a splash
v. to interweave branches for a hedge

PLASMA plaz'mə
n. part of the blood
n. whey

PLASTIC plas'tik
n. a synthetic material
adj. capable of being molded
adj. being able to create

PLATE plāt
n. a dish
n. an illustration
n. silverware
n. a denture

PLAIT plāt, plat
n. a braid

PLAT plat
n. a plot of land

PLATFORM plat'fōrm
n. a raised flooring
n. a body of principles; program

PLATY plā'tē
adj. of thin, flat pieces of rock

PLATY plat'ē
n. a kind of fish

PLAY plā
n. a drama
n. fun, amusement
v. to perform music

PLEASE plēz
v. to satisfy

PLEAS
n. excuses
n. appeals

PLEDGE plej
n. a solemn vow
v. to drink to the health of

PLIGHT plīt
n. a bad situation
v. to pledge to marry

PLOT plot
n. the plan of a book or play
n. a small piece of ground
v. to plan evil
v. to draw a map

PLUCK pluk
n. bravery
v. to pull off

PLUG plug
n. a filling
n. part of an electrical system

n. pressed tobacco
v. to boost

PLUM plum
n. a kind of fruit

PLUMB
adj. vertical, straight

PLUMBAGO plum bā'gō
n. a drawing in lead
n. a kind of plant

PLUME ploom
n. a feather
v. to pride oneself

PLUMP plump
adj. not thin
v. to fall heavily
v. to fill out hollow cheeks
v. to pat pillows

PLURAL ploor'əl
adj. of more than one

PLEURAL
adj. of a membrane of the lungs

PLUSH plush
n. a kind of fabric
adj. luxurious

PLY plī
n. one thickness or layer, as in wood
v. to use
v. to pursue

PNEUMATIC nū mat'ik
n. a kind of tire
adj. spiritual

POACH pōch
v. to trespass in order to hunt
v. to cook in hot liquid
v. to mix with water, as clay

POACHER pō'chər
n. one who trespasses
n. a kind of fish
n. a kind of pan

POCKET pok'it
n. a pouch in clothing
n. financial resources
n. a cavity, as in a wall
v. to conceal or suppress

POD pod
n. pea or bean cover
n. a small herd of seals or whales
n. a small flock of birds

PODIUM pō'di um
n. a platform
n. a foot

POEM pō'əm
n. verse
n. a symbol of beauty

POIGNANT poin'yənt
adj. moving, sincere
adj. sharp, acrid to the smell

POINT point
n. a sharp end
n. a mark of punctuation
n. a position, spot
n. a hint
v. to direct with a finger

POISE poiz
n. balance, self-control
n. suspense, wavering

POKE pōk
v. to prod or push
v. to go slowly
n. a bag or sack
n. a brim on a bonnet

POKER pōk'ər
n. a rod for stirring a fire
n. a kind of card game

POLE pōl
n. a long piece of wood or metal
n. an opposite
n. an extremity of the axis of a sphere
n. (u.c.) a native of Poland

POLL
n. the registering of votes
v. to crop, clip, shear
n. the back of the head

POLICY pol'i sē
n. a course of action adopted
n. an insurance contract

POLISH pol'ish
v. to rub to a shine

POLISH pōl'ish
adj. (u.c.) of Poland

POLLARD pol'ərd
n. a tree with cut-off branches
n. an animal with no horns

POMMEL pum'əl
n. part of a saddle
PUMMEL
v. to beat or thrash

POMPON pom'pon
n. a kind of ornament of dress
n. a small flower

PONE pōn
n. a kind of bread made from
cornmeal
n. card player on the dealer's right

PONY pō'nē
n. a small horse
n. a small glass for liquids
v. to pay one's debts

POOL pool
n. puddle, pond
n. a shared facility
n. stakes of some games
n. a kind of game

POOP poop
n. part of the stern of a vessel
v. to become out of breath

POOR pōr
n. impoverished
PORE
n. a tiny opening in the skin or a leaf
v. to study, meditate
POUR
v. to make flow

POP pop
v. to make a short explosive sound
v. to come or go quickly
n. a kind of drink

POPPIED pop'ēd
adj. covered with poppies
adj. listless

PORT pōrt
n. a place where ships load and
unload
n. the left side of a vessel
n. a kind of wine

PORTER pōrt'ər
n. one who carries luggage
n. a doorkeeper
n. a dark ale

POSE pōz
v. to assume a position or character
v. to embarrass or baffle

POSH posh
adj. luxurious
interj. expression of disgust

POSITION pə zi'shən
n. place, situation
n. status
n. job

POSITIVE poz'i tiv
adj. definite, sure
adj. emphasizing what is laudable
adj. of the north pole of a magnet

POSSESSED pə zest'
adj. spurred by madness
adj. poised, self-possessed

POSSESSIVE pə zes'iv
adj. desirous of having
n. a term used in grammar

POST pōst
n. an upright support
n. the mail
n. a position of duty
v. to bring to public notice
v. to hasten, trot

POSTER pōst'ər
n. a placard
n. a horse kept for hire

POSTURE pos'chūr
n. the carriage of the body as a whole
v. to act in an affected manner

POT pot
n. a kind of container
n. money bet at one time
n. marijuana
n. a fat belly

POTHER poth'ər
n. uproar, fuss
n. a choking cloud
v. to worry

POTTLE pot'əl
n. a two-quart tankard
n. wine and liquor

POUF poof
n. puff of hair
n. a hassock

POUNCE pouns
v. to swoop
v. to grasp
v. to emboss metal
v. to rub the surface of hats with sandpaper

POUND pound
v. to strike repeatedly with force
n. British money unit
n. an enclosure for animals
n. 16 ounces avoirdupois
n. 12 ounces troy weight

POUT pout
v. to look sullen
n. a kind of fish

POUTER pout'ər
n. one who pouts
n. a kind of pigeon

POWER pou'ər
n. ability
n. strength
n. sway, authority

PRACTICE prak'tis
n. custom, repeated performance
n. the business of a doctor or lawyer

PRAGMATIC ·prag mat'ik
adj. of the practical
adj. busy
adj. interfering, dogmatic

PRAIRIE prā'rē
n. a land tract
n. a steam locomotive

PRAISE prāz
n. applause, eulogy

PRAYS
v. petitions or offers thanks to God

PREYS
n. victims
v. makes raids

PRANK prank
n. a trick
v. to dress up, show off

PRECEDENT pres'i dent
n. an example based on experience

PRECEDENT pri sēd'ənt
adj. earlier

PRECIOUS presh'əs
adj. costly, valuable
adj. affected, overly fastidious

PRECIPITATE pri sip'i tāt
v. to bring about suddenly
v. to rain, snow, or hail

PRECISION pri sizh'ən
n. accuracy, strictness

PRECISIAN
n. an English Puritan

PRECISIVE pri sī'siv
adj. separating a person or thing from others
adj. characterized by accuracy

PREDICATE pred'i kit
n. the verb of a sentence

PREDICATE pred'i kāt
v. to declare, assert

PREEN prēn
v. to trim or dress with the beak (of birds)
v. to be proud

PREGNANT preg'nənt
adj. with child
adj. full of meaning

PREMISES prem'i sez
n. propositions, assumptions
n. a tract of land and its buildings

PRESENCE prez'əns
n. attendance or company

PRESENTS
n. gifts

PRESENT prez'ent
n. a gift
adv. at this time

PRESENT prez ent'
v. to give a gift
v. to introduce

PRESENTLY prez'ent lē
adv. soon
adv. now

PRESERVE pri serv'
v. to keep alive
v. to cook fruits with sugar

PRESS pres
n. newspapers, reporters
v. to act with steadily applied force
v. to force into service
v. to iron

PRESUME pri sūm'
v. to take for granted, suppose
v. to overstep, act with impertinence

PRETENSION pri ten'shən
n. a claim or title to something
v. to apply tension before concrete is poured

PRETTY prit'ē
adj. pleasing to the eye
adv. very
adv. moderately

PRIDE prīd
n. a high opinion of one's self

PRIED
v. separated with difficulty

PRIMATE prī'māt
n. a mammal, including man, the apes, and monkeys

PRIMATE prī'mit
n. a bishop

PRIME prīm
adj. of the first importance
n. the period of perfection in a life
v. to make ready, as for painting

PRIMER prim'ər
n. a primary book for children

PRIMER prī'mər
n. a device used in firing powder

PRINCIPAL prins'i pəl
n. a chief or head
adj. most important

PRINCIPLE
n. an accepted rule of action

PRINT print
v. to reproduce words or pictures
n. a picture made from a block pla
n. a design on fabric

PRIOR prī'ər
adj. earlier
n. an officer in a monastery

PRIVATE prī'vit
adj. personal, particular
n. an enlisted soldier

PRIVY priv'ē
n. an outhouse
adj. private, secret

PRIZE prīz
n. a reward
v. to value, appreciate

PRIES
v. inquires impertinently

PROBE prōb
v. to search, question
n. a device used on some aircraft

PROCURE prō kūr'
v. to get by special effort
v. to pander, act as a pimp

PROFANE prō fān'
adj. ungodly, heathen
adj. common, vulgar

PROFESSION prə fesh'ən
n. vocation, employment
n. declaration of faith

PROFILE prō'fīl
n. a picture of the side of a head
n. a written piece on a personality

PROFIT prof'it
n. pecuniary gain

PROPHET
n. a person who speaks for God

PROJECT proj'ekt
n. a plan, scheme

PROJECT pro jekt'
v. to predict, estimate

PROMINENT prom'i nənt
adj. easily seen, conspicuous
adj. projecting
adj. famous, eminent

PROMISCUOUS prō mis'kū əs
adj. unchaste
adj. jumbled, consisting of parts brought together without order

PROMPT prompt
adj. quick or able
v. to help an actor with his lines
v. to urge

PRONE prōn
adj. disposed, liable
adj. with face or palms downward
adj. lying flat
n. a kind of sermon

PROPER prop'ər
adj. suitable

PROPPER
n. one who or that which supports someone or something

PROPERTY prop'ər tē
n. possessions, land
n. attribute or characteristic

PROSAIC prō sā'ik
adj. commonplace, dull
adj. of prose rather than poetry

PROSE prōz
n. the usual form of language; not poetry

PROS
n. professionals

PROSPECT pros'pekt
n. outlook for the future
n. a view, scenery

PROTHESIS proth'ə sis
n. an added sound to the beginning of a word
n. a table for Holy Communion in the Eastern Church

PROTOCOL prō'tō col
n. etiquette
n. the draft of a treaty

PRUNE proon
n. a kind of plum
v. to cut off twigs or branches

PRY prī
v. to raise or move by leverage
v. to look closely
v. to inquire impertinently

PSALTER sal'tər
n. the book of Psalms

SALTER
n. one who makes or sells salt

PUDDING pood'ing
n. a kind of dessert
n. a fender on some ships

PUDDLING pud'ling
n. the act of one who wades in a small pool
n. the act of melting pig iron

PUFF puf
n. a short, quick blast, as of wind
n. a kind of pastry
v. to inflate

PUG pug
n. a kind of dog
n. a pugilist
v. to mix with water for paste

PULP pulp
n. the fleshy part of fruit
n. a magazine printed on cheap paper

PULPIT pool'pit
n. a platform in a church
n. a safety rail on a small boat

PULSE puls
n. the throb of the heart
n. edible seeds of some plants

PUMP pump
n. a machine for lifting fluids
n. a kind of shoe

PUNCH punch
n. a blow with the fist
n. a kind of drink
n. a kind of tool

PUNCHEON pun'chun
n. a large cask
n. a slab of wood

PUNK punk
n. a light for fires
n. an inexperienced boy
n. a petty criminal

PUPIL pū'pil
n. a student
n. part of the eye

PURCHASE per'chəs
v. to acquire by payment
n. leverage
n. a firm grip or grasp

PURSE pers
n. a pocketbook
n. a sum of money offered as a prize
v. to pucker

PURSUE per sū'
v. to follow in order to harm
v. to continue a course of action

PUTTER put'ər
n. a kind of golf club
v. to dawdle

PUTTER pŏŏt'ər
n. one who puts a shot

PYTHON pī'thon
n. a spirit or demon
n. a kind of snake

Q

Q kū
n. seventeenth letter of the English alphabet

CUE
n. a hint
n. a pole used in billiards or pool

QUEUE
n. a pigtail
n. a line of people

QUACK kwak
n. the sound made by a duck
n. a pretender in medicine

QUADRILLE kwo dril'
n. a kind of dance
n. a kind of card game

QUAIL kwāl
n. a kind of bird
v. shrink with fear

QUAKE kwāk
n. an earthquake
v. to tremble from fear

QUALIFY kwol'i fī
v. to make competent
v. to modify or limit

QUALITY kwol'i tē
n. an attribute
n. character with respect to excellence
n. high social position

QUARREL kwo'rel
n. an angry dispute
n. a small pane of glass

QUARRY kwo'rē
n. a pit from which stone is mined
n. an object of search or attack

QUART kwärt
n. one-fourth gallon
n. one-eighth peck
n. a sequence of cards

QUARTER kwär'tər
n. one-fourth
n. a U.S. coin
n. housing accommodations
n. mercy

QUARTZ kwärtz
n. a common mineral

QUARTS
n. certain measures

QUASH kwosh
v. to quell, subdue
v. to make void

QUEEN kwēn
n. a female monarch

QUEAN
n. a shrew, hussy

QUICK kwik
adj. prompt, rapid
n. living persons
n. sensitive flesh

QUILL kwil
n. a large feather
n. a hollow stem for rolling yarn
n. a writing pen

QUIRK kwerk
n. a mannerism
n. a sudden twist or turn
n. a kind of enclosure

QUIT kwit
v. to stop
adj. released from obligation

QUIVER kwiv'ər
n. a case for arrows
v. to shake

R

R ar
n. eighteenth letter of the English alphabet

ARE
v. part of the verb *to be*

RABAT rə bat'
n. a clerical vest

RABAT rab'ət
n. a piece of imperfectly fired pottery

RABBIT rab'it
n. a kind of animal

RABBET
n. a groove on a board

RAREBIT
n. a kind of cheese dish

RABBLE rab'əl
n. a disorderly crowd
n. a kind of tool for a furnace

RABID rab'id
adj. afflicted with rabies; mad
adj. furious
adj. irrationally extreme

RACE rās
n. a contest of speed
n. tribe, family
n. a ginger root

RACER rā'sər
n. one who or that which races
n. a kind of snake

RACK rak
n. a framework
n. agony
n. a pace of a horse
v. to strain in mental effort

WRACK
n. wreck, ruin

RACKET rak'it
n. a loud noise
n. a bat used in some games
n. a dishonest scheme

RACY rā'sē
adj. lively, animated
adj. risqué

RADIANT rā'dē ənt
adj. shining, bright
adj. emitted by radiation

RADIATE rā'dē āt
v. to move like rays
v. to project joy

RADICAL rad'i kəl
adj. of the root, basic
adj. favoring drastic social or political reforms

RAFFLE raf'əl
n. a kind of lottery
n. rubbish

RAFT raft
n. a floating platform
n. a great quantity

RAFTER raf'tər
n. a timber that supports a roof
n. a flock of turkeys

RAG rag
n. a torn old piece of cloth
v. to tease
v. to play ragtime music

RAGE rāj
n. fury
n. vogue, fashion

RAIL rāl
n. a fence or fence part
n. a kind of bird
v. to complain

RAIN rān
n. a shower from clouds

REIGN
v. to rule

REIN
n. part of a harness

RAISE rāz
v. to lift

RAYS
n. beams of light

RAZE
v. to tear down

RAKE rāk
n. a tool used in gathering leaves or hay
n. a roué
v. to incline
v. to hunt (as a dog) with nose close to the ground
v. to fly after game (as a hawk)

RAKISH rāk'ish
adj. smart, jaunty
adj. dissolute

RALLY ra'lē
n. a mass meeting
v. to bring into order again
v. to recover partially from illness
v. to ridicule

RAM ram
n. a male sheep
v. to drive or force by heavy blows

RAMBLER ramb'lər
n. one who wanders aimlessly
n. a kind of rose

RAMIFICATION ram i fi kā'shən
n. a branch
n. a consequence

RAMP ramp
n. a sloping surface between two levels
v. to act violently, rage

RAMPANT ram'pant
adj. violent, raging
adj. standing on the hind legs

RANCOR rank'ər
n. bitter ill-will, hatred

RANKER
adj. more repugnant

RANGE rānj
n. extent or scope
n. row, line, or series of persons or things
n. a kind of stove
n. a tract of land for grazing

RANK rank
n. social or official position
n. a row of things or persons
adj. utter, absolute
adj. having an unpleasant taste or smell

adj. growing with great vigor

RAP rap
v. to strike with a quick, light blow
n. the least bit

WRAP
n. a coat or cloak

RAPE rāp
v. to seize, carry off by force
n. act of forcing a woman to have sexual intercourse
n. a kind of plant used for animals food
n. squeezed grapes

RAPT rapt
adj. absorbed, delighted

WRAPPED
v. covered closely

RARE rair
adj. unusual, choice
adj. slightly cooked

RASH rash
adj. hasty, reckless
n. a skin eruption
n. a number of occurrences in a period of time

RASHER rash'ər
n. a serving of bacon
n. a kind of fish
adj. more reckless

RASPY ras'pē
adj. harsh, grating
adj. easily annoyed

RAT rat
n. a kind of animal
n. a scoundrel
v. to betray one's associates
n. a kind of hairpiece

RATE rāt
n. relative condition or quality
n. charge, cost
n. degree of speed
v. to scold

RATHER rath'ər, räth'ər
adv. in some degree
adv. more willingly
adv. more truly

RATING rāt'ing
n. a classification
n. a scolding

RATIONALIZE rash'ən ə līz
v. to explain away one's actions
v. to use reason

RATTLE rat'əl
v. to give out a series of short, sharp sounds
v. to confuse
n. a baby's toy

RATTLING rat'ling
n. something that rattles
n. ratline
adj. remarkably good
adv. very

RAVE rāv
v. to talk wildly, rage
n. an enthusiastic review of a work of art
n. a sidepiece of a wagon

RAVEL rav'əl
v. to disentangle
v. to tangle

RAVEN rāv'ən
n. a kind of bird
RAVEN rav'ən
v. to eat greedily

RAVING rāv'ing
adj. frenzied
adj. remarkable

RAW rau
adj. uncooked
adj. painfully open
adj. unprepared, rough

RAY rā
n. a narrow beam of light
n. part of a straight line
n. a kind of fish
RE
n. the second note in the musical scale

RAZOR rāz'ər
n. a shaving tool
RAISER
n. one who or that which lifts

REACH rēch
v. to arrive
v. to stretch out

READ rēd
v. to look at and understand words
REED
n. a kind of wild grass
n. a musical pipe

READ red
v. did read
RED
n. a color
n. a communist
n. the condition of operating at a loss
REDD
v. to tidy
n. nest of trout or salmon

READY red'ē
adj. prepared for action or use
adj. agreeable, willing
adj. keen, clever

REAL rēl
adj. true, actual
REEL
n. part of a fishing pole
n. a kind of dance or its music
v. to sway under a blow

REAM rem
n. 500 sheets of paper
v. to enlarge a hole with a special tool

REAR rēr
n. the back of something
v. to support, care for a child
v. to rise on hind legs, as a horse

REASON rē'zən
n. a basis or cause
n. sound judgment
n. rationalization

REBATE rē'bāt
n. partial refund
REBATE rē'bāt, rab'it
n. rabbet

RECALL ri caul'
v. to remember
v. to repeal, annul
v. to summon to return

RECAP rē'cap
v. to add rubber to a worn tire
v. to sum up

RECEDE rē sēd'
v. to go or move away; retreat
v. to give back

RESEED
v. to plant again with seeds

RECEIVER ri sē'vər
n. one who or that which receives
n. part of the telephone

RECEPTACLE ri sept'ə cl
n. a container
n. an electrical outlet

RECESS rē'ses
n. a play period
n. a bay or alcove in a room

RECITE ri cīt'
v. to repeat words from memory
v. to count, enumerate
v. to count again

RECOIL rē koil'
v. to draw back, flinch
v. to come back, rebound

RECOMMEND rek ə mend'
v. to approve
v. to advise

RECORD ri kord'
v. to set down, as in writing, in order
to keep

RECORD rek'ərd
n. the highest or best ever
n. a phonograph disk

RECOVER rē cuv'ər
v. to cover again
v. to regain something lost

RECREATE rē'crē āt
v. to reproduce, remake

RECREATE rek'rē āt
v. to relax and enjoy

REDOLENT red'ə lent
adj. fragrant
adj. reminiscent

REDRESS rē'dres
n. atonement
v. to dress again

REDUCE rē dūs'
v. to bring down to a smaller extent
v. to degrade, vanquish

REEFER rē'fər
n. a short coat of thick cloth
n. a marijuana cigarette

REEK rēk
n. a strong, unpleasant smell

WREAK
v. to inflict, as punishment

REEVE rēv
n. an officer of a town or district
v. to pass a ship's rope through a hole
or ring
n. the female ruff

REFINED ri fīnd'
v. made free from impurities, as metal
adj. polite, well-bred
adj. subtle, precise

REFLECT ri flekt'
v. to cast back from a surface; to
mirror
v. to think, ponder, meditate

REFORM ri form'
n. the improvement of what is wrong
REFORM rē'form'
v. to form again

REFRAIN ri frān'
n. chorus, part of a verse
v. to abstain, cease

REFUND ri fund'
v. to repay
REFUND rē'fund'
v. to fund anew

REFUSE ref'ūs
n. trash, garbage
REFUSE ri fūz'
v. to decline to accept

REGAL rē'gəl
adj. royal
n. a kind of reed organ

REGALE ri gāl'
v. to entertain, delight
REGALE ri'gā'lē
n. a right formerly claimed by some
kings

REGARD ri gärd'
v. to observe
v. to esteem

REGISTER rej'is ter
n. a book of records
v. to show an emotion

REGRATE ri grāt'
v. to buy up in order to sell again
v. to redress stone work

REHEARSE ri hers'
v. to practice for a performance
v. to tell the facts or particulars of

REJOIN rē join'
v. to come again into company; reunite
v. to answer; esp. to counterreply

RELATED ri lāt'əd
v. told a story of happenings
adj. kin

RELATIVE rel'ə tiv
n. kinsman
adj. comparative

RELEASE ri lēs'
v. to let go; free
v. to rent again

RELIEF ri lēf'
n. something that lessens pain or grief
n. a kind of sculpture

REMARK ri märk'
v. to say casually
v. to notice

REMISSION rē mish'ən
n. pardon
n. relaxation

REMIT ri mit'
v. to send money
v. to relax, abate

REMOTE ri mōt'
adj. far apart in space or time
adj. unlikely
adj. aloof, withdrawn

REMOUNT rē mount'
v. to get up on again
n. a fresh horse

REMOVE ri moov'
v. to take away or off
v. to send away
v. to kill

RENAISSANCE ren'a sons
n. a rebirth
n. (u.c.) a period of history in Europe

RENDER rend'ər
v. to give, supply
v. to demonstrate
v. to yield
v. to melt fat

RENEW rē nu'
v. to resume
v. to mend

RENOUNCE ri nouns'
v. to give up voluntarily
v. to repudiate

RENT rent
n. money paid by a tenant
n. a slit

REP rep
n. a kind of fabric
n. an amount of radiation

REPAIR ri pair'
v. to mend
v. to go, as to a place

REPAST ri past'
n. a meal

REPASSED rē'past'
v. passed back again

REPEL ri pel'
v. to drive or force back
v. to cause distaste

REPELLENT ri pel'ənt
n. protective solution, as from mosquitoes
adj. repulsive, causing aversion

REPENT ri pent'
v. to feel sorry for past actions

REPENT rē'pənt
adj. creeping, as a vine

REPERTORY rep'ər tōr'ē
n. a kind of theatrical company
n. a storehouse

REPLACE ri plās'
v. to substitute for
v. to repay
v. to put back

REPORT ri pōrt'
n. a statement of an event
n. a loud noise, as from a gun
n. fame
v. to accuse

REPOSE ri pōz'
v. to lie and be at rest
v. to lie dead
v. to put confidence in a person or thing

REPRESENT rep'ri zent'
v. to symbolize
v. to act in the place of
REPRESENT rē'pri zent'
v. to present again

REPRESS ri pres'
v. to keep under control
v. to crush
REPRESS rē pres'
v. to press again

REPRODUCE rē'prō dūs'
v. to make a copy
v. to bear offspring

REPROVE ri proov'
v. to rebuke
REPROVE rē proov'
v. to prove again

REQUIRE ri kwīr'
v. to need
v. to demand

REQUITE ri kwīt'
v. to repay, reward
v. to revenge

RESALE rē'sāl
n. the act of selling a second time
RESAIL
v. to sail back or again

RESEARCH ri serch'
n. diligent inquiry into a subject
RESEARCH rē search'
v. to search for again

RESERVATION res ər vā'shun
n. the act of keeping back
n. public land held for native American Indians

RESERVE ri zerv'
n. coldness of manner, silence
v. to keep back, hold
RESERVE rē'serv'
v. to serve again

RESIDENCE rez'i dəns
n. a dwelling place
RESIDENTS
n. those who live in a specified place
n. doctors in a stage of medical training

RESIGNED ri zīnd'
v. gave up a position
adj. submissive

RESIST ri zist'
v. to strive against
v. to refrain from reluctantly

RESOLUBLE ri zol'ū bəl
adj. capable of being settled, as an argument
adj. able to be dissolved again

RESOLUTION rez ō loo'shun
n. a formal expression of opinion
n. firmness of purpose, strength

RESOLVE ri zolv'
n. firmness of purpose
v. to determine by will
v. to separate, break up
v. to dispel doubts

RESORT ri zort'
n. a place for a vacation
v. appeal for aid
RESORT rē'sort'
v. to sort again

RESOUND ri zound'
v. to make an echoing sound
v. to be famed or celebrated
RESOUND rē sound'
v. to sound again

RESOURCE rē sōrs'
n. a source of supply
n. cleverness, ingenuity

RESPECT ri spekt′
n. honor, reverence
n. a detail, feature

RESPOND ri spond′
v. to answer in words
v. to match
n. a kind of pilaster

RESPONSIBLE ri spon′si bəl
adj. liable
adj. competent
adj. solvent

REST rest
n. sleep or inactivity
n. remainder

WREST
v. to twist, pull, jerk

RESTIVE rest′iv
adj. nervous, unquiet
adj. stubborn

RESUME ri zoom′
v. to go on with again

RÉSUMÉ rā′zoo mā′
n. a summary

RETAIL rē′tāl
n. the sale of goods

RETAIL ri tāl′
v. to repeat in detail

RETAIN ri tān′
v. to keep possession of
v. to hire a lawyer

RETCH rech
v. to try to vomit

WRETCH
n. a person of base character

RETIRE ri tīr′
v. to withdraw; go to bed
v. to stop working

RETIRE rə tē rā′
n. a ballet step

RETIRING ri tīr′ing
v. withdrawing into privacy
adj. shy

RETORT ri tort′
n. a severe or witty reply
n. a kind of glass used in a laboratory

RETRACE rē′trās′
v. to trace again, as lines

RETRACE ri trās′
v. to go back over, as with steps or memory

RETRACT ri trakt′
v. to draw back
v. to deny

RETREAD rē′tred
v. to recap a tire
v. to tread again

RETREAT ri trēt′
n. withdrawal from an enemy
n. a place of quiet

RETROCEDE re trə sēd′
v. to retire, go back
v. to cede back

RETURN ri tern′
v. to go or come back
v. to reply
v. to replace
v. to repay
n. income

REVEAL ri vēl′
v. to make known, disclose
n. a part of a door or window

REVERE ri vēr′
v. to venerate
n. a lapel

REVERSE ri vers′
adj. opposite
n. mishap

REVIEW ri vū′
n. a critical report
n. a viewing of the past

REVUE
n. a group of dances or songs

REVOLT ri vōlt′
v. to rebel
v. to feel disgust

REVOLUTION rev ə loo′shən
n. a political overthrow
n. movement in a circular course

REVOLVE ri volv′
v. to rotate
v. to think about

RHYME rīm
n. words in a poem that sound similar
RIME
n. a coating of tiny ice particles

RIB rib
n. a bony part of the body
v. to tease

RIBBON rib'ən
n. a woven band of fine material
RIBBAND
n. a strip of wood or metal used in shipbuilding

RICH rich
adj. wealthy
adj. (of food) full of spices, sweets, or butter

RICK rik
n. a haystack
n. a frame to hold boxes or barrels

RIDDLE rid'əl
n. a kind of puzzle
v. to pierce with many holes

RIDER rī'dər
n. one who is carried on something
n. an addition to a document

RIDGE rij
n. a long, narrow elevation of land
n. the back of an animal

RIFFLE rif'əl
n. a ripple
v. to shuffle cards

RIFLE rī'fəl
n. a kind of gun
v. to ransack and rob

RIGHT rīt
adj. fair, true
adj. opposite of left
adj. politically conservative
RITE
n. a ceremony
WRIGHT
n. a workman
WRITE
v. to put words on paper

RIGOR rig'ər
n. severity
n. hardship
RIGGER
n. one who tends the rigging of ships

RIND rind
n. the outer coat of animals or plants
n. a support for an upper millstone

RING ring
n. a circle for the finger
n. a group of persons with like ideas
v. to give forth a sound, as a bell
WRING
v. to twist with force

RIP rip
v. to tear apart or cut
v. to go at great speed

RIPPLE rip'əl
n. a small wave on water
n. a device for removing seeds from flax or hemp

RISE rīz
v. to get or go up
v. to succeed
v. to puff up, as yeast
RYES
n. certain grains

RIVER riv'ər
n. a large natural stream
RIVER rī'vər
n. a person who tears apart

RIVET riv'ət
n. a kind of metal pin
v. to hold (the eye, attention) firmly

ROACH rōch
n. a kind of insect
n. a kind of fish
v. to clip the mane of a horse

ROAD rōd
n. a street, highway
RODE
v. did ride
ROWED
v. did row (a boat)

ROAM rōm
v. to wander
ROME
n. (u.c.) a city in Italy

ROCK rok
n. a mass of stone
v. to sway to and fro
n. a kind of music
ROC
n. a mythical bird

ROCKET rok'ət
n. a space vehicle
n. a device containing combustibles
n. a kind of plant

ROCKY rok'ē
adj. firm, steadfast
adj. shaky
adj. unfeeling

ROD rod
n. a stick
n. part of the retina

ROIL roil
v. to stir up sediment
v. to irritate, vex

ROLE rōl
n. the part an actor plays
ROLL
n. a kind of bread
n. a list
v. to move on wheels

ROLLER rōl'ər
n. a cylindrical body
n. a kind of pigeon

ROMANCE rō mans'
n. a love story
adj. (u.c.) of languages based on Latin

ROOK rŏŏk
n. a kind of crow
n. a piece in chess

ROOKIE rŏŏk'ē
n. a novice, first-year athlete
ROOKY
adj. full of rooks

ROOM room, rŏŏm
n. part of a house

n. capacity
n. scope
RHEUM room
n. a cold

ROOT root
n. part of a plant, tooth, or hair
n. origin
v. to turn up the soil
v. to search
v. to encourage a team
ROUTE
n. a way or road for travel

ROOTER root'ər
n. animal that roots, as with a snout
n. a follower, supporter

ROSARY rō'zə rē
n. prayer beads
n. a rose garden

ROSÉ rōz
n. a kind of flower
v. got up
ROSÉ rō zā'
n. a kind of wine
ROES rōz
n. some deer
ROWS
v. does row
n. straight lines

ROSETTE rō'zet'
n. a rose-shaped ribbon
n. a leopard's spot
n. a kind of plant disease

ROTATE rō'tāt
v. to cause to go through a cycle of changes
v. to wheel, whirl

ROTE rōt
n. routine
n. the sound of waves breaking on the shore
WROTE
v. did write

ROTTEN rot'ən
adj. decaying, bad-smelling
adj. treacherous

ROUGH ruf
adj. not smooth
adj. noisy, impolite
RUFF
n. an old-fashioned collar
n. a kind of fish
v. to trump at cards

ROULETTE roo let'
n. a game of chance
n. an engraver's tool

ROUND round
adj. ring-shaped
n. a kind of dance
adj. roughly correct

ROUNDER round'ər
n. one who makes a circuit
n. a drunkard
adj. more round

ROUSE rouz
v. to stir or wake up
v. to excite
ROWS
n. quarrels

ROUT rout
v. to defeat
v. to poke, search
ROUTE rout, root
n. a way or road for travel

ROVE rōv
v. to amble, stray
v. passed a rope through
v. to form twisted strands, as of wool
or cotton

ROVER rōv'ər
n. a wanderer
n. a pirate

ROW rō
v. to propel a boat by oars
ROE
n. a kind of deer
n. a mass of fish eggs

ROYAL roi'əl
adj. of a king or queen
adj. bigger in size and quality

RUB rub
v. to move one thing on the surface of

something else
n. difficulty

RUBBER rub'ər
n. a kind of elastic material
n. an eraser
n. an overshoe
n. a series of games in card playing

RUCK ruk
n. a large number; mass
v. to fold or wrinkle

RUDE rood
adj. impolite
adj. rough
ROOD
n. a crucifix
n. one-fourth acre
RUED
v. regretted

RUE roo
v. to regret
n. a kind of plant with yellow flowers
ROUX
n. a kind of cooking sauce

RUFFLE ruf'əl
n. a kind of trimming
v. to disorder, rumple
n. a low, continuing beat of a drum

RUGGED rug'id
adj. rocky, hilly
adj. austere
adj. strong and tough

RULER rool'ər
n. a person who governs
n. a measuring stick

RUMINATE roo'mi nāt
v. to meditate, ponder
v. to chew the cud

RUMP rump
n. the hind part of an animal
n. remaining members of a legislative
body after most have gone

RUN run
v. to go quickly by moving the legs
v. to change color in water
n. a ladder, as in stockings

RUNE roon
n. a poem, song, or verse
n. part of an old alphabet

RUNG rung
n. a step of a ladder
v. was made to sound, as a bell

WRUNG
v. did wring

RUNLET run'let
n. a small stream
n. a small cask

RUNNER run'ər
n. a messenger
n. a blade, as on a sled
n. a long, narrow rug

RUSH rush
v. to hasten, run
n. a grasslike herb

RUSSET rus'it
n. a reddish brown
n. a kind of apple

RUSTY rust'ē
adj. oxidized, as metal
adj. forgetful
adj. stubborn

RUT rut
n. a track or groove in the ground
n. a period of sexual activity in some
animals
n. a fixed mode of procedure

RYE rī
n. a cereal grass
n. a Gypsy gentleman

WRY
adj. twisted, crooked

S

S es
n. nineteenth letter of the English
alphabet

ESS
n. something curved like an S

SABLES sā'bəlz
n. certain fur-bearing animals
n. mourning garments

SABOT sab'ō
n. a wooden shoe
n. a soft metal ring at the base of a
projectile

SACK sak
n. a large bag
n. a kind of wine
v. to loot, plunder

SAC
n. a baglike part of an animal or plant

SACQUE
n. a loose-fitting jacket

SACRAL sā'krəl
adj. of sacred rites
adj. of the sacrum

SACRIFICE sak'rə fīs
n. an offering to a god
n. a loss in selling something below
its value

SAD sad
adj. unhappy
adj. deplorably bad

SADDLE sad'əl
n. a seat for a rider on a horse
n. a cut of meat
n. a strip of leather on a shoe
v. to load as if with a burden

SAFETY sāf'tē
n. the state of being free from harm
or risk
n. a base hit in baseball

SAGE sāj
n. a wise man
n. a kind of herb

SAIL sāl
n. canvas rigging on a boat or ship

SALE
n. something sold, sometimes at
reduced prices

SAILER sāl'ər
n. a vessel propelled by sails

SAILOR
n. a seaman
n. a kind of straw hat

SAKE sāk
n. cause, purpose, or end

SAKE sä'kē
n. a Japanese drink

SAKI
n. a kind of monkey

SALAMANDER sal'ə mand ər
n. a kind of lizard
n. a kind of portable stove

SALIENT sā'lē ənt
adj. prominent, striking
adj. leaping or jumping

SALLOW sal'ō
adj. of a sickly, pale color
n. a willow

SALLY sal'ē
n. a sudden activity
n. a clever, witty remark

SALMON sam'ən
n. a kind of fish
n. light yellowish-pink color

SALOON sal oon'
n. a bar
n. a room on a ship for the use of passengers

SALT sault
n. a seasoning
n. an old sailor
n. wit, pungency

SALUTE sal ūt'
n. gesture of respect
n. a kind of gold coin

SALVE sav
n. a soothing ointment
v. to salvage

SAMPLER sam'plər
n. a piece of needlework
n. a collection of selections or models

SANDAL sand'əl
n. a kind of shoe
n. sandalwood

SANDY sand'ē
adj. of the nature of tiny grains of rock
adj. of a yellowish-red color

SANE sān
adj. having a sound, healthy mind

SEINE
n. a fishing net
n. (u.c.) a river in France

SANGUINE sang'gwin
adj. cheerful, hopeful
adj. blood red

SAP sap
n. the juice of a woody plant
v. to weaken, deplete
n. a deep, narrow trench

SARDINE sär dēn'
n. a kind of fish

SARDINE sär'dīn
n. a kind of gem

SASH sash
n. a band or scarf
n. part of a window

SATELLITE sat'el īt
n. a body that revolves around a planet
n. an obsequious follower

SATURATE sat'ū rāt
v. to soak thoroughly
v. to destroy a target

SATYR sā'tər
n. half-man, half-goat of mythology
n. a lecher
n. a kind of butterfly

SAVE sāv
v. to rescue, keep safe
prep. except, but

SAVER sāv'ər
n. one who saves

SAVOR
n. a particular taste or smell

SAVORY sā'və rē
adj. pleasant in taste or smell
n. a kind of mint

SAW sau
n. a kind of tool
v. did see
n. a maxim

SAY sā
v. to speak
n. an old-fashioned fabric

SCAB skab
n. the crust on a healing wound
n. a worker who refuses to act with a labor union

SCABIOUS skā'bē əs
adj. covered with scabs
adj. pertaining to scabies
n. a kind of herb

SCABROUS skab'rəs
adj. having a rough surface
adj. full of difficulties
adj. indecent, obscene

SCALD skauld
n. a burn caused by hot liquid or steam
adj. scabby

SCALES skālz
n. balances for weighing purposes
n. graduated series
n. flat, horny plates covering fish
v. climbs up or over

SCALLOP skal'əp
n. a kind of marine animal
n. a series of half-circles on material
n. a thin, pounded piece of meat

SCAMP skamp
n. a rascal
n. a kind of fish

SCAN skan
v. to examine minutely
v. to read hastily
v. to examine the meter of verse

SCAPULAR skap'ū lər
adj. of the shoulder blade
n. a loose, sleeveless garment
n. a kind of bandage

SCAR skär
n. the mark left by a healed sore
n. a cliff
n. a low rock in the sea

SCARAB ska'rəb
n. a kind of beetle
n. a kind of gem

SCARF skärf
n. a long, narrow piece of material
n. a strip of skin of a whale
n. a tapered piece of timber

SCARIFY ska'rə fī
v. to make scratches
v. to hurt by unkind criticism

SCAT skat
v. to go off hastily
n. a kind of card game

SCATHE skāth
v. to attack with criticism
v. to hurt, as by scorching

SCATOLOGY skat ol'ə jē
n. the study of obscenity
n. the study of fossil excrement

SCAVENGE skav'enj
v. to cleanse from filth, as a street
v. to gather something usable from discarded material

SCENE sēn
n. the place where something happens
n. a division of a play
n. any view or picture
n. a display of bad manners

SEEN
v. was looked at

SCHEME skēm
n. a plan of action to be followed
n. a conspiracy

SCHOLAR skol'ər
n. a learned person, esp. in a particular subject
n. a pupil

SCHOLARSHIP skol'ər ship .
n. learning, knowledge acquired by study
n. a sum of money granted to a student

SCHOOL skool
n. a place of instruction, esp. for children
n. a large number of fish or whales
n. any body of persons who agree

SCIENCE sī'əns
n. a branch of knowledge dealing with facts
n. skill

SCION sī'ən
n. a descendant
n. a shoot or twig

SCISSORS siz'ərs
n. a cutting instrument
n. certain holds in wrestling

SCONCE skons
n. a bracket for lights
n. a small detached fort; a shelter
n. the head or skull

SCOOP skoop
n. a ladle
n. a news story that breaks first

SCOOTER skoo'tər
n. a kind of vehicle
n. a kind of duck

SCOPE skōp
n. range of view
n. space for activity
n. length

SCORCH skaurch
v. to affect by burning slightly
v. to criticize severely

SCORE skōr
n. the record of points in a game or test
n. a group of 20

SCOT skot
n. an assessment or tax
n. (u.c.) a native of Scotland

SCOTCH skoch
v. to cut or gash
v. to put an end to
v. to block or prop with a wedge
n. (u.c.) a kind of whiskey
adj. (u.c.) of people of Scotland

SCOUR skour
v. to remove dirt by hard rubbing
v. to range over, as in search

SCOUT skout
n. a person sent out to find information
v. to reject with scorn, despise
n. (u.c.) a member of Girl Scouts or Boy Scouts

SCRABBLE skrab'əl
v. to scratch or scrape
v. to scribble
n. (u.c.) a certain word game

SCRAG skrag
n. the lean end of a neck of veal or mutton
v. to test (spring steel) by bending

SCRAMBLE skram'bəl
v. to climb or move quickly, using one's hands and feet
v. to cook foods that have been mixed
v. to make messages
v. to make messages incomprehensible

SCRAP skrap
n. a bit, fragment
n. a fight, quarrel

SCRAPE skrāp
v. to smooth by rubbing
v. to mar the surface
n. a bad situation
v. to draw the foot back while making a bow

SCRATCH skrach
v. to mar by rubbing with something rough
v. to erase, cancel
n. a scrawl

SCRATCHY skrach'ē
adj. causing a slight grating noise
adj. haphazard
adj. causing itching
adj. covered with scratches

SCREAK skrēk
v. to screech
v. to creak

SCREAM skrēm
v. to utter a loud cry
v. to be conspicuous
n. something hilariously funny

SCREED skrēd
n. a long essay
n. a kind of wooden ship

SCREEN skrēn
n. anything that shelters, protects, or conceals
n. motion pictures

SCREW skroo
n. a kind of metal fastener
v. to distort
v. to coerce

SCRIBBLE skri'bəl
v. to write carelessly
v. to tear apart wool fibers

SCRIBE skrīb
n. one who acts as a penman
v. to mark or score wool with a pointed instrument

SCRIPT skript
n. handwriting
n. a manuscript for the theater

SCROLL skrōl
n. a roll of paper with writing or pictures on it
n. a form of ornamentation
n. the curved head of a violin

SCRUB skrub
v. to rub hard in washing
n. low trees or shrubs
v. to cancel a mission flight
n. a mongrel

SCRUPLE skroo'pəl
n. qualm, compunction
n. a unit of weight

SCUD skud
v. to run or move quickly
v. to cleanse a hide of hair or dirt

SCUFF skuf
v. to mar by scraping
v. to shuffle
n. a flat-heeled slipper

SKULL skul
n. the bony part of the head

SCULL
n. a kind of oar
n. a kind of boat

SCUTTLE skut'əl
v. to abandon
n. a deep basket for carrying coal
v. to hurry
n. a small hatch on a ship

SEAL sēl
n. an emblem used as evidence of authority
n. a kind of water animal
n. any material that tightly closes anything

SEAM sēm
n. the line formed by sewing together pieces of cloth

SEEM
v. to appear to be or do

SEAMAN sē'mən
n. sailor

SEMEN
n. fluid of the male reproductive organ

SEAR sēr
v. to char
v. to make callous
n. part of a pistol

SEER
n. a prophet
n. one who observes

SERE
adj. dry, withered

SEASON sē'zən
n. one of the four divisions of the year
v. to add spices or herbs to food
v. to become mature, experienced

SEASONABLE sē'zən ə bəl
adj. suitable for the time of year
adj. opportune, well-timed

SEAT sēt
n. something to sit on, as a chair
n. the buttocks
n. authority

SECOND sek'ənd
adj. the next after the first
n. support of a motion before the vote
n. a backer
n. the sixtieth part of a minute

SECONDARY sek'ən de'rē
adj. of minor importance
n. a kind of feather

SECOND-HAND sek'ənd hand'
adj. obtained from others or from books

SECOND HAND
n. part of a watch or clock

SECRETARY sek'ri tā'rē
n. one who handles office correspondence
n. an official
n. a kind of desk

SECRETE sē krēt'
v. (in a cell or gland) to release a substance
v. to hide, conceal

SECTION sek'shən
n. a part that is cut off or separated
n. an incision

SECULAR sek'ū lär
adj. of worldly, not sacred, matters
adj. continuing through long ages

SECURE sē kūr'
adj. free from danger
v. to get hold of, obtain

SEDUCE si dūs'
v. to lead astray, corrupt
v. to win over, attract

SEED sēd
n. the propagative part of anything
n. offspring
v. to arrange players in an athletic match

CEDE
v. to yield

SEEDY sē'dē
adj. containing many seeds
adj. shabby, run-down

SEEP sēp
n. a kind of jeep
v. to ooze

SEETHE sēth
v. to soak
v. to boil
v. to be excited

SEIZE sēz
v. to grasp by force

C'S
n. certain letters

SEAS
n. oceans

SEES
v. looks at

SEMBLANCE sem'blans
n. an unreal appearance
n. a likeness, copy

SEMINAL sem'i nəl
adj. having possibilities of future development
adj. consisting of semen

SEND send
v. to emit

SCEND
v. to heave, as a boat in a swell

SENILE sē'nīl
adj. characteristic of old age, esp. decline in mental faculties
adj. of topographical features advanced in erosion

SENSE sens
n. practical intelligence
n. faculty, as sight or hearing
v. to become aware of

CENSE
v. to burn incense

CENTS
n. coins

SCENTS
n. odors

SENSIBLE sens'ə bəl
adj. intelligent
adj. conscious
adj. capable of being perceived by the senses

SENTENCE sent'ens
n. a unit in grammar
v. to condemn to punishment

SEQUENCE sē'kwens
n. a succession, series
n. result

SERENE se rēn'
adj. calm, peaceful
adj. most high or august

SERIES sē'rēs
n. sequence

CERES
n. (u.c.) an ancient Roman goddess

SERIOUS sēr'ē əs
adj. characterized by deep thought
adj. grave, somber
adj. giving cause for apprehension

SERPENTINE ser'pen tēn
adj. winding like a snake
n. a common mineral

SERUM sē'rum
n. the pale yellow liquid of blood
n. an antitoxin

SERVE serv
v. to wait upon
v. to start the play, as in tennis
v. to do duty, as a soldier or juror
v. to suffice

SERVICE ser'vis
n. help, aid
n. the armed forces
n. a set of dishes

SET set
v. to put in a particular place
v. to put a value on something
v. to sink
v. to harden
n. a clique
n. a division in some games
adj. stubborn

SETBACK set'bak
n. a reverse or defeat
n. a form of architecture

SETTER set'ər
n. one who or that which sets
n. a kind of dog

SETTING set'ing
n. the act of one who or that which sets
n. environment
n. china, silver, glassware at table

SETTLE set'əl
v. to appoint, fix, agree
v. to pay
v. to colonize
v. to compose
v. to subside
n. a kind of bench

SEVERAL sev'ər əl
adj. more than two but fewer than many
adj. individual

SEVERE si vēr'
adj. harsh, strict
adj. simple, plain

SEWER soo'ər
n. a conduit

SUER
n. one who sues

SEWER sō'ər
n. one who or that which sews (stitches)

SOAR
v. to fly

SORE
adj. painful

SEX seks
n. gender

SECTS
n. groups of particular religious faiths

SHADE shād
n. darkness, shadow
n. a ghost
n. a slight difference, as of color
n. a blind for a window

SHADOW shad'ō
n. a dark figure cast by interception of light
n. shelter
n. hint
n. an inseparable companion

SHADY shād'ē
adj. indistinct
adj. disreputable

SHAFT shaft
n. a long pole
n. a well-like passage, as for an elevator
n. an unkind remark

SHAG shag
n. rough, matted hair or wool
n. a kind of bird
n. a kind of dance
v. to fetch

SHAKE shāk
v. to waver
v. to tremble
v. to clasp hands

SHAMBLES sham'bəlz
n. a scene, place, or thing in disorder
v. walks awkwardly, shuffles

SHANGHAI shang'hī
v. to enroll (a sailor) for crew by illegitimate means
n. a kind of chicken
n. (u.c.) a city in China

SHANK shank
n. leg
n. a connecting shaft
n. the early or latter part of a period of time

SHANTY shan'tē
n. a crude hut or house

SHANTEY
n. a sailor's song

SHARD shärd
n. a fragment of pottery
n. eggshell

SHARE shair
v. to divide equally
n. part of a plow

SHARK shärk
n. a kind of sea animal
n. a cheater

SHARP shärp
adj. having a cutting edge or piercing point
adj. clever, shrewd

SHAVE shāv
v. to cut or trim closely
v. to reduce, deduct from

SHEAR shēr
v. to clip off, as wool or hair

SHEER
adj. vertical
adj. transparently thin
adj. utter
adj. unmixed
v. to swerve

SHEAVE shēv
v. to bind together in a bundle
n. a wheel with a grooved rim

SHED shed
n. a rude hut used for storage
n. a strongly built structure
v. to release
v. to repel
v. to take off

SHE'D shēd
v. she did, she would, she had

SHEEP shēp
n. a kind of animal
n. a meek person

SHEET shēt
n. a covering for a bed
n. a rope or chain for a sail

SHELL shel
n. a hard outer covering
n. a long, narrow racing boat
n. a pie crust

SHE'LL shēl
v. she will

SHELLAC shə lak'
n. a kind of varnish
v. to defeat

SHIFT shift
v. to move from one place to another
v. to get along by indirect methods
v. to change gears
n. a period of work

SHINER shīn'ər
n. one who or that which glows with light
n. a black eye
n. several kinds of fish

SHINGLES shing'əlz
n. thin pieces of wood or slate, esp. for roofs
n. a kind of skin disease
n. some haircuts

SHINNY shin'nē
n. a kind of hockey game
v. to climb by drawing oneself upward

SHIP ship
n. a vessel or plane
v. to transport
v. to take in water over the sides of a boat

SHIRR sher
v. to bake eggs in a shallow dish
v. to gather cloth on three parallel threads

SHIVER shiv'ər
v. to shake or tremble
v. to break or split into fragments

SHOAL shōl
n. a place where water is shallow
n. a school of fish
n. an exposed sand bank

SHOCK shok
n. a sudden or violent blow
n. a sudden, violent disturbance
n. a group of sheaves
adj. shaggy, as hair

SHOE shoo
n. covering for the foot

SHOO
v. to drive away

SHONE shōn
v. did shine

SHOWN
v. was demonstrated

SHOOK shŏŏk
n. a set of staves for a barrel
v. did shake

SHOOT shoot
v. to use one of several weapons
v. to put forth buds
v. to move or send swiftly

CHUTE
n. a slope
n. a channel
n. a parachute

SHORE shōr
n. land by the water's edge
v. to support with post or beam

SHOT shot
n. a discharge
n. a photograph
adj. streaked with color
adj. ruined

SHORT shaurt
adj. not long
adj. curt
adj. scanty
adj. crisp and flaky, as pie crust

SHOULDER shōl'dər
n. part of the body
n. edge of a road

SHOWER shou'ər
n. a brief fall, as of water or snow

SHOWER shō'ər
n. one who or that which shows

SHREW shroo
n. a woman of violent temper
n. a kind of animal

SHROUD shroud
n. a winding cloth for a corpse
n. any of several ropes or wires on a vessel
v. to hide from view

SHRUB shrub
n. a bush
n. a kind of drink

SHRUG shrug
v. to raise the shoulders
n. a short sweater

SHUFFLE shuf'əl
v. to move clumsily
v. to mix cards

SHUT shut
v. to close
v. to confine
v. to exclude

SHY shī
adj. bashful
n. a quick, sudden throw

SIAMESE sī'am ēz'
n. (u.c.) a native of Siam
n. (u.c.) a kind of cat
n. a twin born joined
n. an inlet outside a building to be used in case of fire

SICK sik
adj. ill
adj. nauseated

SIC
v. to encourage to attack

SICKLE sik'əl
n. a curved tool for cutting grass

SECKEL
n. a kind of pear

SIDE sīd
n. one of two or more surfaces
n. a team
n. line of descent

SIGHED
v. did sigh

SIDECAR sīd'kär
n. a small car attached to a motorcycle
n. a kind of cocktail

SIDELINE sīd'līn
n. an additional occupation
n. one of the two boundaries of a sports field

SIDETRACK sīd'trak
v. to move a train from the main track
v. to distract

SIDEWINDER sīd'wīnd ər
n. a blow from the side
n. a kind of rattlesnake

SIEGE sēj
n. a persistent effort to overcome
n. a flock of herons

SIEVE siv, sēv
n. a strainer
n. a person who cannot keep a secret

SIGHT sīt
n. vision
n. a view
n. something unusual
n. any of various viewing devices

CITE
v. to quote

SITE
n. a location

SIGMOID sig'moid
adj. shaped like the letter *C*
adj. shaped like the letter *S*
adj. of part of the intestine

SIGN sīn
n. an indication
n. a signal
v. to affix one's name

SINE
n. part of a triangle

SIGNATURE sig'nə chər
n. one's handwritten name
n. a theme song

SIGNET sig'nit
n. a small seal, as in a ring

CYGNET
n. a young swan

SIGNIFY sig'ni fī
v. to be a sign of, to mean
v. to be of importance

SILENCE sī'lens
n. absence of sound
n. secrecy

SILK silk
n. fiber made from the cocoon of the silkworm
n. the beard of an ear of corn

SILKEN silk'ən
adj. made of silk
adj. smoothly ingratiating

SILVER sil'vər
n. a kind of metal
adj. eloquent

SILVERFISH sil'vər fish
n. a kind of fish
n. a kind of insect

SIMA sī'mə
n. a layer of rocks rich in silica
n. part of a cornice

SIMMER sim'ər
v. to cook in liquid below the boiling point
v. to be in a state of subdued activity

SIMPLE sim'pəl
adj. plain, uncomplicated
adj. ignorant
adj. guileless

SIMPLY sim'plē
adv. easily, plainly
adv. merely
adv. wholly
adv. foolishly

SINCE sins
adv. from then till now
adv. because

SINGER sing'ər
n. a vocalist

SINGER sinj'er
n. one who or that which singes

SINGLE sing'əl
adj. one only
adj. sincere
adj. isolated
v. to select

SINGULAR sing'ū lər
adj. unusual
adj. rare
adj. not plural

SINISTER sin'i stər
adj. bad, wicked
adj. of or on the left side

SINK sink
n. a wash basin
v. to fall to a lower level
v. to enter the mind

SINUS sī'nəs
n. a cavity in the skull
n. a curve or bend

SIREN sī'rən
n. a warning device
n. a beguiling woman
n. a kind of salamander

SISTER sist'ər
n. a female sibling
n. a nun
adj. similar, as of ships

SIT sit
v. to be seated
v. to pose
v. to be a baby sitter
v. to be located

SITUATION sit ū ā'shun
n. location
n. employment
n. state of affairs

SIZE sīz
n. bulk
n. number
n. measure
n. a filler for cloth or paper

SIGHS
v. lets out breath audibly

SKATE skāt
v. to go on ice with special equipment for the feet
n. a kind of sea animal

SKEIN skān
n. a length of yarn on a reel
n. a flock of geese in flight

SKETCH skech
n. a hastily drawn picture
n. a short play or essay

SKID skid
n. a plank or bar used in moving heavy goods
v. to slide without rotating

SKIFFLE skif'əl
n. a form of jazz
v. to dress stone

SKIM skim
v. to remove something from liquids
v to glide along
v. to read hastily

SKIMMER skim'ər
n. a strainer
n. a kind of hat
n. a kind of bird

SKIMP skimp
v. to be frugal; scrimp
v. to do or perform hastily; scamp

SKINNER skin'ər
n. dealer in hides or pelts
n. driver of draft animals
n. tractor driver

SKIP skip
v. to leap lightly
v. to be absent
v. to advance, as in school or business

SKIPPER skip'ər
n. captain of a vessel or team
n. a kind of insect

SKIRT skert
n. part of a dress or coat
v. to border or edge
v. to avoid

SKIVVY skiv′ē
n. a man's cotton T-shirt
SKIVY
n. a female servant

SKULK skulk
v. to hide for an evil reason
n. a pack or group of foxes

SLACKS slaks
n. trousers
v. is careless, loose

SLAKE slāk
v. to refresh
v. to make less active
v. to cause disintegration of lime

SLAM slam
v. to shut forcefully
n. the winning of all (or all but one) tricks in cards

SLASH slash
v. to cut, as with a knife
n. a tract of swampy ground

SLATE slāt
n. a kind of rock used in roofing and tiling
n. a list of candidates
v. to scold

SLAVE slāv
n. a bond servant
n. a kind of flash bulb

SLAVER slāv′ər
n. a dealer in slaves
n. a slave ship
SLAVER slav′ər
v. to slobber

SLAVISH slāv′ish
adj. submissive
adj. imitative

SLAY slā
v. to kill
SLEIGH
n. a sled

SLEDGE slej
n. a sled
n. a large hammer

SLEEPER slēp′ər
n. one who dozes, naps
n. a block that lies horizontally
n. a sleeping car
n. merchandise that sells slowly

SLEEVE slēv
n. the part of a garment that covers the arm
n. an envelope for a phonograph record

SLEIGHT slīt
n. skill, dexterity
SLIGHT
adj. slender, small

SLICK slik
adj. smooth, glossy, slippery
n. a kind of magazine

SLICKER slik′ər
n. an oilskin raincoat
n. a big-city dweller
adj. more slippery

SLIDE slīd
v. to slip, skid
n. a small plate of glass used in photography and laboratories
n. a landslide

SLIDER slīd′ər
n. a fast pitch in baseball
n. a kind of turtle

SLIGHT slīt
v. to ignore, snub
adj. small, not important

SLIM slim
adj. slender, thin
adj. insignificant

SLING sling
n. a weapon for hurling stones
n. a strap or bandage
n. a kind of drink

SLINK slink
v. to go in a furtive manner
v. to bring forth young prematurely, esp. of cows

SLIP slip
v. to flow, glide
v. to be lost
v. to err
n. a piece cut from a plant
n. a space for a vessel to dock in
n. an undergarment of women
n. a paper form

SLOE-EYED slō'īd
adj. having dark eyes
adj. having slanting eyes

SLOP slop
v. to spill or splash
n. feed for swine
n. cheap, ready-made clothing

SLOPPY JOE slop ē jō'
n. an overlarge sweater
n. a kind of sandwich

SLOT slot
n. a narrow slit or notch
n. a place, as in a sequence
n. the track or trail of a deer

SLOTH slauth
n. laziness
SLOTH slōth
n. a kind of animal

SLOUGH slou, sloo
n. a swamp
SLEW sloo
v. did slay
SLUE
v. to turn around
SLOUGH sluf
v. to cast off, as skin by a snake
v. to discard in card games

SLOW slō
adj. not quick
SLOE
n. the blackthorn

SLUG slug
n. a snaillike animal
n. a counterfeit coin
n. a piece of crude metal
v. to hit hard

SLUR sler
v. to speak carelessly
v. to slander

SLUSH slush
n. watery mire
n. silly, emotional talk or writing

SMACK smak
v. to strike sharply with the open hand
n. a taste, suggestion
n. a kind of fishing vessel

SMART smärt
v. to feel a sharp local pain
adj. clever, intelligent
adj. chic

SMASH smash
v. to break to pieces, shatter
n. financial ruin

SMEAR smēr
v. to spread or daub
v. to vilify

SMELT smelt
n. a kind of fish
v. had or noticed an odor
v. to fuse or melt ore

SMILE smīl
n. a quiet laugh
v. to express approval
v. to express derision

SMOKE smōk
n. visible vapor from burning
v. to use tobacco
v. to cure meat

SMOLDER smōld'ər
v. to burn without flame
v. to suppress emotion

SMOOTH smooth
adj. not rough
adj. fluent

SMUG smug
adj. conceited
adj. smooth, sleek

SMUT smut
n. a particle of soot
n. obscenity
n. a disease of some plants

SNAG snag
n. an obstacle or impediment
n. a stump of a tooth

SNAKE snāk
n. a reptile
n. a treacherous person
v. to wind, twist

SNAIL snāl
n. a kind of mollusk
n. a lazy person
n. a spiral disc

SNAP snap
n. a catch or fastener
v. to crack, click
v. to move quickly
adj. easy

SNARE snair
n. a trap, usually a noose
n. a string on a snare drum

SNARL snarl
n. a tangle
v. to growl angrily

SNATCH snach
v. to try to seize suddenly
v. to kidnap
n. a brief bit of something, as
conversation

SNEAKER snēk'ər
n. a kind of shoe
n. one who is furtive

SNIP snip
v. to cut with a quick stroke
n. a small or insignificant person

SNIPE snīp
n. a kind of bird
v. to shoot from a hidden position
v. to criticize, esp. anonymously

SNOOK snook
n. a kind of fish
n. a gesture of defiance

SNORE snōr
v. to breathe audibly during sleep
n. part of a pump

SNOUT snout
n. muzzle of an animal
n. nozzle or spout

SNOW snō
n. icy precipitation
n. faults on television screens
n. a kind of sailing vessel

SNOWBALL snō'baul
n. a ball of snow
n. a kind of flowering shrub
v. to grow or become larger

SNOWSHOE snō'shoo
n. a frame for the feet, used on deep
snow
n. an orange-yellow color

SNOWY snō'ē
adj. covered with snow
adj. immaculate

SNUB snub
v. to treat with disdain
v. to check, as a horse or boat
adj. (of the nose) short, turned-up

SNUFF snuf
n. a pinch of tobacco that is inhaled
v. to extinguish, as a candle

SNUG snug
adj. cozy
adj. concealed

SO sō
adv. thus
adv. very
adv. therefore
n. the fifth tone in the musical scale

SEW
v. to attach by stitches

SOW
v. to plant seeds

SOW sou
n. an adult female swine
n. a kind of channel or basin

SOAK sōk
v. to saturate, steep
v. to penetrate into the mind or
feelings
n. a drunkard

SOBER sōb'ər
adj. temperate
adj. quiet, dull
adj. rational

SOCIAL sō'shəl
adj. pertaining to friendly relations
adj. pertaining to achieving better
conditions for people

SOCK sok
n. a short stocking
n. comedy
v. to strike or hit hard

SODDEN sod'ən
adj. soaked, saturated
adj. dull, stupid

SOFT soft, sauft
adj. not hard
adj. dulcet, sweet
adj. sympathetic
adj. submissive

SOGGY sog'ē
adj. sodden, soaked
adj. dull, stupid

SOIL soil
n. part of the earth's surface
v. to make unclean
v. to feed green fodder to horses

SOLD sōld
v. did sell
SOLED
v. mended a shoe

SOLDER sod'ər
n. an alloy
SODDER
n. one who applies turf to land

SOLE sōl
n. the bottom of the foot
n. a kind of fish
SOUL
n. the spirit

SOLEMN sol'əm
adj. mirthless
adj. sacred

SOLUTION sə lū'shən
n. an explanation or answer
n. a mixture of two or more
substances

SOLVENT sol'vent
adj. able to pay all debts
adj. having the power of dissolving
n. something that solves or explains

SOMBER som'bər
adj. murky, cloudy
adj. melancholy

SOME sum
adj. of an unspecified number
SUM
n. a total

SOMERSAULT sum'ər sault
n. an overturn of the body
n. a reversal, as of opinion

SON sun
n. a male child
SUN
n. a heavenly body
SUNN
n. fiber from a kind of shrub

SOP sop
n. a piece of food used for dipping
into liquid
n. a bribe

SORDID saur'did
adj. filthy
adj. stingy
adj. depraved

SORE sōr
adj. physically painful
adj. mentally painful
SOAR
v. to fly upward

SORREL so'rəl
n. a reddish brown horse
n. a kind of plant with edible leaves

SORRY so'rē
adj. regretful
adj. worthless
adj. painful

SOUND sound
n. noise, tone
adj. whole, healthy
v. to measure depth
n. a narrow passage of water

SOUR sour
adj. acid, tart
adj. peevish

SOUSE sous
v. to plunge into liquid
n. a drunkard
n. pickled pig's feet

SPACE spās
n. extent of time
n. extent of area

SPADE spād
n. a kind of tool

SPAYED
v. made neutral, as an animal

SPADES spādz
n. tools for digging
n. one of the four suits in a deck of cards

SPAN span
n. a variable unit of distance
v. to pass or extend over
n. a pair of horses

SPANK spank
v. to slap on the buttocks
v. to move rapidly

SPAR spär
n. a mast or boom on a boat
v. to attack or defend, as in boxing

SPARE spair
v. to save from strain, pain, or annoyance
adj. thin, lean
n. something extra

SPARK spärk
n. a fiery particle
n. a lover, suitor

SPAT spat
n. a petty quarrel
v. did spit
n. a kind of foot gear
n. young oysters

SPAY spā
v. to remove ovaries of an animal
n. a three-year-old male red deer

SPEAR spēr
n. a kind of weapon
n. a sprout
v. to stab

SPIER
n. an architectural screen

SPECTACLES spek'tə kəls
n. large public shows
n. eyeglasses

SPELL spel
v. to write or say the letters of a word
n. charm, incantation
n. an interval of space or time

SPELT spelt
v. did spell
n. a kind of wheat

SPENCER spen'sər
n. a short, close-fitting jacket
n. a large gaff sail

SPEND spend
v. to pay out money
v. to exhaust

SPERM sperm
n. male reproductive cell
n. a solid from the sperm whale used for candles or medicines

SPHERE sfēr
n. a round body or mass
n. a particular social walk of life

SPHERICS sfer'iks
n. mathematics of numbers on a sphere
n. a method of weather forecasting

SPICA spī'kə
n. a kind of bandage
n. (u.c.) a star in Virgo

SPICY spīs'ē
adj. flavored with pepper, cloves, etc.
adj. naughty, risqué

SPIDER spīd'ər
n. a small insect
n. a frying pan
n. a device for pulverizing soil

SPIKE spīk
n. a large, naillike fastener
n. a young mackerel
n. an ear, as of wheat

SPILL spil
v. to allow to run or fall from a container
n. a slender piece of wood or paper used to light fires

SPIN spin
v. to make thread or yarn
v. to whirl
v. to tell a story

SPINDLE spind'əl
n. a rod used in spinning
v. to grow tall and slender

SPINE spīn
n. backbone
n. strength, stamina

SPINNER spin'ər
n. one who or that which spins
n. a kind of lure used in fishing

SPIRE spīr
n. a steeple
n. a blade or spear of grass
n. a coil

SPIER
n. one who watches or discovers

SPIRIT spi'rit
n. the soul
n. a ghost
n. humor, mood

SPIRITUAL spir'it ū əl
adj. religious

SPIRITUEL
adj. light and airy

SPIT spit
v. to eject saliva
n. an island of sand
n. a bar used in cooking

SPITS spits
v. ejects saliva

SPITZ
n. a kind of dog

SPLASH splash
v. to wet by dashing water or mud
n. a patch of color or light

SPLAT splat
n. part of a chair back
n. noise made by slapping

SPLAY splā
v. to spread out, extend
v. to disjoin
n. a kind of window

SPLIT split
v. to divide, separate
n. a small bottle of wine

SPLUTTER splut'ər
v. to talk rapidly
v. to spatter, as a liquid

SPOILS spoilz
v. damages or harms
v. rots
n. booty

SPOKE spōk
n. part of a wheel or ladder
v. did speak

SPONGE spunj
v. to soak up liquid
n. a kind of marine animal
v. to wash off
n. a bandage
n. a kind of pudding

SPOON spoon
n. an eating utensil
n. a golf club with a wooden head

SPORT spōrt
n. an athletic activity
n. laughing stock
n. mutation

SPOT spot
n. a speck, stain
n. a place
n. one of several playing cards
v. to locate

SPOTTER spot'ər
n. a disk on a target
n. an observer
n. one who removes spots in dry cleaning

SPOUT spout
v. to emit a stream or jet
n. a kind of dumbwaiter

SPRAY sprā
n. a jet of fine particles
n. a single twig or branch
n. a group of cut flowers

SPREAD spred
v. to unfold
v. to apply a thin coating
v. to radiate
v. to publish

SPRIG sprig
n. a small spray of a plant
n. a young fellow

SPRING spring
n. a season
v. to dart forward or upward
v. to become bent or cracked

SPRUCE sproos
n. a kind of tree
adj. neat, dapper

SPRUE sproo
n. an accumulation of waste metal
n. a kind of tropical disease

SPUR sper
n. a goad, as for horses
n. a short shoot bearing flowers
n. a mountain ridge

SPURIOUS spū′rē əs
adj. counterfeit
adj. of illegitimate birth

SPURT spert
n. a sudden gush, as of liquid
n. an increase of effort, as in racing

SQUAB skwob
n. a young pigeon
n. a soft cushion

SQUALL skwaul
n. a sudden gust of wind
v. to cry loudly

SQUARE skwair
n. a rectangle
n. plaza, park
v. to pay off, as a debt
adj. balanced

SQUASH skwosh
n. a kind of vegetable
v. to crush
v. to splash

SQUAT skwot
v. to crouch, sit on one's heels
v. to draw water astern of a vessel

SQUEEZE skwēz
v. to press together
v. to hug
v. to merge

SQUIB skwib
n. a short and witty saying
n. a firecracker broken in the middle

SQUINT skwint
v. to look with the eyes partly closed
n. a small opening in a church wall

SQUUSH skwush
v. to squash
v. to squish

STAB stab
v. to pierce or wound
n. a brief attempt

STABLE stāb′əl
n. shelter for horses
adj. firm, steady

STACK stak
n. a pile, as of hay or straw
n. a vertical duct
n. a great many

STAFF staf
n. a stick, pole, or rod
n. sustenance
n. a group of employees
n. the five lines used in writing music
n. a temporary plaster

STAG stag
n. an adult male deer
n. a castrated swine
adj. for or of men only

STAGE stāj
n. a particular period in development
n. the platform in a theater
n. stagecoach
v. to plan activity

STAGGERED stag′ərd
v. walked unsteadily

STAGGARD
n. a four-year old male deer

STAID stād
adj. proper, serious

STAYED
v. remained

STAIR stair
n. a step

STARE
v. to gaze fixedly

STAKE stāk
n. a pointed stick
n. a bet
n. a post to which persons were
bound for torture

STEAK
n. a cut of meat

STALE stāl
adj. not fresh
v. (of livestock) to urinate

STALK stauk
n. the stem of a plant
v. to walk with stiff strides
v. to pursue, as in hunting

STALL staul
n. a small compartment
n. a trick used to delay or deceive
v. to come to a standstill

STAMP stamp
n. postage on mail
n. type, character
v. to bring the foot down

STAND stand
v. to stop, remain upright
n. a piece of furniture
n. a location

STANDARD stand'ərd
n. an approved model
n. a flag

STANDING stand'ing
n. rank or status
adj. still, not flowing
adj. continuing without cessation

STAPLE stā'pəl
n. a short piece of wire
n. a principal raw material, as food

STAR stär
n. a heavenly body
n. a five-pointed figure
n. a well-known actor or musician

STARCH stärch
n. a carbohydrate
n. stiffness of manner

STARK stärk
adj. sheer, utter, complete
adj. dreary
adj. rigid

START stärt
v. to begin
v. to set out
v. to give an involuntary jump
v. to found

STATE stāt
n. the condition of a person or thing
n. a commonwealth
v. to declare

STATIC stat'ik
n. electrical interference
adj. of a fixed or stationary condition

STATION stā'shən
n. a stopping place
n. a position, office, or rank

STATIONARY stā'shə nair'ē
adj. not moving

STATIONERY
n. writing paper

STAUNCH staunch
v. to stop the flow of blood
adj. firm, steadfast

STAVE stāv
n. part of a barrel
n. a rung of a ladder
n. alliteration
n. a verse of a poem or song

STAY stā
v. to remain
v. to hinder, delay
n. a brace
n. a strong rope

STEADY sted'ē
adj. firmly placed or fixed
adj. regular in movement

STEAL stēl
v. to take without permission
v. to sneak out or in

STEEL
n. a metal

STELE stēl'ē
n. an upright stone slab

STELE
n. a cylinder of some growing plants

STEAMER stēm'ər
n. a kind of ship
n. a kind of cooking vessel

STEEP stēp
v. to soak in water, infuse
adj. having a high slope

STEER stēr
n. a castrated male bovine
v. to guide
v. to follow a course of action

STEM stem
n. stalk of a plant
n. part of a watch
n. part of a word
n. bow of a ship
v. to arise, originate
v. to stop, restrain
v. to make headway

STEP step
n. a movement of the foot
n. a support for the foot; stair
n. rank, degree

STEPPE
n. a vast, treeless plain

STERN stern
adj. firm, strict
n. the aft part of a vessel

STICH stik
n. a verse or line of poetry
n. the last trick in some card games

STICK
n. a piece of wood
v. to pierce, stab
v. to adhere

STICKER stik'ər
n. an adhesive label
n. a worker in a slaughterhouse
n. a kind of wooden piece

STICKY stik'ē
adj. adhesive
adj. hot and humid
adj. awkwardly difficult

STIFF stif
adj. rigid, firm
adj. obstinate
adj. rigidly formal
adj. clumsy

STIFLE stī'fəl
v. to smother
v. to prevent
n. a knee joint in a horse

STIGMATA stig mä'tə
n. marks of disgrace
n. holy marks of some Christian visionaries

STILL stil
adj. quiet
adj. remaining in place
adv. as yet
n. a distilling apparatus

STILT stilt
n. a pole used in walking above ground
n. a kind of bird

STILTED stilt'ed
adj. pompous, formal
adj. raised above the ground on poles

STINGER sting'ər
n. an animal or plant having an organ to prick or wound
n. a kind of cocktail
n. an unkind joke

STINGY stin'jē
adj. not generous

STINGY sting'ē
adj. having a sting

STINT stint
v. to limit, restrict
n. a kind of sandpiper

STIPULATE stip'ū lāt
v. to require as an essential condition
adj. having certain plant leaves

STIR ster
v. to mix with a curving movement
v. to move in a slight way
v. to move briskly

STITCH stich
n. the smallest unit of sewing
n. a sudden, sharp pain
n. the least bit of anything

STOCK stok
n. a supply of goods on hand
n. line of descent
n. a kind of paper
n. broth
n. repertory theater
n. shares in a company
n. livestock
n. a stem in grafting a plant

STOCKING stok'ing
n. a covering for the foot and leg
v. hoarding

STOCKS stoks
n. a pillory
n. shares, as in a business

STODGY stoj'ē
adj. heavy, dull
adj. unduly formal

STOLE stōl
n. a kind of scarf
v. did steal

STOMACH stum'ək
n. part of the body
v. to tolerate

STONY stōn'ē
adj. having rocks or pebbles
adj. unfeeling

STOOL stool
n. a seat without arms or back
n. a decoy
n. a bowel movement
n. a bishop's seat

STOOP stoop
v. to bend the head and shoulders over
n. a small porch

STORE stōr
n. a retail establishment
v. to put away for some time

STORIED stōr'ed
adj. recorded in history or legend
adj. having floors

STORM staurm
n. a heavy rain accompanied by thunder and wind
v. to attack, as in battle

STORY stō'rē
n. a narrative, tale
n. a level of a building

STOUT stout
adj. heavy, fat
adj. brawny, sinewy
adj. stubborn
n. an alcoholic drink

STOVE stōv
n. a heating or cooking piece of equipment
v. broke into a barrel or cask

STRAIGHT strāt
adj. not curved or askew
adj. honorable

STRAIT
n. a narrow passage of water

STRAIGHTEN strāt'en
v. adjust, put to rights

STRAITEN
v. to put into financial difficulties

STRAIN strān
v. to stretch, tighten
v. to pour through a filter
n. a muscle injury
n. hereditary character, tendency, or trait

STRAND strand
v. to leave ashore
n. a rope or coil
n. a lock of hair
n. the land bordering a body of water

STRAPPED strapt
v. whipped with a belt or the like
adj. needy, wanting

STRAPPING strap'ing
adj. powerfully built
n. straps, collectively

STRAW strau
n. a dry stem of grain or grass
n. trifle, least bit

STREAM strēm
n. a flowing body of water or air
v. to hang loose

STRESS stres
n. emphasis, significance
n. strain
n. beat, as in music or poetry

STRIKE strīk
v. to deal a blow
v. to lower a flag
v. to find oil or gold
v. to stop work so as to get better terms

STRIKER strīk'ər
n. a protesting worker
n. clapper on a bell
n. certain army or navy men

STRING string
n. a slender cord
n. a group of animals belonging to one owner
v. to kill by hanging

STRINGER string'ər
n. a part-time reporter for a newspaper
n. a kind of cord used in fishing

STRIP strip
v. to uncover
n. a long narrow piece, as of cloth or metal
n. a comic strip

STRIPE strīp
n. a band of a different nature from the rest
n. style, variety, kind
v. to whip with a lash

STRIPPER strip'ər
n. a kind of dancer
n. a kind of harvesting machine

STROKE strōk
n. a blow
v. to rub gently
n. an attack of paralysis
n. beat, rhythm

STROLLER strōl'ər
n. a person who takes a leisurely walk
n. a vehicle for small children
n. a vagrant

STRONG straung
adj. mighty
adj. brave
adj. brilliant
adj. smelly

STRUCTURE struk'tūr
n. system, form
n. edifice, as a building or dam

STRUM strum
n. a strainer
v. to play lightly on a stringed instrument

STRUT strut
n. wood beam used under a roof
v. parade oneself, swagger

STUB stub
n. a short projecting part, stump
v. to strike accidentally against an object

STUD stud
n. a knob or nailhead used in decorating
n. a stallion
n. a narrow piece of wood used in building walls
v. to scatter at intervals

STUDY stud'ē
n. reading, learning, thought
n. a library, den

STUFF stuf
n. material
n. foolish ideas
v. to cram full

STUMBLE stum'bəl
n. a moral blunder
v. to trip, walk unsteadily

STUMP stump
n. a short remnant, as of a tree or tooth
v. to embarrass, render at a loss
v. to walk clumsily

STUN stun
v. to make dizzy or unconscious
v. to astonish

SOOT
n. fine particles found in smoke

SUITE swēt
n. a connected series of rooms
SWEET
adj. not sour

SULKY sul'kē
adj. sullen, ill-humored
n. a kind of one-horse carriage

SULLEN sul'ən
adj. moody, bad-tempered
adj. overcast, cloudy

SULTRY sul'trē
adj. hot and close or moist
adj. characterized by or arousing
passion

SUMMARY sum'ə rē
n. a brief outline
adj. direct, prompt, often impatient
SUMMERY
n. of, like, or for summer

SUMMER sum'ər
n. a season of the year
n. a beam or lintel

SUNDAE sun'dā
n. a kind of dessert
SUNDAY
n. (u.c.) the first day of the week

SUNK sungk
v. did sink
adj. of a structure less than a deck
above the main deck

SUP sup
v. to eat the evening meal
v. to sip

SUPINE soo'pīn
adj. lying on the back
n. the infinitive of a verb

SUPPLIANCE sə plī'əns
n. the act of furnishing a lack
SUPPLIANCE sup'lē əns
n. appeal, plea

SUPPLY sə plī'
v. to furnish

SUPPLY sup'lē
adj. in a supple manner

SUPREME soo prēm'
adj. of the highest quality or rank
n. a kind of bowl

SURF serf
n. the swell of the sea
SERF
n. a slave

SURFACE ser'fis
n. any face of a body or thing
v. to rise to the surface
adj. via land or sea

SURGE serj
n. a strong forward movement
v. to slacken a rope
SERGE
n. a kind of fabric

SUSPECT sus pekt'
v. to believe to be guilty
v. to believe to be likely; guess

SUSPENSION sə spen'shən
n. a temporary withholding
n. undissolved particles
n. that which is hung

SUSPICION sə spish'ən
n. belief in the existence of guilt
n. a slight trace, hint

SWAG swag
n. loot
n. a festoon, wreath
n. a low place in a tract of land

SWALLOW swol'ō
v. to eat, drink
v. to suppress
n. a kind of bird

SWAMP swomp
n. marshy ground
v. to render helpless

SWARM swärm
n. a group of honeybees
v. to climb with legs and arms; to shin

SWASH swosh
v. to splash
v. to swagger

STUNNING stun'ing
v. causing loss of consciousness or strength
adj. of striking beauty

STUNT stunt
n. a display of skill
v. to slow down growth, dwarf

STY stī
n. a pen for swine
n. a small boil on the eye

STYLE stīl
n. a mode of living or dressing
n. characteristics, as in writing or painting
n. an ancient writing tool, stylus
v. to call by a title

STILE
n. steps over a fence
n. a rail used in carpentry

SUBBASE sub'bās
n. the lowest part of a column or pillar

SUBBASS
n. one of the pedal stops of an organ

SUBJECT sub'jikt
n. a theme, course of study
n. part of a sentence in grammar
n. one who owes allegiance to his government

SUBJECT sub ject'
v. to bring under control
v. to lay open, expose

SUBMIT sub mit'
v. to yield, obey
v. to proffer, as a plan for approval

SUBSERVIENT sub ser'vē ənt
adj. obsequious
adj. useful in promoting a purpose

SUBSTANCE sub'stans
n. that of which a thing consists
n. theme
n. wealth

SUBSTANTIVE sub'stən tiv
n. a noun
adj. essential
adj. of considerable amount

SUBTERRANEAN sub tər ā'nē ən
adj. underground
adj. secret

SUBTILIZE sut'əl īz
v. to sublimate
v. to refine

SUBTLE sut'əl
adj. delicate, faint, mysterious
adj. skillful, crafty

SUCCEED suk sēd'
v. to attain a goal
v. to follow

SUCCOR suk'ər
n. aid

SUCKER
n. a lollipop
n. a kind of fish

SUCCUBOUS suk'ū bəs
adj. having overlapping leaves

SUCCUBUS
n. a demon in female form

SUCH such
adj. like or similar
adj. not specified
adj. being as stated

SUEDE swād
n. a kind of finish for leather

SWAYED
v. moved to and fro

SUFFER suf'ər
v. to feel pain
v. to allow

SUFFRAGE suf'rij
n. the right to vote
n. a kind of prayer

SUGGEST sug jest'
v. to advise, propose
v. to hint, imply

SUIT soot
n. a form of dress
n. legal prosecution
n. one of the four sets in a deck of cards
v. to be appropriate
v. to woo: *press suit·*

SWATH swoth
n. the space covered by the stroke of a scythe

SWATHE swoth, swāth
v. to enfold, bandage

SWAY swā
v. to move to and fro
v. to dominate

SWEAR swair
v. to declare
v. to curse

SWEAT swet
v. to perspire
v. to work hard
v. to employ at low wages

SWEATER swet'ər
n. a knitted article of clothing
n. an employer who underpays

SWEEP swēp
v. to use a broom
v. to gaze over
n. a steady driving motion
n. a trailing motion

SWIFT swift
adj. quick
n. a kind of bird

SWILL swil
n. kitchen refuse given to swine
n. a deep drink of liquid

SWIM swim
v. to move one's body through water
v. to be dizzy

SWINDLED swind'əld
v. did cheat someone
adj. a kind of cut jewel

SWING swing
v. to move or sway to and fro
v. to hit at with hand or hand-held instrument

SWITCH swich
n. a flexible rod
n. a device that turns electric current off and on
n. a hairpiece
n. a turning or changing

SWORD sōrd
n. a kind of weapon

SOARED
v. flew upward

SYMBOL sim'bəl
n. sign; something used for something else

CYMBAL
n. a kind of musical instrument

SYMPATHETIC sim pə thet'ik
adj. compassionate
adj. pertaining to part of the nervous system

SYNCOPATE sin'kō pāt
v. to accent weak musical beats
v. to elide words

SYNTHETIC sin thet'ik
adj. artificial
adj. of a whole formed by separate elements
adj. of a type of language

SYSTEM sis'tem
n. a combination of parts making a whole
n. the universe
n. the entire body

T

T tē
n. the twentieth letter of the English alphabet

TEA
n. a kind of plant
n. a kind of drink
n. an afternoon party

TEE
n. a small peg, in golf

TI
n. a note in the musical scale

TAB tab
n. a small flap, strap, or loop
v. to name

TABARET tab'ə rit
n. a kind of fabric
n. an embroidery frame

TABBY tab'ē
n. a kind of cat
n. an old maid
n. a kind of fabric

TABERNACLE tab'ər nak əl
n. a temporary dwelling
n. a place of worship
n. a raised support for a mast

TABLATURE tab'lə tūr
n. a space or surface, with orderly arrangements
n. a system of music notation

TABLE tā'bəl
n. a certain kind of furniture
n. an arrangement of words or numbers
n. a plateau
v. to postpone
v. to exhibit a set of facts

TABLEAU tab'lō
n. a representation of a picture
n. a method used in the game of solitaire

TABLET tab'let
n. a writing pad
n. a small, flat cake, as of a drug

TABLOID tab'loid
n. a small newspaper
n. a summary

TACITURN tas'i tern
adj. quiet
adj. gloomy
adj. stern

TACK tak
n. a short nail
n. a stitch
n. gear for horses
v. to change the course of a ship

TACKLE tak'əl
n. equipment, as for fishing
n. a mechanism used in lifting or leveling
n. a football player
v. to undertake to solve
v. to harness a horse

TACT takt
n. a keen sense of what to do or say

TACKED
v. stitched

TAG tag
n. a label or loop
n. the last words of a speech or act
n. a traffic ticket
n. a torn piece, tatter
n. a running game
v. to follow closely

TAGLINE tag'līn
n. a catchword
n. a cable on a crane

TAIL tāl
n. to hindmost part of an animal
n. the reverse of a coin

TALE
n. a story
n. a lie

TAILGATE tāl'gāt
n. a board at the back of a truck or stationwagon
n. a style of playing the trombone
v. to follow too close to another car

TAILOR tā'lər
n. one who makes suits and coats
n. a stroke of a bell indicating a death

TAILPIECE tāl'pēs
n. an end piece
n. a small design at the end of a chapter
n. part of a violin or viola

TAIPAN tī'pan
n. the head of a foreign business in China
n. a kind of snake

TAKE tāk
v. to acquire
v. to suppose
v. to endure
v. to charm
v. to need
v. to have the intended result, as an inoculation

TALENT tal′ənt
n. a natural ability
n. an ancient unit of weight or money

TALLBOY taul′boy
n. a chest of drawers on a stand
n. a tall chimney pot

TALUS ta′ləs
n. anklebone
n. a slope

TAMBOUR tam′boor
n. a drum or drum player
n. an embroidery frame
n. a flexible shutter

TAME tām
adj. domesticated
adj. meek
adj. dull
adj. cowardly

TAMMY tam′ē
n. a fabric used in linings
n. a cloth mesh used in straining

TAMPER tam′pər
v. to meddle
n. one who or that which forces down with light strokes

TAMPON tam′pon
n. a plug of cotton
n. a two-headed drumstick

TAN tan
v. to make a hide into leather
v. to make brown, as by the sun

TANG tang
n. a strong taste or flavor
n. a long strip on a chisel or knife
n. a sharp ringing sound

TANGENT tan′jent
adj. touching, meeting
n. a straight line forming an angle

TANK tank
n. a large container for liquid or gas
n. a kind of combat vehicle

TANTO tän′tō
adv. a musical direction; *too much*
n. a Japanese dagger

TAP tap
v. to strike with light blows
n. a faucet
n. the withdrawal of fluid in surgery
n. a piece that makes a heel or sole thicker
v. to bug, as a telephone

TAPER tā′pər
n. a small candle
v. to become smaller

TAPIR
n. a kind of animal

TAPPER tap′ər
n. a telegraph key
n. one who cuts screw threads

TARGET tar′gət
n. anything fired at
n. a disc-shaped signal at a railroad station

TARO tär′ō
n. root of some plants

TAROT
n. a playing card used in fortune telling

TARRY ta′rē
v. to delay, linger

TARRY tä′rē
adj. of or like tar

TARSUS tär′səs
n. part of the foot
n. part of the eyelid

TART tärt
n. a small pie
adj. sharp

TARTAN tär′tən
n. a striped woolen cloth
n. a kind of ship

TARTAR tär′tər
n. a deposit on the teeth
n. a savage person

TASSEL tas′əl
n. a pendent ornament
n. corn silk

TASTE tāst
v. to savor, test flavor
n. a liking for something
n. a sense of the beautiful

TATTER tat'ər
n. a torn piece
n. one who makes lace

TATTOO tat oo'
n. a pattern marked on the skin
n. a signal for soldiers or sailors
n. a knocking

TATTY tat'ē
adj. vulgar
n. a kind of window screen

TAUNT taunt
v. to mock, jeer
adj. well-rigged, as a mast

TAUT taut
adj. tense, rigid
adj. tidy, neat

TAUGHT
v. did teach

TAW tau
n. a kind of marble used in a game
v. to make a hide into white leather

TAX tax
n. sum of money imposed by government
v. to make demands on
v. to accuse

TACKS
n. small nails
v. changes direction

TEAL tēl
n. a kind of duck
n. a green-blue color

TEAM tēm
n. a group of players
n. draft animals harnessed together

TEEM
v. to abound
v. to swarm
v. to empty, pour out

TEAR tēr
n. a drop of liquid in the eye

TIER
n. a level, layer
n. a kind of rope

TIRE tīr
n. a wheel covering
v. to become weary

TEAR tēr
n. a drop of liquid in the eye

TEAR tair
v. to pull apart

TARE
n. a kind of weed
n. the weight of a receptacle

TEASE tēz
v. to vex, annoy
v. to separate fibers or hairs

T's
n. some letters

TEAS
n. afternoon parties

TELL tel
v. to narrate, announce
n. an artificial mound

TELLER tel'ər
n. a clerk in a bank
n. one who narrates

TEMPER tem'pər
n. a state of mind
v. to toughen metal or glass

TEMPLE tem'pəl
n. a place of worship
n. part of the forehead
n. part of a loom

TEMPORAL tem'pər əl
adv. of time
adv. of present life
adv. of the temple bone

TENANT ten'ənt
n. one who rents

TENENT
adj. adapted for holding, as hairs on insects' feet

TEND tend
v. to be willing to do something
v. to care for

TENDER ten′dər
adj. soft or delicate
v. to make a formal offer
n. a small boat

TENOR ten′ər
n. a male singer
n. continuous progress
n. the subject of a metaphor

TENSE tens
adj. stretched tight
n. the time expressed by a verb

TENT tent
n. a portable shelter
n. a roll, as of cotton used in surgery

TERM term
n. a period of time with set limits
v. to apply a name to

TERMINAL term′ə nəl
adj. situated at the end
n. a railroad station and its yards

TERRIER te′ri ər
n. a breed of dog
n. an anti-aircraft missile
n. a kind of law book

TEST test
n. an examination
n. the hard shell of some invertebrates

TESTAMENT tcst′ə mənt
n. a legal will
n. an agreement between God and man

TESTER tes′tər
n. one who examines
n. a canopy over a bed
n. a coin of old England

TEXAS tek′səs
n. a deckhouse
n. (u.c.) a state

THATCH thach
n. a kind of roof cover
n. a head of hair

THE ᵼhē, ᵼh
definite article (see A): particular person or thing

THEE ᵼhē
pron. thou

THEN ᵼhen
adv. at that time
adv. next in order of time or place

THENCE ᵼhens
adv. from that place
adv. from that time

THERE ᵼhair
adv. in that place
adv. to that place

THEIR
pron. belonging to them

THEY'RE
v. they are

THICK thik
adj. not thin
adj. close-packed
adj. mentally slow

THINNER thin′ər
n. something that dilutes
adj. less fat

THIRST therst
n. need of liquid
n. eager desire

THOLE thōl
n. a pin for an oar
n. a place for sacrifices in ancient Greek temples

THRASH thrash
v. to flog
v. to plunge about wildly
v. to force a vessel against the wind

THRASHER thrash′ər
n. one who flogs
n. a kind of bird

THREAD thred
n. a fine cord used in sewing
v. to move carefully through a passage

THROAT thrōt
n. part of the body
n. a narrow passage
n. part of a shoe

THRONE thrōn
n. chair or seat of a sovereign, bishop, etc.

THROWN
v. was cast away

THROUGH throo
prep. in at one end and out the other
prep. having reached the end
prep. by way of

THREW
v. did throw

THROW thrō
v. to hurl or cast
v. to unseat
v. to shape on a potter's wheel
v. to bring forth young (of domestic animals)

THROE
n. a pang, strong emotion

THRUM thrum
v. to play a stringed instrument
n. an end of warp threads in a loom

THRUSH thrush
n. a kind of bird
n. a kind of disease

THUMB thum
n. one of the fingers
v. to glance quickly through a book

THWART thwart
v. to oppose successfully
n. a seat across a boat

TIC tik
n. a sudden muscle spasm

TICK
n. the cloth case of a mattress
n. a slight click or tap
n. a bloodsucking arachnid

TICKET tik'it
n. a card of admission or fare
n. a list of candidates

TICKLE tik'əl
v. touch lightly; itch
v. to amuse

TIDE tīd
n. the rise and fall of waters

TIED
v. fastened together

TIE tī
v. to fasten together
n. a cravat

TYE
n. a kind of chain

TIGER tī'gər
n. a kind of animal
n. a kind of fish

TIGHT tīt
adj. not easily moved or opened
adj. stingy

TIGRESS tī'gris
n. a female tiger

TIGRIS
n. (u.c.) a river in Asia

TIL til
n. the sesame plant

'TIL
conj. until

TILL
prep. until
n. a money box or drawer
v. to plow

TILLER til'ər
n. a farmer
n. a bar on a rudder
n. a sapling

TILT tilt
v. to cause to slope or slant
v. to charge with a lance
n. an awning

TIMBAL tim'bəl
n. a kettledrum

TIMBALE
n. a shell of batter used in cooking

TIMBER tim'bər
n. wood of growing trees
n. personal quality

TIMBRE
n. the quality of a sound

TIME tīm
n. past, present, or future
n. occasion
n. period, space

THYME
n. a kind of herb

TINKER'S DAM ting'kərs dam
n. something of no worth
n. a barrier used by plumbers

TINNY tin'ē
adj. of or like tin
adj. sounding twangy

TINSEL tin'səl
n. shiny strips
n. showy pretense

TIP tip
n. a top or end
n. a useful hint
n. a light blow, tap
n. a small sum of money in exchange for service
v. to tilt

TYPP
n. a pound of yarn threads

TIPPLE tip'əl
v. to drink
n. a device that tips a freight car

TISSUE tish'oo
n. a material of animals and plants
n. soft paper
n. a woven fabric

TIT tit
n. a kind of bird
n. a teat

TITI tē'tē
n. a kind of monkey
n. a kind of shrub

TITLE tīt'əl
n. name or rank
n. championship
n. a legal right

TO too
prep. not from, toward

TOO
adv. also
adv. overly

TWO
n. a cardinal number

TOAD tōd
n. a kind of animal

TOWED
v. pulled or dragged

TOAST tōst
n. bread browned by heat
v. to honor someone with raised glasses
v. to warm

TOE tō
n. part of the foot
v. to drive a nail obliquely

TOW
v. to haul, drag
n. fiber of flax, hemp, or jute

TOILET toi'let
n. a bathroom fixture
n. dress or costume

TOILS toilz
v. works hard
n. a net for trapping game

TOKEN tō'kən
n. a symbol
adj. slight, minimal

TOLD tōld
v. did tell

TOLLED
v. rang a large bell

TOLL tōl
v. to ring a large bell
n. an extent of loss, damage, or suffering
n. a payment, as for use of a highway

TOLE
n. decorated metalware

TON tun
n. 2,000 pounds

TUN
n. a large cask

TONE tōn
n. quality of a sound
n. quality of a color
n. quality of body organs

TONER tō'nər
n. a kind of pigment
n. one of the workers in a paint factory

TONGS tongs
n. an instrument used in lifting, as firewood
n. certain Chinese secret societies

TONGUE tung
n. part of the mouth
n. part of a shoe
n. language of a particular people

TOOL tool
n. a hand-held instrument
n. a design on a book's cover
n. a person manipulated by another

TULLE
n. a netlike fabric

TOOTH tooth
n. one of the teeth
n. taste, fondness

TOP top
n. the highest point or part
n. a spinning toy
n. a stroke that hits the ball above its center
v. to surpass

TOPAZ tō'paz
n. a yellow gemstone
n. a kind of bird

TOPE tōp
n. a kind of shark
n. a kind of dome
v. to drink too much

TOPI tō pē'
n. a kind of sun hat or helmet: *topee*
n. a kind of antelope

TOPPER top'ər
n. one who excels
n. a kind of coat

TORCH taurch
n. a light to be carried
n. to apply a mixture to a roof

TORE tōr
v. ripped apart
n. a kind of circle; *torus*

TORQUES tôrks
n. something that causes rotation

TORQUES tôr kwēz'
n. a collar

TORT taurt
n. a wrongful act

TORTE
n. a rich cake

TORTOISE tôr'təs
n. a kind of turtle
n. a fortification

TOSS taus, tos
v. to throw
v. to fling about
v. to mix a salad

TOT tot
n. a small child
v. to add

TOUCH tuch
v. to put the hand or finger on something so as to feel
v. to affect with emotion
v. to border

TOUCHY tuch'ē
adj. cranky, irritable
adj. easily ignited, as timber

TOUGH tuf
adj. strong, hard to break

TUFF
n. a kind of volcanic rock

TOWARD tōrd
prep. in the direction of
adj. in progress, coming soon

TOWER tou'ər
n. a part of some buildings
v. to rise above

TOWER tō'ər
n. one who or that which pulls

TOWHEAD tō'hed
n. a head of very light hair
n. a sand bar in a river

TOY toi
n. a plaything
v. to dally amorously

TRACE trās
n. a surviving mark of a former agent or event
v. to copy a picture by using transparent paper
v. to go back

TRACK trak
n. railroad line
n. evidence that something has passed
v. to follow a trail

TRACT trakt
n. a region, district
n. a brief publication

TRACKED
v. followed a trail

TRAFFIC traf'ik
n. movement of vehicles or people in an area
n. trade, buying and selling

TRAIL trāl
v. to drag behind
v. to track
n. a running vine

TRAIN trān
n. railroad cars and engine
n. a body of followers
n. a long part of a skirt
v. to instruct

TRAIT trāt
n. a personal characteristic
n. a pen or pencil stroke

TRAM tram
n. a truck on rails in a mine
n. restraint
n. a kind of silk

TRAMP tramp
n. a vagabond
v. to walk with a firm step

TRANSFIX trans fiks'
v. to pierce with a pointed weapon
v. to make motionless with amazement or awe

TRANSFORMATION trans fər mā'shən
n. change in form or nature
n. a wig

TRANSLATE trans'lāt
v. to turn from one language into another
v. to move a bishop from one see to another

TRANSMISSION trans mish'ən
n. part of a car
n. broadcasting, as by radio

TRANSPIRE trans pīr'
v. to occur, become known
v. to sweat

TRAPPER trap'ər
n. one who catches animals for their fur
n. one who tends the door of a mine

TRAPPY trap'ē
adj. tricky
adj. (of a horse) moving with legs lifted high

TRAPS traps
n. snares
n. curves in pipes
n. percussion instruments in dance bands
n. some forms of rocks
v. dresses richly

TRAVELER trav'əl ər
n. one who goes from one place to another
n. a metal ring on a boat

TRAVERSE trə vers'
v. to pass or move along or over
v. to obstruct

TRAY trā
n. a flat container

TREY
n. a playing card with three pips

TREAD tred
v. to walk, trample
v. (of a male bird) to copulate

TREAT trēt
v. to discuss
v. to give food or presents

TREBLE treb'əl
adj. triple
adj. high in pitch

TREMBLER trem'blər
n. one who or that which shakes
n. a kind of bird

TRENCHER trench'ər
n. one who digs narrow ditches
n. a kind of tray for food

TRIBUNE trib'ūn
n. one who defends the rights of the people
n. a raised platform for a speaker

TRICE trīs
n. a short time, an instant
v. to pull with a rope

TRICK trik
n. an action intended to cheat
n. a prank
n. the cards played in one round

TRICKY trik'ē
adj. skilled
adj. uncertain

TRIED trīd
v. attempted
adj. tested and proved good
adj. subjected to worry, trouble

TRIFLE trī'fəl
n. something of little value
n. a kind of dessert
v. to waste time

TRIGGER trig'ɛr
n. part of a firearm
n. a stimulus

TRIM trim
v. to make neat by clipping
v. to adorn

TRIP trip
n. a voyage
v. to stumble

TRIVET triv'it
n. a stand to go under a hot plate
n. a kind of knife

TRIVIAL triv'ē əl
adj. unimportant
adj. (of names of animals) specific

TROLL trōl
n. a kind of dwarf
v. to sing in a full, rolling voice
v. to fish with a moving line

TROOP troop
n. a company, group

TROUPE
n. a company of actors or singers

TROT trot
n. a gait of an animal
n. a kind of fishing line

TROY troi
adj. computed by a system of weights
n. (u.c.) an ancient city

TRUCK truk
n. a vehicle
n. vegetables raised for the market
n. odds and ends
n. a bargain

TRUMP trump
n. a playing card of the winning suit
n. a trumpet

TRUMPETER trump'ə tər
n. one who plays a certain wind instrument
n. a kind of bird

TRUNK trungk
n. the main stem of a tree
n. a box or chest
n. torso
n. a kind of telephone line

TRUSS trus
n. a supporting frame used in building
v. to tie, bind, fasten

TRUST trust
n. belief, confidence
n. a large business monopoly

TRUSSED
adj. bound, tied

TRY trī
v. to attempt
v. to render fat

TRYING trī'ing
v. attempting
adj. annoying, difficult

TUB tub
n. a kind of container
n. a band around a mast

TUBER too'bər
n. a potato
n. one who uses hollow cylinders

TUBEROSE toob'rōz
n. a kind of flowering plant
TUBEROSE too'bə rōs
adj. having qualities of tubers

TUCKS tuks
n. folds made in sewing
v. puts into a small place

TUX
n. dinner jacket, tuxedo

TUMBLER tumb'lər
n. one who does leaps and turns
n. part of a lock
n. a kind of drinking glass
n. a kind of pigeon

TUNA toon'ə
n. a kind of fish
n. a kind of fruit

TUNE toon
n. a melody
v. to adjust a motor or musical instrument

TOON
n. a kind of tree

TURF terf
n. a layer of grassy earth
n. peat, esp. as material for fuel

TURKEY ter'kē
n. a kind of bird
n. (u.c.) a country in both Asia and Europe

TURN tern
v. to rotate, reverse
v. to metamorphose
v. to fashion, mold

TERN
n. a kind of bird
n. a set of three

TURNOUT tern'out
n. a gathering
n. manner or style

TURNOVER tern'ō vər
n. upset
n. change
n. a kind of bread or pastry

TURNSOLE tern'sōl
n. a kind of flower
n. a purple dye: litmus

TURRET tur'it
n. a small tower
n. part of a gun mount

TURTLE ter'təl
n. a kind of reptile
n. a kind of pocket in a sail

TWANG twang
v. to speak with a nasal tone
v. to let fly an arrow

TWILL twil
n. a kind of woven fabric

'TWILL
v. it will

TWINKLE twink'əl
v. to shine with a flickering gleam
n. the time required for a wink

TWISTER twist'ər
n. one who or that which winds or coils
n. a whirlwind

TWIT twit
v. to tease
n. a weak place in yarn

TWITCH twich
v. to tug or jerk
n. a noose for horses

TYPE tīp
n. kind, class, group
n. printed characters

U

U ū
n. twenty-first letter of the English alphabet

EWE
n. female sheep

YEW
n. kind of tree or shrub

YOU
pro. second person singular or plural

ULTRAMARINE ul'trə ma rēn'
n. a blue pigment
adj. beyond the sea

ULTRAMONTAINE ul'trə mon'tān
adj. beyond the mountains
adj. supporting the belief of papal supremacy

UMBRAGE um'brij
n. offense, annoyance
n. leaves that afford shade

UNAFFECTED un ə fek'tid
adj. sincere, genuine
adj. unaltered

UNBOLTED un bōl'tid
adj. not fastened
adj. not sifted, as grain

UNBUTTON un but'ən
v. to unfasten
v. to end a silence

UNCTUOUS ung'choo əs
adj. oily, greasy
adj. excessively pious

UNDERBELLY un'dər bel'ē
n. the lower abdomen
n. the area most vulnerable to attack

UNDERCOAT un'dər cōt'
n. a jacket worn under another
n. a paint or sealer

UNDERCUT un'dər kut'
v. to cut under or away
v. to sell at a lower price

UNDERGO un'dər gō'
v. to experience
v. to suffer

UNDERGROUND un'dər ground'
n. the place below the surface of the earth
n. a secret organization

UNDERHAND un'dər hand'
adj. secret and crafty
adj. done with the hand below the shoulder and the palm forward

UNDERMINE un'dər mīn'
v. to tunnel beneath
v. to attempt to subvert by stealth

UNDERSHOT un'dər shot'
adj. having projecting lower teeth
adj. driven by water passing beneath

UNDERSIZE un'dər sīz'
adj. smaller than the normal
adj. (of minerals) passing through a mesh

UNDERTAKER un'dər tāk'ər
n. a mortician
n. one who attempts

UNDERWORLD un'dər werld'
n. the criminal element in society
n. a region below the surface, as of the earth

UNDERWRITE un'dər rīt'
v. to sign one's name
v. to guarantee capital for
v. to insure

UNDISTINGUISHED un di sting'gwisht
adj. without apparent differences
adj. mediocre

UNDO un doo'
v. to erase
v. to destroy

UNDUE
adj. excessive
adj. not owed

UNDONE un dun'
adj. not accomplished
adj. unfastened

UNEARTH un erth'
v. to dig up
v. to inquire into

UNFAILING un fāl'ing
adj. dependable
adj. endless

UNFOLD un fōld'
v. to spread out
v. to explain

UNFROCK un frok'
v. to deprive of ecclesiastical rank
v. to strip of a frock

UNGUARDED un gar'did
adj. undefended
adj. open, frank
adj. indiscreet

145

UNGULA ung′gū lə
n. a part cut from a cone
n. a nail, claw, hoof

UNHAPPY un hap′ē
adj. sad
adj. unsuitable

UNHEALTHY un helth′ē
adj. sickly
adj. dangerous

UNHINGE un hinj′
v. to remove from hinges
v. to upset, disorient

UNIFORM ū′ni form
adj. consistent
n. a style of fashion of dress

UNION ū′nyn
n. combination, association
n. part of a flag

UNIT ū′nit
n. a single thing or person
n. a body of soldiers

UNITY ū′nit ē
n. the state of being one
n. one of the three principles of playwriting

UNIVERSAL ū ni ver′səl
adj. of all or the whole
adj. noting any of various tools

UNMOLD un mōld′
v. to destroy the shape of
v. to take out of a mold

UNNATURAL un nat′ūr əl
adj. not genuine
adj. extremely cruel or evil

UNOCCUPIED un ok′ū pīd
adj. empty, vacant
adj. idle

UNPACK un pak′
v. to remove contents
v. to reveal

UNREAL un rēl′
adj. imaginary
UNREEL
v. to unwind

UNSAID un sed′
v. retracted something said
adj. unstated

UNSAVORY un sāv′ər ē
adj. tasteless or insipid
adj. morally offensive

UNSUNG un sung′
adj. not uttered by singing
adj. not celebrated

UNTHOUGHT un thaut′
v. dispelled from the mind
adj. not anticipated

UNUSED un ūzd′
adj. not put into use
UNUSED un ūst′
adj. not accustomed

UNWARPED un worpt′
adj. not warped
adj. impartial

UNWASHED un wosht′
adj. not cleansed
n. the rabble

UP up
adv. to, toward, or in a more elevated position
adj. informed

UPGRADE up′grād
v. to augment grade, rank, or position
adj. uphill

UPLIFT up′lift
n. spiritual exaltation
n. a brassiere

UPON up on′
prep. up and on
prep. on the occasion of

UPPER up′ər
adj. higher
n. part of a shoe

UPRIGHT up′rīt
adj. raised upward
adj. honest, righteous

UPRISE up′rīz
v. to slope upward
v. to come into prominence

UPRISING up rī′ zing
n. a revolt
n. an ascent

UPSET up set′
v. to overturn
v. to disturb mentally or emotionally

UPSTAGE up stāj′
v. to move toward the back of the stage
v. to behave snobbishly

UPTAKE up′tāk
n. understanding
n. a lifting

UPWARD up′werd
adv. toward a higher place or source
adv. more

URANIC ū ran′ik
adj. containing uranium
adj. celestial

URCHIN er′chin
n. a small boy
n. a kind of sea animal

USANCE ū′sans
n. a length of time
n. income from wealth

USE ūs
n. the act of putting into service

USE ūz
v. to put into service
v. to habituate

EWES
n. female sheep

UTILITIES ū til′ə tēz
n. useful things
n. public services
n. stocks and bonds

UTTER ut′ər
v. to speak or pronounce
adj. complete, total

V

V vē
n. twenty-second letter of the English alphabet

VEE
adj. shaped like a V

VACUUM vak′ūm
n. emptiness
n. a kind of machine used for cleaning

VAIN vān
adj. proud
adj. worthless

VANE
n. device indicating wind direction

VEIN
n. a blood vessel

VALANCE va′lens
n. a short piece of drapery

VALENCE
n. a kind of chemical quality

VALE vāl
n. a valley

VAIL
v. to lower

VEIL
n. something that covers or conceals

VALET val′it
n. a manservant
n. a clothes rack

VALUE val′ū
n. merit, worth
n. degree of lightness in a color

VALVE valv
n. a device for controlling the flow of liquid or air
n. a kind of half-shell

VAMP vamp
n. part of a shoe
n. a seductive woman
n. an accompaniment to jazz

VAN van
n. the forefront
n. a covered vehicle

VANITY van′i tē
n. conceit
n. worthlessness
n. a dressing table

VAPOR vā′pər
n. a visible exhaltation, as fog or smoke
v. to boast

VARNISH vär′nish
v. to give wood or metal a glossy surface
v. to deceive

VAULT vault
n. an arched structure
v. to leap or spring

VEER vēr
v. to change direction
v. to slacken or let out

VEHICLE vē′i kəl
n. a conveyance
n. the object of a metaphor

VEND vend
v. to peddle
v. to publish

VENEER ven ēr′
n. a thin layer of wood
n. a superficially pleasing appearance

VENOM ven′əm
n. snake poison
n. malice

VENT vent
n. an outlet
n. a kind of slit in a coat
v. to give public utterance to

VERGE verj
n. edge, rim
v. to incline
n. limited scope

VERONICA və ron′i kə
n. a kind of plant
n. a pass used in bullfighting
n. an image of the face of Christ

VERTICAL ver′ti kəl
adj. upright
adj. of the consolidation of related businesses

VERY ve′rē
adj. extremely
adj. precise
adj. sheer, utter

VESSEL ves′əl
n. a ship or aircraft
n. an artery, vein, or the like
n. a container

VEST vest
n. a sleeveless garment
v. to pass into possession

VESTRY ves′trē
n. part of a church building
n. a committee of elected church members

VEXED vekst
adj. annoyed
adj. tossed about, as waves

VIABLE vī′ə bəl
adj. capable of living
adj. vivid, real
adj. workable

VIBRATION vī brā′shən
n. the act of moving to and fro
n. an emotional response

VICAR vik′ər
n. a clergyman
n. a deputy

VICE vīs
n. an evil practice

VISE
n. a kind of grasping tool

VICE vī′sē
prep. instead of

VIEW vū
n. sight, vision
n. opinion, theory

VILLAIN vil′ən
n. a scoundrel

VILLEIN
n. a serf-freeman in the Middle Age

VINTAGE vin′tij
n. wine from a particular crop
n. age
adj. representing high quality of a past era

VIOLA vē ō′lə
n. a kind of stringed instrument

VIOLA vī′ō lə
n. a flowering plant

VIPER vī'pər
n. one of several snakes
n. a spiteful person

VIRGIN ver'jin
n. a female who has not had sexual intercourse
adj. without alloy
adj. from the first pressing (oil) or smelting (metal)

VIRGINAL ver'jə nəl
adj. pure, unsullied
n. a harpsichord

VISITANT viz'i tənt
n. a visitor
n. an occasional mood or emotion

VIXEN viks'ən
n. a female fox
n. an ill-tempered woman

VOLAR vō'lər
adj. of or pertaining to palm of hand or sole of foot
adj. used in flight

VOLT vōlt
n. a unit of electrical charge
n. a turning movement of a horse

VOLUME vol'ūm
n. a book
n. loudness
n. an amount of space

VOLUNTEER vol'ən tēr'
n. one who offers his services
n. an unexpected plant, as in a garden

VULGAR vul'gər
adj. indecent
adj. common
adj. spoken by the people generally

W

W doub əl ū
n. the twenty-third letter of the English alphabet

UU
n two *U*'s spelled together

WAD wäd
n. a small mass, lump, or ball
n. a mass of manganese oxide minerals

WADE wäd
v. to walk in water

WEIGHED
v. determined the heaviness of something

WADERS wäd'ərs
n. several long-legged birds
n. high boots

WAG wag
n. a wit, rogue
v. to move rapidly from side to side or up and down

WAGE wāj
n. salary
v. to carry on, as war

WAHOO wä'hoo
n. a kind of shrub or tree
n. a kind of fish

WAIL wāl
n. a mournful cry of grief, pain, or despair

WALE
n. a welt

WAIST wāst
n. part of the body
n. a blouse

WASTE
n. desolate country, desert
v. to fritter away

WAIT wāt
v. to linger

WEIGHT
n. amount of heaviness
n. power

WAITER wāt'ər
n. a man who serves at table
n. a tray

WAIVE wāv
v. to relinquish, defer

WAVE
n. a swell of the sea
n. a signal made by fluttering something, as a hand

WAIVER wā'vər
n. a relinquishment of some right or interest
WAVER
v. to sway, hesitate

WAKE wāk
v. to become roused from sleep
n. a vigil by the body of a dead person
n. the track of waves left by a ship or boat

WALES wālz
n. streaks or ridges
n. (u.c.) part of the United Kingdom

WALK wauk
v. to go or travel by foot
n. a branch of activity
n. an enclosed pen for domestic animals

WALKER wauk'ər
n. a hiker
n. a support for babies or invalids

WALL waul
n. an upright structure of a building
n. the outmost layer of an object, as a blood cell

WALLEYE waul'ī
n. a kind of fish
n. an eye that appears out of focus

WALLFLOWER waul'flou ər
n. a kind of plant
n. an unpopular girl

WALLOW wäl'ō
v. to move with difficulty
v. to luxuriate

WAN wän
adj. lacking color
adj. lacking competence

WANE wān
v. to decline in power, importance
WAIN
n. a farm wagon or cart

WANTON wän'tən
adj. headstrong
WON TON wän tän
n. a kind of Chinese food

WARBLE waur'bəl
v. to sing with trills
n. a kind of tumor on an animal's back

WARD waurd
n. a division of a city, town, or hospital
n. a person who is under the protection of another
v. to turn aside, prevent
WARRED
v. fought

WARDER waur'dər
n. a watchman, guard
n. a staff of office

WARES wairz
n. articles for sale
WEARS
v. has on clothing

WARM waurm
adj. having moderate heat
adj. enthusiastic
adj. furious

WARP waurp
v. to bend or twist out of shape
v. to fertilize land by inundation

WASH wosh
v. to cleanse, as by action of water
v. to erode
n. swill; hogwash

WASHER wosh'ər
n. a machine for laundry
n. a flat ring used to prevent leaks

WATCH woch
n. a portable timepiece
v. to be on the lookout

WATTLE wotl
n. a lobe on the throat of some birds
v. to bind, wall, fence with poles

WAX waks
n. a substance secreted by bees
v. to increase, grow

WAY wā
n. manner, fashion
n. a path
adv. away

WEIGH
v. to find the heaviness of something
v. to ponder

WHEY
n. milk serum

WE wē
pro. nominative plural of I

WEE
adj. very small

WEAK wēk
adj. not strong

WEEK
n. seven days

WEAL wēl
n. a wale or welt

WE'LL
v. we will, we shall

WEAR wair
v. to carry clothing on the body
v. to exhaust

WEASEL wē'zəl
n. a kind of animal
v. to evade a duty

WEATHER weth'ər
n. atmospheric conditions
v. to come safely through danger

WETHER
n. a castrated male sheep

WEAVE wēv
v. to interlace wool or threads to form
  fabric

WE'VE
v. we have

WEB web
n. a net woven by a spider
n. a kind of membrane

WED wed
v. to marry

WE'D wēd
v. we had, we should, we would

WEEDS wēds
n. useless plants
n. mourning garments

WEEPER wēp'ər
n. one who cries
n. a loose-hanging object

WEIR wēr
n. a small dam

WE'RE
v. we are

WERE wer
v. part of the verb to be

WELD weld
v. to fuse metals
n. a kind of flower
v. to bring into harmony

WELLED
v. gushed up

WELL wel
n. a hole drilled for water
adj. healthy
adv. happily
adv. carefully

WELSH welsh
v. to cheat by not paying one's debts
n. (u.c.) the people of Wales

WELT welt
n. a ridge on the body, as from a whip
n. a leather cloth or strap

WELTER welt'ər
v. to roll or tumble about
v. to lie drenched in blood
v. to become deeply involved

WHIFF hwif
n. a slight gust of wind
n. a kind of fish

WHIP hwip
v. to strike, lash
v. to beat eggs, cream
v. to unite
v. to wind

WHIPLASH hwip'lash
n. the lash of a whip
n. a neck injury

WHISK hwisk
v. to sweep
v. to hurry
v. to beat eggs, cream

WHIST hwist
n. a certain card game
interj. hush!

WHISTLE hwis'əl
v. to make a sound by forcing breath through the lips
v. to whiz by

WHISTLER hwis'lər
n. one who whistles
n. one of several birds

WHITE-HOT hwīt'hot'
adj. extremely hot
adj. extremely emotional

WHITEWASH hwīt'wosh
n. a kind of thin paint
v. to cover faults of others

WHITING hwīt'ing
n. a kind of fish
n. ground-up chalk

WHIZ hwiz
n. an especially able person
v. to make a buzzing sound
v. to move rapidly

WHOSE hooz
pro. of whom or which

WHO'S
v. who is

WHY hwī
adv. for what reason?
interj. oh, my!

WIDOW wid'ō
n. a woman whose husband has died
n. a short last line of a paragraph

WILL wil
n. power of the mind
n. a legal testament
v. am, is, are about to

WILT wilt
v. to become limp
n. a kind of plant disease

WIND wind
n. air in motion

WIND wīnd
v. to bend, turn, or twist

WINED
v. drank wine

WINDOW win'dō
n. an opening in a wall
n. metal strips dropped to confuse radar

WINDY wind'ē
adj. airy
adj. talkative

WINGS wings
n. flying devices
n. a badge worn by airmen

WINK wink
v. to close one eye
n. an instant
n. a disk used in a kind of game

WINNOW win'ō
v. to free grain from impurities
v. to analyze

WIRE wīr
n. a thin string of metal
n. a telegram

WISP wisp
n. a small bundle of hay or hair
n. a small person or thing

WITH with, with
prep. accompanied by

WITHE
n. a willow twig
n. a partition in a chimney

WITHERS with'ərz
v. shrivels, fades
n. part of the back of some animals

WOE wō
n. sorrow

WHOA hwō, wō
interj.: stop!

WOLF woolf
n. a kind of animal
n. a discord in music
v. to eat hungrily

WONT waunt
n. custom, habit

WON'T wōnt
v. will not

WOOD wood
n. stems, branches of trees or bushes

WOULD
v. part of the auxiliary verb *will*

WORD werd
n. a unit of speech
n. a promise

WORK werk
n. toil, employment
n. a fortification

WORKER werk′ər
n. one who works
n. a female ant, bee, wasp, or termite

WORLD werld
n. the earth or globe
n. the human race
n. the universe

WORM werm
n. a creeping animal
n. a contemptible person
n. a spiral pipe
v. to get by persistent efforts

WORN wōrn
v. part of the verb *to wear*
adj. exhausted

WORRY wu′rē
v. to fret, fidget
v. to seize by the throat with the teeth

WORSTED wŏos′tid
n. firmly twisted yarn
WORSTED wers′təd
v. got the better of

WORT wert
n. malt used in making beer
n. a plant, herb, or vegetable
n. the whortleberry

WOUND woond
n. an injury
WOUND wound
v. did wind

WRECK rek
n. something in a state of ruin
RECK
v. to take heed

WROUGHT raut
adj. worked
adj. shaped by beating with a hammer

Y

YAK yak
n. a kind of ox
v. to talk a lot

YANK yank
v. to pull, jerk
n. (u.c.) Yankee

YANKEE yank′ē
n. (u.c.) a native of New England
n. a kind of sail

YAP yap
v. to yelp, bark
YAPP
n. a kind of bookbinding

YARD yärd
n. an outdoor area
n. three feet

YARN yärn
n. thread
n. an adventure story

YAW yau
v. to change from a straight course
n. a kind of skin lesion

YEAST yēst
n. a leaven for dough
n. foam

YELLOW yel′ō
n. a color
adj. cowardly

YEN yen
n. a coin of Japan
n. a desire

YET yet
adv. now; thus far
adv. but; on the contrary

YIELD yēld
v. to bear, supply
v. to submit

YOKE yōk
n. a kind of harness
YOLK
n. the yellow part of an egg
n. a grease from the skin of a sheep

YORE yōr
n. long ago
YOUR
pro. belonging to you
YOU'RE yūr
v. you are

Z

ZIP zip
n. energy, vim
v. to fasten with a zipper

ZOMBIE zom'bē
n. a ghost
n. a kind of drink
ZOMBI
n. a snake god

ZOOM zoom
v. to move quickly with a humming
noise
n. a kind of lens for a camera

ZING zing
n. enthusiasm
v. to move with a sharp noise

PART II

BRUISERS

BRUISERS

Bruisers are almost-homonyms, words that are so much alike that they are easily confused, either in speech or in writing. This confusion comes about in various ways. Some of the causes are untrained reading habits, inability to distinguish between sounds, tendencies to reverse letters, and poor vocabulary. These very causes create reading problems for many children.

But they can be conquered. The child who has any such problems should study each word phonetically; say each sound, blend it into other sounds, say the word, then write the word. By this method, *disassemble* will not be confused with *dissemble,* since it has been found to have four syllables while the second word has only three. Clear consonant sounds will differentiate between *plaintiff* and *plaintive;* clear vowel sounds between *bed* and *bid.* I urge any reader who is in any way confused by new words - as most of us are - to adopt the slow but rewarding phonetic approach.

And add your own *Bruisers.* (This list is only a guidepost to the goal, it doesn't pretend to be complete.) For instance when I was learning to read, I was utterly confused by an account of someone's travels with a *bureau.* It was a *burro.*

If you can be both lighthearted and persevering, you will find joy in the complexity of words.

PART II

BRUISERS

A

ABASE ə bāse'
v. to reduce or lower, humble
A BASE
n. a support

ABATE ə bāt'
v. to lessen
A BAIT
n. a lure

ABBESS ab'is
n. a superior in a convent
ABYSS ə bis'
n. a deep space, chasm

ABET ə bet'
v. to help, aid
A BET
n. a wager

ABLATION ab lā'shən
n. removal
OBLATION o blā'shən
n. a religious offering

ABOARD ə bōrd'
adv. on a train, ship, or plane
A BOARD
n. a plank

ABOUND ə bound'
v. to occur in large numbers
A BOUND
n. a jump

ABRADE ə brād'
v. to erode
A BRAID
n. a plait, trimming

ABREAST ə brest'
adv. side by side
A BREAST
n. part of the body

ABRIDGE ə brij'
v. to shorten, diminish
A BRIDGE
n. a structure over a river, etc.

ABROAD ə braud'
adv. overseas

A BROAD
adj. a wide (something)

ACCIDENCE ak'si dəns
n. the essentials of a subject

ACCIDENTS ak'si dənts
n. unfortunate happenings

ACCIDENT ak'si dənt
n. mischance
OCCIDENT ok'si dənt
n. (u.c.) the West

ACCOMPLICE ə kom'plis
n. a person who helps another in a crime
ACCOMPLISH ə kom'plish
v. to carry out, finish

ACCRUE ə kroo'
v. to add, as interest on money
A CREW
n. a group of workers
ECRU ā'kroo
n. a light tan color

ACQUAINT ə kwānt'
v. to inform
v. to introduce
A QUAINT
adj. an old fashioned (something)

ACQUIRE ə kwīr'
v. to get, own
A CHOIR
n. a chorus

ACROSS ə kraus'
adv. from one side to the other
A CROSS
n. a disagreeable (person)

ACUTE ə kūt'
adj. sharp
A CUTE
adj. an attractive (person)

ADAPT ə dapt'
v. to adjust
ADEPT ə dept'
adj. skillful
ADOPT ə dopt'
v. to take as one's own

ADDRESS ə dres'
n. place where one lives
A DRESS
n. an article of clothing

ADIEU ə dū'
interj. farewell!
ADO ə doo'
n. fuss, trouble

ADORE ə dōr'
n. to love
A DOOR
n. an opening

ADVERT ad vert'
v. to refer
AVERT ə vert'
v. to prevent

ADVICE ad'vīs
n. suggestion
ADVISE ad'vīz
v. to give a suggestion

AENEID i nē'əd
n. (u.c.) a poem by Vergil
ENNEAD en'ē ad
n. a group of nine persons or things

AFFECT ə fekt'
v. to influence
v. to pretend
EFFECT
n. a result

AFFIRM ə firm'
v. to state as true
A FIRM
n. a partnership

AFFLUENT af'loo ənt
adj. rich, abundant
EFFLUENT ef'loo ənt
adj. flowing out or forth

AFFORD ə fōrd'
v. to be able to pay for
A FORD
n. a shallow part of a river

AFFRONT ə frunt'
v. to insult, abuse
A FRONT
n. a foremost part of anything

AGAIN ə gen'
adv. once more
A GAIN ə gān'
n. an addition, advantage

AHEAD ə hed'
adv. before
A HEAD
n. part of the body

ALAS ə las'
interj. how sad!
A LASS
n. a girl

ALEE ə lē'
adv. away from the wind
ALLAY ə lā'
v. to calm, quiet

ALLEY al'ē
n. a narrow roadway
ALLY al'ī
n. partner

ALIGHT ə līt'
v. to settle, descend
A LIGHT
n. a lamp

ALIGN ə līn'
v. to arrange in a line
A LINE
n. a long mark

ALLAY ə lā'
v. to calm, quiet
A LAY
adj. of the church but not the clergy

ALLEGE ə lej'
v. to declare
A LEDGE
n. a narrow shelf

ALLOT ə lot'
v. to divide by lot, distribute
A LOT
n. a piece of land

ALLUDE ə lood'
v. to refer casually
ELUDE
v. to escape

A LEWD
adj. an indecent (something)

ALMS ämz
n. gifts to the poor

ARMS ärmz
n. parts of the body

ALOFT ə loft′
adv. high up

A LOFT
n. a room with a sloping roof

ALONE ə lōn′
adj. separate, apart

A LOAN
n. something lent

ALONG ə long′
prep. from one end to the other

A LONG
adj. a not short (something)

AMASS ə mas′
v. to collect

A MASS
n. a church service

AMAZE ə māz′
v. to astonish

A MAZE
n. a puzzle

AMEN ä men′
interj. so be it!

AMEND ə mend′
v. to change for the better

AMISS ə mis′
adv. out of order

A MISS
n. a girl

AMOUNT ə mount′
n. sum total

A MOUNT
n. a riding horse

AMPLE am′pəl
adj. large, liberal

AMPULE am′pūl
n. a sealed glass used in medicine

AMUSE ə mūz′
v. to entertain

A MUSE
n. a goddess of the arts

ANEW ə nū′
adv. once more

A NEW
adj. a fresh (something)

ANGEL ān′jel
n. a spirit with wings

ANGLE an′gel
n. a corner

ANKLE ank′əl
n. part of the body

ANNOYS ə noiz′
v. pesters, irritates

A NOISE
n. a loud sound

ANT ant
n. a kind of insect

AUNT ant, aunt
n. mother's or father's sister

ANTE an′tē
pref. before

ANTI an′tī
pref. against

APIECE ə pēs′
adv. each

A PIECE
n. a bit

A PEACE
n. a truce

APLENTY ə plen′tē
adj. enough of

A PLENTY
n. a lot of (something)

APPARENT ə pā′rent
adj. visible

A PARENT
n. a mother or father

APPEAL ə pēl′
n. a request

A PEAL
n. a ringing of bells

A PEEL
n. a rind

APPEAR ə pēr'
v. to come into view
A PEER
n. a nobleman
A PIER
n. a wharf

APPOINT ə point'
n. to name, select
A POINT
n. a sharp end

APPOSITE ap'ə zit
adj. pertinent
OPPOSITE op'ə zit
adj. facing

APPRISE ə prīz'
v. to inform
A PRIZE
n. a reward

AQUIVER ə kwiv'ər
adj. trembling
A QUIVER
n. a container for arrows

AREA är'ē ə
n. space, land
ARIA är'ē ə
n. a song
A REAR ə rēr'
n. a back
ARREAR
n. state of being behind

ARISE ə rīz'
v. to spring, flow
A RISE
n. a swelling

AROSE ə rōz'
v. got up
A ROSE
n. a kind of flower

AROUND ə round'
adv. nearly
A ROUND
adj. a circular (something)

ARRAIGN ə rān'
v. to accuse

A RAIN
n. a shower
A REIGN
n. a sovereign's authority

ARRANGE ə rānj'
v. to place in order
A RANGE
n. a stove

ARRAY ə rā'
v. to dress up
A RAY
n. a beam of light

ARREST ə rest'
v. to seize and hold
A REST
n. a time of repose

ASIDE ə sīd'
adv. apart, away from
A SIDE
n. a surface

ASLEEP ə slēp'
adj. not awake
A SLEEP
n. a deep nap

ASOCIAL ā sō'shəl
adj. selfish
A SOCIAL
n. a party

ASPECT as'pekt
n. appearance, nature
ASPIC as'pik
n. a kind of jelly

ASPIRE ə spīr'
v. to hope, yearn
A SPIRE
n. a steeple

ASSAIL ə sāl'
v. to attack
A SAIL
n. rigging on some boats

ASSAULT ə sault'
n. an attack
A SALT
n. a sailor

ASSAY ə sā'
v. to try or test
ESSAY es'ā
n. a prose writing

ASSIGN ə sīn'
v. to give
A SIGN
n. a notice

ASTERN ə stern'
adv. behind a boat
A STERN
adj. a strict (person)

ASTRAY ə strā'
adj. away from that which is right
A STRAY
n. a lost person or animal
ESTRAY
n. anything that has strayed

ASTRIDE ə strīd'
adj. seated, as on horseback
A STRIDE
n. a long step

ATOLL at'ol
n. a coral reef
AT ALL at ol'
adv. in the least

ATONE ə tōn'
v. to make up for
A TONE
n. a sound

ATOP ə top'
adj. on or at the top
A TOP
n. a toy

ATRIP ə trip'
adj. (of a snail) in position
A TRIP
n. a journey

ATROPHY a'tro fē
n. a wasting away of the body
A TROPHY ə trō'f ē
n. a keepsake

ATTACK ə tak'
v. to fight against

A TACK
n. a small nail

ATTIRE ə tīr'
n. dress
A TIRE
n. a wheel covering

ATTRIBUTE a'trib ūt
n. a quality
A TRIBUTE ə trib'ūt
n. a gift of thanks

ATTUNE ə toon'
v. to adjust
A TUNE
n. a melody

AVAIL ə vāl'
v. to be of use
A VALE
n. a valley
A VEIL
n. netting

AVERSE ə vers'
adj. unwilling
A VERSE
n. part of a poem

AWAIT ə wāt'
v. to expect
A WAIT
n. a rest period
A WEIGHT
n. a device to measure heaviness

AWAKE ə wāk'
adj. alert, not sleeping
A WAKE
n. a time of mourning

AWARD ə waurd'
v. to give as due
A WARD
n. an adopted child

AWARE ə wair'
adj. alert
A WARE
n. a piece of goods

AWAY ə wā'
adv. from here to there

A WAY
n. a path, route

AWEIGH
adj. (of an anchor) free from the bottom

B

BALM bäm
n. a resinous substance

BOMB bom
n. an explosive device

BANQUET bang′kwit
n. a feast

BANQUETTE bang ket′
n. a long bench

BATHOS bā′thos
n. anticlimax

PATHOS pā′thos
n. pity

BAUBLE bau′bəl
n. a trinket

BUBBLE bub′əl
n. a round body of gas in a liquid

BAZAAR bə zär′
n. a market place

BIZARRE bi zär′
adj. unusual, odd

BELLOW bel′ō
v. to cry like a bull or cow

BELOW bi lō′
adj. under

BLOW blō
v. to breathe upon

BERET be rā′
n. a kind of cap for the head

BERRY be′rē
n. a kind of fruit

BESIDE bi sīd′
prep. at the side of

BESIDES bi sīdz′
adv. moreover

BIANNUAL bī an′ū əl
adj. occurring twice a year

BIENNIAL bī en′ē əl
adj. happening every two years

BOARDER bōrd′ər
n. lodger

BORDER baurd′ər
n. rim

BORE bōr
n. a tiresome person

BOOR boor
n. a rude, clownish person

BORN baurn
adj. brought forth by birth

BORNE bōrn
v. did bear

BOURN boorn
n. limit

BORROW bo′rō
v. to take and promise to give back

BURROW bu′rō
n. a hole in the ground

BOUILLON bool′yən
n. a kind of broth

BULLION bool′yən
n. gold or silver

BOY boi
n. a male child

BUOY boo′ē
n. a float in the water

BRAN bran
n. a cereal

BRAND brand
n. a kind, grade

BRASSIERE brə zēr′
n. a woman's undergarment

BRAZIER brā′zher
n. a metal receptable

BREATH breth
n. air taken into the lungs

BREATHE brēth
v. to take oxygen into the lungs

BRETON bret′ən
n. (u.c.) a native of Brittany

BRITAIN brit′ən
n. (u.c.) England

BRITON brit'on
n. (u.c.) a native of England

BROOM broom, br͝oom
n. a brush with which to sweep

BROUGHAM broom, brōm
n. a kind of closed carriage

BUREAU bū'rō
n. a chest of drawers

BURRO bu'rō
n. a donkey

BUSINESS biz'nis
n. a trade

BUSYNESS biz'ē nis
n. activity

BYPASS bī'pas
n. a way around a place

BYPAST bī'past
adj. bygone

C

CABAL kə bal'
n. a group of plotters

CABLE kā'bəl
n. a heavy rope

CALM käm
adj. quiet

CLAM klam
n. a kind of sea creature

CALVARY kal'və rē
n. (u.c.) the place where Jesus was crucified

CAVALRY kav'əl rē
n. mounted soldiers

CANADA kən yä'də
n. a dry riverbed

CANADA kan'ə də
n. (u.c.) a nation in North America

CANAPE kan'ə pā'
n. a small sandwich

CANOPY kan'ə pē
n. an awning

CANDID kan'did
adj. frank, sincere

CANDIED kan'dēd
adj. sweet

CANNON can'ən
n. a mounted gun

CANON kan'yən
n. a deep valley

CAPTOR kap'tər
n. one who has taken by force

CAPTURE kap'chər
v. to take prisoner

CARD kärd
n. a piece of stiff paper

CORD kaurd
n. a thin rope

CAREFUL kair'ful
adj. watchful, exact

CARFUL kär'ful
n. a crowded car

CARIES kā'rēz
n. tooth decay

CARRIES ka'rēz
v. transports

CAROUSAL kə rou'zəl
n. a noisy feast

CAROUSEL ka'rə sel'
n. a merry-go-round

CARTON kär'tən
n. a large cardboard box

CARTOON kär toon'
n. a sketch or drawing

CATCH kach
v. to reach after and get

KETCH kech
n. a sailing vessel

CELERY sel'ər ē
n. a kind of vegetable

SALARY sal'ər ē
n. payment for work done

CELLA sel'ə
n. part of a classical temple

CELLAR sel'ər
n. an underground room

CENSOR sens'ər
n. one who examines literature and art for their morals

CENSURE sen'shər
v. to blame, disapprove

CENTER sen'tər
n. the middle

CENTAUR sen'tor
n. a half-man, half-horse mythical being

SENDER sen'dər
n. one who sends

CERTAIN ser'tən
adj. sure

CURTAIN ker'tən
n. a cloth, as at a window

CHARY cha'rē
adj. careful, shy

CHERRY che'rē
n. a kind of fruit

CHATTER chat'ər
v. to talk rapidly

SHATTER shat'ər
v. to smash, break

CHEATER chē'tər
n. a fake, liar

CHEETAH chē'tə
n. a kind of wild cat

CHEF shef
n. head cook

CHIEF chēf
n. head of a tribe

CHESS ches
n. a game for two

CHEST chest
n. part of the body

CHIN chin
n. part of the face

SHIN shin
n. the front of the leg

CHOLER kol'ər
n. anger

COLLAR
n. something worn around the neck

CHOLERA kol'ər ə
n. a kind of disease

CHORAL kōr'əl
adj. of a choir

CHORALE kō ral'
n. a group of singers

CORAL ko'rəl
n. a sea animal

CIRRUS si'rəs
n. a kind of cloud

SCIRRHUS skir'əs
n. a hard tumor or cancer

CLEAVER klēv'ər
n. a heavy knife

CLEVER klev'ər
adj. witty, bright

CLEF klef
n. a sign used in music

CLEFT kleft
n. a split

CLIMACTIC klī mak'tik
adv. pertaining to a climax

CLIMATIC klī mat'ik
adj. of or pertaining to climate

CLOTH klauth
n. fabric

CLOTHE klōth
v. to dress

COAL kōl
n. black fuel

COLD kōld
adj. not warm

COLIC kol'ik
n. a stomach ache

COLLECT kol'ekt
n. a kind of prayer

COLLAGE kō läzh'
n. an art technique

COLLEGE kol'ij
n. an institution of higher learning

COLLAR kol'ər
n. something worn around the neck
COLOR kul'ər
n. hue, tint
COMA kō'mə
n. a state of unconsciousness
COMMA kom'ə
n. a punctuation mark (,)
COMMAND kə mand'
v. to order
COMMEND kə mend'
v. to praise
COMMANDEER kom ən dēr'
v. to seize
COMMANDER kom an'dər
n. one who orders
COMMENCE kə mens'
v. to begin
COMMENDS kə mendz'
v. praises
CONSOLE kən sōl'
v. to comfort
CONSUL kon'səl
n. an official to a foreign government
CONTEND kən tend'
v. to struggle, strive
CONTENT kon tent'
adj. satisfied
CO-OP kō'op
n. a cooperative organization, as a store or dwelling
COOP koop
n. a cage or pen
COOPED koopt
v. caged up
CO-OPT kō'opt
v. to elect into a body
CORAL ko'rəl
n. skeleton of a sea animal
CORRAL kə ral'
n. a pen for horses
CORD kaurd
n. a thin rope
CORED kōrd
v. eliminated the center, as of fruit

CORPS kōr
n. a group of persons acting together
CORPSE kaurps
n. a dead body
COUGH kauf
v. to expel air
CUFF kuf
n. the edge of a sleeve
COURTESY kert'ə sē
n. polite behavior
CURTSY kert'sē
n. a bow by women in some dances
COWARD kou'ərd
n. one who is not brave
COWHERD kou'hərd
n. one who tends cows
CREDIBLE kred'ə bəl
adj. believable
CREDITABLE kred'it ə bəl
adj. praiseworthy
CROCHET krō shā'
n. a kind of needlework
CROTCHET kroch'it
n. whimsy, oddity
CROQUET krō kā'
n. a kind of game
CROQUETTE krō ket'
n. a kind of fried food
CRUMBLE krum'bəl
v. to break into crumbs
CRUMPLE krum'pəl
v. to wrinkle
CURE kūr
v. to make well
CURÉ kū'rā
n. a parish priest
CUTIN kū'tin
n. part of the surface of plants
CUT-IN kut'in
n. a still scene in motion pictures
CYCLE sī'kəl
n. circle, wheel
SECKEL sek'əl, sik'əl
n. a kind of pear

SICKLE si'kəl
n. a blade for cutting grass

CYNIC sin'ik
n. one who thinks selfishness guides people
SCENIC sē'nik
adj. having beautiful scenery

CYNOSURE sin'ə sür
n. something that attracts attention
SINECURE sin'ə kür
n. an office that requires little work

D

DAIRY dā'rē
n. a place where milk and cream are produced
DIARY dī'rē
n. a record of daily events

DEAD ded
adj. no longer living
DEED dēd
n. an action

DEADEN ded'ən
v. to weaken, dull
DEAD-END ded' end'
n. a street closed at one end

DEAFENED def'ənd
v. made unable to hear
DEFEND də fend'
v. to protect

DEBIT deb'it
n. the record of a debt
DEBT det
n. something owed

DECADE dek'ad
n. a series of ten
DECAYED dē kād'
adj. rotten

DECANT di kant'
v. to pour out gently
DECENT dē'sent
adj. proper
DESCANT des'kant
n. a melody

DESCENT di sent'
n. a downward slope

DECEASE di sēs'
v. to die
DISEASE di zēz'
n. illness

DECLAIM di klām'
v. to make a formal speech
DISCLAIM dis klām'
v. to repudiate

DECRY di krī'
v. to discredit
DESCRY di skrī'
v. to detect

DEFER di fer'
v. to put off until later
DIFFER dif'ər
v. to be unlike

DEFUSE dē fūz'
v. to remove a fuse (from a bomb)
DIFFUSE di'fūz
v. to scatter

DEFY di fī'
v. to resist
DEIFY dē'i fī
v. to make a god of

DELEGATE del'ə gāt
n. a representative
DELICATE del'ə kit
adj. soft, fragile

DEMEAN di mēn'
v. to lower in dignity
DEMESNF
n. an estate

DEMON dē'mən
n. a spirit
DIAMOND dī'a mund
n. a gem

DEMUR di mer'
v. to object
DEMURE di mūr'
adj. shy, modest

DENS denz
n. caves

DENSE dens
adj. crowded

DEPRECATE dep'rə kāt
v. to express disapproval
DEPRECIATE di prē'shē āt
v. to lessen the value of (money)

DESPERATE des'per it
adj. having little or no hope
DISPARATE dis pa'rit
adj. different

DEVICE di vīs'
n. a trick
DEVISE di vīz'
v. to plan

DICE dīs
n. small cubes used in games
DIES dīz
v. stops living

DINGHY ding'gē
n. a small boat
DINGY din'jē
adj. shabby, dull

DISASSEMBLE dis ə sem'bəl
v. to take apart
DISSEMBLE di sem'bəl
v. to conceal

DISBURSE dis bers'
v. to pay out money
DISPERSE dis pers'
v. to scatter

DISCOMFIT dis kum'fit
v. to defeat utterly
DISCOMFORT dis kum'fərt
n. uneasiness

DISCUS dis'kus
n. a round disk for throwing
DISCUSS dis kus'
v. to talk over or write about

DIVERS dī'verz
n. those who dive
DIVERSE dī vers'
adj. unlike

DODGE doj
v. to move aside

DOGE dōj
n. a former officer of Venice

DOER doo'ər
n. an active person
DOOR dōr
n. an entrance

DOGGY dau'gē
n. a small dog
DOGIE dō'gē
n. a motherless calf

DONG dong
n. a sound of a bell
DUNG dung
n. manure

DOSE dōs
n. a quantity of medicine
DOZE dōz
v. to nap

DOUSER dou'sər
n. one who drenches
DOWSER dou'zər
n. a wand that bends over water

DRAUGHT draft
n. a current of air
DROUGHT drout
n. dry weather

DUMB dum
adj. silent or stupid
DUM-DUM dum'dum'
n. a kind of bullet

E

EITHER ē'ther, ī'ther
adj. one or the other
ETHER ē'ther
n. a chemical used in medicine

ELL el
n. an extension of a house
'LL l
v. contraction of *will*

ELSE els
adj. other or in addition to
L'S elz
n. more than one *l*

EMIGRATE em′ə grāt
v. to leave for another country
IMMIGRATE im′ə grāt
v. to come to another country

EMIT i mit′
v. to expel, exhale
OMIT ō mit′
v. to leave out

ENERVATED en′ər vāt id
adj. enfeebled
INNERVATED i ner′vāt ed
adj. stimulated through the nerves

ENSURE en sūr′
v. to secure
INSURE in sūr′
v. to guarantee against loss

ENVELOP en vel′əp
v. to surround
ENVELOPE en′vel ōp
n. a wrapper, as for a letter

EPIC ep′ik
n. a kind of poem or book
EPOCH ep′ok
n. a particular period of time
ERA ē′rə
n. a period of time
ERROR e′rər
n. a mistake

ERS ers
n. a kind of plant used for forage
ERRS erz
v. mistakes

ETHIC eth′ik
n. a body of moral principles
ETHNIC eth′nik
adj. pertaining to a culture group

EXCEPTIONABLE ik sep′shən ə bəl
adj. liable to objection
EXCEPTIONAL ik sep′shə nəl
adj. unusual

EXECUTER eks′ə kūt ər
n. one who puts to death according to law
EXECUTOR ig zek′ū tər
n. one who performs a duty

EXERCISE eks′ər sīz
v. to train the body or mind
EXORCISE eks′or sīz
v. to expel an evil spirit

EXPANDS eks pands′
v. grows bigger
EXPANSE eks pans′
n. a wide area

EXTANT eks′tant
adj. in existence
EXTENT eks tent′
n. length, scope

EYES īz
n. organs of sight
ICE īs
n. frozen water

F

FACE fās
n. the front part of the head
PHASE fāz
n. a stage in a process of development
FACIAL fā′shəl
adj. of the face
FACILE fa′sil
adj. moving with ease
FAIRY fā′rē
n. a small imaginary being
FAERIE fā′ər ē
n. imaginary land of fairies
FERRY fe′rē
n. a boat that carries people or cars

FALSE fauls
adj. erroneous
FAULTS faults
n. flaws

FARM färm
n. land used to grow food
FORM form
n. shape
FROM frum
prep. away, off

FARMER färm′ər
n. one who works the land

FORMER form'ər
adj. earlier

FARTHER fär'ŧħer
adj. more remote

FATHER fä'ŧħer
n. male parent

FURTHER fer'ŧħer
v. to promote

FEASTER fēs'tər
n. one who eats a good meal

FESTER fes'tər
v. to form pus

FECKLESS fek'lis
adj. feeble

FLECKLESS flek'lis
adj. without spots or freckles

FIBBER fib'ər
n. one who tells a small lie

FIBER fīb'ər
n. a thread

FIEND fēnd
n. a devil

FIND find
v. to discover

FILE fīl
n. a narrow tool

PHIAL, VIAL fī'əl, vī'əl
n. a small container for liquids

FILLIP fil'ip
n. a tap or stroke

FLIP flip
adj. pert, smart

FINAL fīn'əl
adj. last in place, order, or time

FINALE fi nal'ē
n. the last piece, division, etc., in
music

FINENESS fīn'nis
n. state or quality of being fine

FINESSE fi nes'
n. subtlety

FLAUNT flaunt
v. to display boldly

FLOUT flout
v. to ignore

FLEES flēz
n. runs away

FLEECE flēs
n. wool coat of some animals

FOREWORD fōr'werd
n. preface

FORWARD for'werd
adv. ahead

FUNERAL fū'nər əl
n. a ceremony for the dead

FUNEREAL fu nēr'ē əl
adj. mournful

FUNNY fun'ē
adj. amusing

PHONY fō'nē
adj. not genuine

FURRY fer'ē
adj. covered with fur

FURY fū'rē
n. great anger

G

GABBLE gab'əl
v. to talk idly

GABLE gā'bəl
n. part of a roof

GALLON gal'ən
n. four quarts

GALLOON gə loon'
n. a kind of braid

GALLOP gal'əp
n. a fast ride on horseback

GALOP
n. a kind of fast dance

GAMIN gam'ən
n. street urchin

GAMINE gam ēn'
n. a tomboy

GEE jē
v. to turn a horse to the left

GHEE gē
n. a kind of liquid butter

GENIUS jē'nyus
n. high intelligence
GENUS jē'nəs
n. kind, set, class

GENTEEL jen tēl'
adj. polite, stylish
GENTILE jen'tīl
adj. not Jewish
GENTLE jen'təl
adj. kind, mild

GERMAN jer'mən
adj. having the same parents
GERMANE jer mān'
adj. apt, suited, relevant

GIB gib
n. a male cat
JIB jib
n. a kind of sail

GLACÉ glo'sā
adj. frozen or frosted food
GLASS glas
n. a hard, brittle material

GLACIER glā'shər
n. a mass of ice
GLAZIER glā'zhər
n. one who fits windows with glass

GLEAM glēm
n. a flash of light
GLEAN glēn
v. to pick up bit by bit

GOOD go͝od
adj. moral, pure
GOODS go͝odz
n. possessions; fabrics

H

HAIRY hair'ē
adj. having much hair
HARRY ha'rē
v. to harass

HALF haf
n. one of two equal parts
HAVE hav
v. to possess

HALLO hə lō'
v. to cry, as after hunting dogs
HALLOW hal'ō
v. to make holy
HALO hā'lō
n. a nimbus

HANDSOME hand'sum
adj. good-looking
HANSOM han'sum
n. a two-wheeled horse-drawn cart

HAPLY hap'lē
adv. by chance
HAPPILY hap'i lē
adv. with pleasure

HEADDRESS hed'dres
n. a covering for the head
HEADREST hed'rest'
n. a support for the head

HEART härt
n. part of the body
HEARTH härth
n. fireside

HEEL hēl
n. part of the foot
HELL hel
n. a place of torment

HIS hiz
pro. belonging to him
HISS his
v. to make a long s sound

HOARSE hōrs
adj. husky, throaty
HORSE haurs
n. a kind of animal

HOLD hōld
v. to keep, restrain
HOLE hōl
n. an opening

HUMAN hū'mən
adj. of mankind
HUMANE hū mān'
adj. merciful
HUNGARY hung'ə rē
n. (u.c.) a country in Europe

HUNGRY hung'grē
adj. having a need for food

HYPERCRITICAL hī pər krit'ik əl
adj. overcritical

HYPOCRITICAL hip ə krit'ik əl
adj. sham

I

IMBRUE im broo'
v. to stain with blood

IMBUE im bū'
v. to inspire, as with opinions

IMPATIENCE im pā'shəns
n. restlessness

IMPATIENS im pā' shē enz
n. a kind of flower

INCREDIBLE in kred'ə bəl
adj. unbelievable

INCREDULOUS in kred'ū lus
adj. skeptical

INGENIOUS in jēn'yəs
adj. inventive

INGENUOUS in jen'ū əs
adj. artless

INSOLATE in'sō lāt
v. to expose to the sun's rays

INSULATE ins'ū lāt
v. to segregate

J

JACAL hə käl'
n. a kind of mud house

JACKAL jak'əl
n. a kind of animal

JALOUSIE jal'ə sē
n. a kind of blind or shutter

JEALOUSY jel'ə sē
n. envy

JEWS jooz
n. (u.c.) a people whose religion is Judaism

JUICE joos
n. the liquid of plant or animal substance

K

KILLED kild
v. caused death

KILT kilt
n. a kind of short skirt

KNELLED neld
v. sounded a bell

KNELT nelt
v. got on one's knees

KNOW nō
v. to understand

NOW nou
adj. at the present time

KNOWN nōn
v. understood

NOUN noun
n. a part of speech

L

LAIR lair
n. a den

LIAR lī'ər
n. one who does not tell the truth

LAME lām
adj. crippled

LAMÉ lä mā'
n. an ornamental fabric

LANGUOR lang'gər
n. lack of spirit

LANGUR lung goor'
n. a kind of monkey

LARVA lär'və
n. young insects

LAVA lä'və
n. fluid rock from a volcano

LATER lāt'ər
adj. more tardy

LATTER lat'ər
adj. being the second mentioned of two

LATH lath
n. a narrow strip of wood
LATHE lāth
n. a kind of machine

LAUD laud
v. to praise
LOUD loud
adj. noisy

LAUNCH launch
n. a kind of boat
LUNCH lunch
n. the midday meal

LENDS lendz
v. makes a loan
LENS lenz
n. part of a camera

LIABLE li'ə bəl
adj. under legal obligation
LIBEL li'bəl
v. to misrepresent damagingly

LIFELONG līf'long
adj. lasting through life
LIVELONG liv'long
adj. (of time) slow in passing

LIGHTENING līt'ən ing
v. making bright
LIGHTNING līt'ning
n. a flash from an electrical storm

LINEAMENT lin'ē ə ment
n. a feature of a face or body
LINIMENT lin'ə mənt
n. unguent

LION li'ən
n. a large animal
LOIN loin
n. a part of the body

LOATH lōth
adj. unwilling
LOATHE lōth
v. to abhor

LOCAL lō'kəl
adj. of a special place

LOCALE lō kal'
n. a place or setting
LOCUS lō'kəs
n. a place
LOCUST lō'kəst
n. a kind of grasshopper

LOOSE loos
adj. not tight
LOSE looz
v. to fail to keep

LOSS laus, los
n. failure to keep
LOST laust, lost
adj. no longer to be found

LOUP loo
n. a half-mask
LOUPE loop
n. a kind of magnifying glass

LOUVAR loo'vär
n. a kind of fish
LOUVER loo'vər
n. a slat over a door or window

LOVE luv
n. affection
LUFF luf
v. to let a sail flap

LUNG lung
n. part of the body
LUNGE lunj
v. to thrust something forward

LYRICIST lēr'i sist
n. one who writes lyrics
LYRIST līr'ist
n. one who plays the lyre

M

MADDENING mad'ə ning
adj. driving to frenzy
MADDING mad'ing
adj. mad

MAGNATE mag'nāt
n. a person of importance
MAGNET mag'nət
n. metal that attracts another

MANDREL man'drəl
n. a spindle on a circular saw

MANDRILL man'dril
n. a kind of baboon

MANNA man'ə
n. divine food

MANNER man'ər
n. custom, style

MARCH märch
v. to walk with measured tread

MARSH märsh
n. low, wet ground

MARGARITE mär'gə rīt
n. a kind of mineral

MARGUERITE mär'gə rēt
n. a daisy

MARITAL ma'ri təl
adj. of marriage

MARTIAL mär'shəl
adj. warlike, brave

MARRY ma'rē
v. to wed

MERRY me'rē
adj. gay, happy

MATE māt
n. one of a pair

MATE mä tä'
n. a kind of tea

MAUVE mōv
n. a bluish purple

MOVE moov
v. to go from one place to another

MEANT ment
v. did mean

MEND mend
v. make whole

MELD meld
v. to merge, blend

MELT melt
v. to become liquid

MENDACITY men das'i tē
n. untruthfulness

MENDICITY men dis'i tē
n. the practice of begging

MENSTRUAL men'stroo əl
adj. monthly

MENSURAL men'shə rəl
adj. pertaining to measure

MILD mīld
adj. gentle

MILE mīl
n. 5,280 feet

MINCE mins
v. to cut or chop

MINTS mints
n. certain candies

MORAL mo'rəl
adj. honest, upright

MORALE mō ral'
n. cheerfulness, zeal

MORE mōr
adj. in greater quantity

MOWER mō'ər
n. one who or that which cuts grass

MORN maurn
n. early day

MOURN mōrn
v. to express sorrow

MOTIF mō tēf'
n. a design that reappears throughout
a work of art

MOTIVE mō'tiv
n. incentive

MOUTH mouth
n. part of the body

MOUTHE mouth
v. to give a long speech

MUCH much
n. a great deal

MUSH mush
n. soft cooked cornmeal

MUCIC mū'sik
n. a kind of acid

MUSIC mū'zik
n. melody

MUSICAL mū'zi kəl
adj. of music

MUSICALE mū zə kal'
n. a program of music for guests

N

NEITHER nē'<del>th</del>er, nī'<del>th</del>er
conj. not either
NETHER ne<del>th</del>'er
adj. below the earth's surface

O

OF uv
prep. from
OFF auf, of
prep. away from

ONCE wuns
adv. at one time
ONES wunz
n. singles

OR aur
conj. (used to connect words)
ORE ōr
n. metal

ORDINANCE aur'di nans
n. rule, law
ORDNANCE aurd'nans
n. cannon or artillery

ORIEL ōr'i əl
n. a bay window
ORIOLE ōr'ē ōl
n. a kind of bird

OWN ōn
v. to possess
WON wun
v. did win

P

PARISH pa'rish
n. an ecclesiastical district
PERISH pe'rish
v. to die unseasonably

PAROLE pə rōl'
n. conditional release
PAYROLL pā'rōl'
n. list of employees

PASTORAL pas'tər əl
adj. rustic
PASTORALE pas tə ral'
n. music with a pastoral subject
PASTURAL pas'chər əl
adj. grassy

PEASANT pez'ənt
n. a rustic
PHEASANT fez'ənt
n. a kind of bird

PERCENT per sent'
n. one one-hundredth part
PRECENT pri sent'
v. to lead a choir
PRESENT pri zent'
v. to give

PERCEPT per'sept
n. knowledge gained through the senses
PRECEPT prē'sept
n. a rule of action

PERFECT per'fekt
adj. without blemish
PREFECT prē'fekt
n. overseer, director

PERFORM per form'
v. to act, do
PREFORM prē'form'
v. to form beforehand

PERQUISITE per'kwi zit
n. an extra fee
PREREQUISITE pri rek'wi zit
n. something required beforehand

PERSECUTE per'si kūt
v. to harass, worry
PROSECUTE pro'si kūt
v. to begin legal proceedings against (someone)

PERSONAL per'sən əl
adj. individual, private
PERSONNEL per son el'
n. all who are employed in one place

PERSPECTIVE per spek'tiv
n. a visible scene extending to a distance

PROSPECTIVE prə spek'tiv
adv. of or in the near future

PERVERSE per vers'
adj. contrary, wayward

PERVERTS per verts'
v. leads astray morally

PICARESQUE pik'ə resk'
adj. of a rogue in some novels

PICTURESQUE pik'tū resk'
eadj. charming, quaint

PIERCE pērs
v. to make a hole in something

PIERS pērz
n. docks, wharves

PILASTER pī'las tər
n. a projection like a column on a wall

PLASTER plas'tər
n. a composition for walls

PILLAR pil'ər
n. a shaft used in building

PILLOW pil'ō
n. a headrest

PIMENTO pi men'tō
n. allspice

PIMIENTO pı myen'tō
n. a garden pepper

PISTOL pis'təl
n. a kind of firearm

PISTOLE pi stōl'
n. a kind of gold coin

PITEOUS pit'ē əs
adj. deserving pity

PITIABLE pit'ē əb əl
adj. evoking pity

PITIFUL pit'i fəl
adj. such as to deserve pity

PLAGUE plāg
n. an epidemic

PLAQUE plak
n. a kind of wall ornament

PLAINTIFF plān'tif
n. one who brings suit in law

PLAINTIVE plān'tiv
adj. expressing sorrow

POEM pō'əm
n. verse

POME pōm
n. a fruit of the apple family

POGROM pə grom'
n. slaughter

PROGRAM prō'gram
n. a playbill

POISE poiz
n. state of balance

POSE pōz
n. a bodily posture

POOR poor
adj. not rich

POUR pōr
v. to let a liquid fall

POSSES pos'ēz
n. men who assist police officers

POSSESS pə zes'
v. to own

POUF poof
n. an arrangement of hair over a pad

PUFF puf
n. a short blast of wind

PRECEDE pri sēd'
v. to go before

PROCEED prō sēd'
v. to go onward after stopping

PRECEDENT pres'i dent
n. a preceding case

PRESIDENT prez'i dent
n. head of a business or country

PRECESSION prē sesh'ən
n. the act of going before

PROCESSION prō sesh'ən
n. an orderly line of people or animals

PRESCRIBE pri skrīb'
v. to dictate

PROSCRIBE prō skrīb'
v. to prohibit

PRESENCE prez'əns
n. attendance, company

PRESENTS prez'ənts
n. gifts

PRICE prīs
n. the cost
PRIZE prīz
n. an award

PRONOUNCE prō nouns'
v. to enunciate, utter
PRONOUNS prō'nounz
n. some parts of speech

PROOF proof
n. evidence
PROVE proov
v. to verify

PROPHECY prof'i sē
n. revelation
PROPHESY prof'i sī
v. to foretell

PROSTATE pros'tāt
n. a gland in men
PROSTRATE pros'trāt
v. to lie face down

PUNCTATION punk tā'shən
n. a tiny point or dot

PUNCTUATION punk tū ā'shən
n. marks used in writing

PUT pŏŏt
v. to place
PUTT put
v. to strike a golf ball gently

Q

QUIET kwī'ət
n. freedom from noise
QUITE kwīt
adv. wholly, truly

R

RACE rās
n. a contest of speed
RAISE rāz
v. to erect

RACER rā'ser
n. one who or that which races
RAZOR rā'zer
n. a tool for shaving

RADISH rad'ish
n. a kind of edible root
REDDISH red'ish
adj. somewhat red

RANKLE rank'əl
v. to cause keen irritation
WRANGLE rang'əl
v. to argue

RATIONAL rash'ən əl
adj. reasonable
RATIONALE rash ən al'
n. a statement of reasons

REALITY rē al'i tē
n. the state of being real
REALTY rē'əl tē
n. real estate

RECENT rē'sent
adj. not long past
RESENT rē zent'
v. to feel insulted

REFECTORY ri fek'tə rē
n. a dining hall
REFRACTORY ri frak'tə rē
adj. stubborn

REFERENCE ref'er əns
n. act of seeking a source
REFERENTS ref'er əns
n. the object to which a term refers

REPERTOIRE rep'ər twär'
n. a stock of plays or songs a
company can perform
REPERTORY rep'ər tō rē
n. a kind of theatrical company

RETCHED rechd
v. tried to vomit
WRETCHED rech'id
adj. unhappy

REVEREND rev'ər ənd
adj. worthy to be revered
REVERENT rev'ər ent
adj. deeply respectful

RHINE rīn
n. (u.c.) a river in Germany

RIND rīnd
n. the outside of a piece of fruit

RIDGED rijd
v. marked with raised strips

RIGID rij'əd
adj. stiff, firmly fixed

RIFFLE rif'əl
n. a ripple

RIFLE rī'fəl
n. a kind of gun

RING ring
n. a circular band for the finger

RINK rink
n. an expanse of ice for skating

RISKY ris'kē
adj. hazardous

RISQUÉ risk ā'
adj. off-color, naughty

ROAR rôr
n. a loud, deep cry

ROWER rō'ər
n. one who rows (a boat)

ROMANCE rō mans'
n. a love story

ROMANS rō'manz
n. (u.c.) people of Rome

ROOMER room'ər
n. a lodger

RUMOR roo'mər
n. gossip

S

SACRED sā'kred
adj. holy

SCARED skaird
adj. frightened

SCARRED skärd
adj. with scars

SALAD sal'əd
n. a dish of fresh vegetables, etc.

SALLET sal'ət
n. a kind of helmet

SALUTE səl ūt'
n. a gesture of respect

SOLUTE sol'ūt
n. a dissolved substance

SANATORIUM san ə tōr'ē əm
n. a kind of hospital

SANITARIUM san i tā'ri əm
n. a health resort

SATIRE sat'īr
n. irony

SATYR sāt'ər
n. a woodland deity

SAVIOR sāv'yər
n. one who delivers

SAVOR sāv'ər
n. a taste or smell

SCION sī'ən
n. a descendant

ZION zī'ən
n. (u.c.) a hill in Jerusalem

SCRIP skrip
n. a scrap of paper

SCRIPT skript
n. handwriting

SEAL sēl
n. a kind of water animal

ZEAL zēl
n. eagerness

SECOND sek'ənd
adj. next after the first

SECUND sē'kund
adj. unilateral

SELFISH sel'fish
adj. caring mostly for oneself

SHELLFISH shel'fish
n. a kind of seafood

SEPTIC sep'tik
adj. infected

SKEPTIC skep'tik
n. a doubter

SEVER sev'ər
v. to cut

SEVERE səv ēr'
adj. harsh

SHORE shōr
n. land by the water's edge
SHOWER shō'ər
n. one who shows
SURE shoor
adj. free from doubt

SILVER sil'vər
n. a kind of metal
SLIVER sliv'ər
n. a splinter

SIMULATE sim'ū lāt
v. to pretend
STIMULATE stim'ū lāt
v. to encourage

SINK sink
n. a wash basin
ZINC zink
n. a kind of metal

SLACK slak
adj. loose
SLAKE slāk
v. to refresh

SMOOTHER smooth'ər
adj. less rough
SMOTHER smuth'ər
v. to suffocate

SOLDIER sōld'yər
n. a member of the army
SOLIDER sol'id er
adj. more firm

SOLID sol'id
adj. firm, stable
STOLID stol'id
adj. unemotional

SOUFFLE soo'fəl
n. a murmuring sound
SOUFFLÉ soo flā'
n. a dish made light with egg whites

SPECIE spē'shē
n. coin
SPECIES spē'shēz
n. a distinct sort or kind

STABILE stā'bēl
n. a piece of sculpture with fixed supports
STABLE stā'bəl
adj. firm, steady

STATUE stat'ū
n. a carved work of art
STATUTE stat'ūt
n. a law

SUE soo
v. to bring civil action
ZOO zoo
n. menagerie

SUPER soo'pər
adj. very good
SUPPER sup'ər
n. an evening meal

SUPPOSITIONS sup ə zish'ənz
n. the act of supposing
SUPPOSITIOUS sup ə zish'əs
adj. formed from supposition

SURPLICE ser'plis
n. a vestment
SURPLUS ser'plus
n. superabundance

T

TEETH tēth
n. more than one tooth
TEETHE tēth
v. to cut teeth

THOROUGH thu'rō
adj. total
THOUGH thō
conj. even if

THOUGHT thaut
n. idea

THROUGH throo
prep. into and then out of
THROW thrō
v. to hurl

TINNY tin'ē
adj. of tin

TINY tī'nē
adj. very small

TIRED tīrd
adj. weary

TRIED trīd
v. attempted

TRACK trak
v. to pursue

TRACT trakt
n. region, district

TRADER trād'ər
n. a businessman

TRAITOR trāt'ər
n. one guilty of treason

TRAIL trāl
v. to drag behind

TRIAL trī'əl
n. proof, test

U

URBAN er'ban
adj. living in a city

URBANE er'bān'
adj. having sophistication

V

VARY vā'rē
v. to change or alter

VERY ve'rē
adv. extremely

VENAL vēn'əl
adj. bribable

VENIAL vē'nē əl
adj. excusable

VERSE vers
n. part of a poem

VERSED verst
adj. skilled

VICE vīs
n. an evil practice

VISE
n. a holding tool

VIRTU ver'too
n. merit in art objects

VIRTUE ver'tū
n. goodness

W

WAILS wālz
v. moans

WALES wālz
n. (u.c.) a part of Great Britain

WHALES hwālz
n. some sea animals

WANT waunt
v. to need

WONT
n. custom, habit

WON'T wōnt
v. will not

WARY wair'ē
adj. watchful

WEARY wē'rē
adj. tired

WEATHER wetẖ'ər
n. state of atmosphere

WHETHER hwetẖ'ər
conj. used with or

WEN wen
n. a kind of tumor

WHEN hwen
adv. at what time?

WHICH hwich
pro. what one?

WITCH wich
n. a woman who does magic

WHILE hwīl
n. a period of time

WILE wīl
n. a trick

WHINE hwīn
v. to complain

WINE wīn
n. a drink made from grapes

WHORE hōr
n. a prostitute

WHO'RE hoor
v. who are?

WICKED wik'id
adj. evil

WICKET wik'it
n. a small door or arch

WREATH rēth
n. a circle of flowers

WREATHE rēth
v. to encircle, as with a wreath